CHRISTIANITY
ON
TRIAL

CHRISTIANITY ☩N TRIAL

ARGUMENTS AGAINST ANTI-RELIGIOUS BIGOTRY

VINCENT CARROLL & DAVID SHIFLETT

Encounter Books
San Francisco

First edition published in 2002 by Encounter Books, an activity of Encounter for Culture and Education, Inc., a nonprofit tax exempt corporation.

Encounter Books website address: www.encounterbooks.com

Cover design by Zen Jam, San Francisco

Manufactured in the United States and printed on acid-free paper.

The paper used in this publication meets the minimum requirements of ANSI/NISO Z39.48-1992 (R 1997)(*Permanence of Paper*).

Library of Congress Cataloging-in-Publication Data

Carroll, Vincent.
    Christianity on trial : arguments against anti-religious bigotry /
Vincent Carroll and David Shiflett.—1st ed.
        p.   cm.
    Includes bibliographical references and index.
    ISBN 1-893554-15-5 (alk. paper)
        1. Apologetics.   2. Church history.   3. Christian ethics—
History.   I. Shiflett, David. II. Title.
BT1250.C33 2002
239—dc21

                                                            2001040778

10   9   8   7

CONTENTS

Introduction

Christianity inhabits a strange space in American life. It is by far the predominant religion in the most religious country in the industrialized world, with more than 90 percent of its citizens professing belief in God and a large majority claiming allegiance to a Christian denomination or sect. Yet Christians are regularly targeted for ridicule and vilification by a significant portion of America's cultural elite, a situation all the more striking in view of the prevailing hypersensitivity toward other religious, ethnic and lifestyle groups. When a presidential aide in the Clinton administration sought to discredit an independent prosecutor, for example, he instinctively denounced the churchgoing attorney as a "religious fanatic"—a career-ending insult had it been directed at a devout Jew or Muslim. The fact that the aide kept his job while the White House refused to issue even a perfunctory apology illustrates the impunity that surrounds casual bigotry against Christians.

In isolation, such put-downs are relatively harmless. The problem is that similarly harsh judgments have become so commonplace and are asserted so aggressively that they threaten to distort Christians' own view of themselves and their past. Perhaps this has already happened. How else to explain the largely passive reception of a sound-bite version of history in which Christians' religious forebears are considered notable mainly for intolerance, superstition and oppression?

Even mainstream news stories, to the extent that they address Christian history at all, often dwell on conflict and controversy. For instance, the 900th anniversary of the Crusaders' conquest of Jerusalem in 1099 occasioned a spate of stories reflecting on Christian culpability in that blood-soaked adventure. The quincentenary of Columbus's first voyage to the New World provoked an even more damning torrent of articles and commentaries on Christian complicity in the demise of America's natives. Allegations against Pope Pius XII regarding his behavior during the Holocaust, no matter how vitriolic, qualify as major news stories more than half a century after World War II. Americans who have scarcely ever cracked a history book are likely to have heard a great deal in the mass media about the church's suppression of Galileo and the horrors of the Inquisition, but next to nothing about Christianity's role in ending infanticide and slavery.

Even the apparent good news of an agreement between Lutherans and Roman Catholics in 1999 to resolve their nearly five-hundred-year doctrinal dispute became, in more than one report, yet another opportunity to recapitulate in grim detail the body count of the Wars of Religion. Perhaps this should not be surprising, since interfaith conflict is probably the most common theme in news coverage of religion. According to a 1999 study by the Garrett-Medill Center for Religion and the News Media in Evanston, Illinois, such conflict "was the main news value" in half of the page-one stories in the four newspapers examined (*New York Times*, *Chicago Tribune*, *USA Today* and *Chicago Sun-Times*). Overall, conflict "was found in 25 percent of the stories about religion, spirituality, or values in daily newspapers, television news, and weekly news magazines."

The moral failings of the clergy, especially Catholic clergy, are also a staple of the media. In early 2000, for example, a widely reprinted series in the *Kansas City Star* asserted that priests were four times more likely to contract AIDS than the general population—a conclusion based on a paltry response to a mail survey that was a laughable parody of social science. Yet because the series vented against such fundamental church policies as priestly celibacy, its empirical defects were largely overlooked by the editors who selected it. Derogatory depictions of Catholic priests have become stereotypical in our media culture. In a 1998 article about a sexual predator among the Catholic clergy (to cite just one of many examples), the *New York Times* permitted the sole expert it quoted to assert that "there's a deep systemic problem in Catholic culture," without so much as raising an editorial eyebrow.

A recent study by the Center for Media and Public Affairs confirms the popularity of that kind of reporting. In a review of religion coverage in the major news magazines, network evening newscasts and the *New York Times* and *Washington Post,* researchers found that the most frequently discussed topic in the 1990s was sexual morality, while a remarkable one in fourteen stories concerned "crimes or other wrongdoing" involving churches or clergy.

It is true that many news organizations have consciously increased their coverage of religion and spirituality in recent years. Some articles on Christianity's role in history have been complex and first-rate, such as *U.S. News & World Report's* cover story in January 2001 entitled "The Year One A.D." It conveyed not only the cultural distance between Roman society and our own, but also the timelessness of many ancient concerns, and it provided reasons why Christianity might prosper in such a world. But when a major story breaks the mold—for instance, when the *New York Times* reported on Professor John L. Heilbron's revelations about the medieval church's unappreciated support of astronomy—it often has a man-bites-dog tone of wonderment. What, forward-looking Christians?

In mainstream news these days, the word "Christian" most often appears in connection with politics. Because the "Religious Right" provides many of the shock troops for one side of today's "culture wars," it encounters sharply abusive rhetoric in return. Politics being what it is, some of this abuse is inevitable, and is relevant to this book only insofar as it veers into a wholesale condemnation of Christians or a large subset of them—and it often does. Minnesota governor Jesse Ventura's gibe that "organized religion is a sham and a crutch for weak-minded people" who "stick their noses in other people's business" was prompted (his office later tried to explain) by animosity toward the Religious Right in particular. The shower of insult directed in recent years at evangelical and fundamentalist Christians is typified by the *Washington Post's* sneer that they are usually "poor, uneducated and easily led." Such pronouncements apparently resonate with a large segment of the population: according to a study published in *Public*

Opinion Quarterly in 1999, a remarkable 37 percent of highly educated white Americans hold "intensely antagonistic feelings" toward fundamentalists.

This book is not about the Religious Right and its agenda. Nor is it about the Religious Left, as represented by, say, the National Council of Churches. Christian ethical thinking draws no well-marked map for the great bulk of public policy questions—whatever some Christians, of both the Right and the Left, occasionally suggest. Christian opinion on such provocative issues as the teaching of evolution, prayer in school and the death penalty spans a wide spectrum of conviction. Let future historians assess the impact of Christians on contemporary politics; our purpose here is to rectify the common distortions of Christianity's role in history and tell the neglected story of its contributions, particularly where these have been most maligned.

For that reason, our discussion is necessarily both broad and selective. It covers much ground, but is not intended to be a condensed history of Christianity, or anything close to it. Rather, it focuses on the favorite topics of Christianity's fiercest critics. They say that Christians have spent the better part of two thousand years suppressing freedom, individual rights and democracy, while choking off science and most other forms of intellectual inquiry. They say that Christian intolerance has been a major cause of war and oppression, and Christian disdain for the natural world a primary force behind environmental degradation.

That such an indictment goes largely unchallenged is surprising, especially when its particulars are either plainly false or so stripped of context as to be purposefully misleading. We refute this sophistry not by whitewashing the past, but by reminding readers of the overlooked side of the ledger: the wide-ranging achievements and works of mercy that are rarely acknowledged in contemporary discussions of Christianity. We also take the provocative step of making comparisons, where appropriate, with other religions and cultures. Thus we argue that the world is better off in many ways for the rise of Christianity, without whose influence the past two millennia quite probably would have been crueler, poorer and more provincial, as well as less democratic, creative and informed—in a word, less civilized.

Anti-Christian bigotry relies on forgetfulness and loss of perspective. Its antidote is historical memory.

— — —

We expect there will be dissension even on our starting point: that Christianity is the target of a notable amount of contempt from cultural elites. Some will assert that quite the opposite is true. In the presidential campaign of 2000, after all, George W. Bush, when asked during a primary debate to name his favorite political philosopher, cited Jesus Christ; and Al Gore, not to be outdone, let it be known that when confronted with an important decision, he asks himself, "What would Jesus do?" Both Bush and Gore endorsed government aid for faith-based social-service programs. And Gore chose a Jewish running mate, Joseph Lieberman, who mentioned God no fewer than thirteen times in his very first campaign speech—to the satisfaction of a number of Christian commentators.

American politicians tend to use religious language even more generously when they find themselves immersed in scandal. At the Religious Leaders' Breakfast in September 1998, for example, President Clinton publicly confessed to sin and asked the American people to forgive him. This prompted Martin E. Marty of the University of Chicago Divinity School to ask, "In what other republic or industrialized nation would the chief executive or prime minister regard himself as a sort of priest who could convoke clergy and then turn himself into a penitent, turning the American people, as a body, into confessors?" The answer, he said, is "none."[1]

Yet there is less here than meets the ear. The pious words of these politicians represent what scholars call "America's civic religion," a tradition involving "platitudes that reaffirm the religious base of American culture despite being largely void of theological significance," to quote Frederick Mark Gedicks.[2] Moreover, as Yale law professor Stephen L. Carter dryly observes, "The platitudes of America's civil religion are expected and accepted—but they are only platitudes."[3] Those politicians who venture beyond the most perfunctory religious expression will be warned that they are breaching the wall of separation between church and state. And even the kind of pious boilerplate that politicians are permitted on the campaign trail, and that journalists dutifully report, often draws indignation or derision in other circumstances.

Those who mount the attacks on Christianity today presumably see themselves as brave dissenters, manning the same ramparts as iconoclasts like H. L. Mencken, who kicked the shins of organized religion in an era when it wielded far more clout. (Mencken once quipped, "Wouldn't it be terrible if I quoted some reliable statistics which prove that more people are driven insane through religion than by drinking alcohol?") Yet the foes of Christianity today have far more comrades in arms than did Mencken, and the tone has changed.

When we speak of today's "anti-Christian bigotry," we are not referring to good-natured joking. Nor are we concerned when idiosyncratic scribblers draw bizarre religious comparisons, such as Christopher Knight of the *Los Angeles Times* describing the image of guerrilla Che Guevara as that of "an ever-youthful demigod. Chesucristo, superstar." Mr. Knight, after all, is an art critic, and is therefore not required to color inside the lines. What we are talking about is the outright mockery and disparagement of Christians and their heritage that appear in the mainstream news and entertainment media, in the arts and academia, far too often to be treated as eccentric outbursts—and that in the aggregate have decisively shaped the prevailing view of Christianity's past.

Why, for example, would the artistic community in New York City rally en masse to defend a play called *Corpus Christi,* which highlights a gay Jesus having sex with his apostles, without expressing a hint of sympathy for those offended by the play's content? Why would the *New York Times,* joining the boosters of *Corpus Christi,* denounce the alleged "bigotry, violence and contempt for artistic expression" of those who protested against the play, but have nothing to say about the playwright's own bigotry and contempt for Christian conviction? *Corpus Christi* may be the most controversial play in recent years, yet by no means the most vicious. *The Cardinal Detoxes,* for example, featured a Catholic cardinal who murders a woman and bribes a judge. *The Most Fabulous Story Ever Told* depicted the Virgin Mary as a lesbian. *Burning Habits* showcased lesbian nuns in scenes reminiscent of the most lurid anti-Catholic tracts of the nineteenth century.

The intention to shock and degrade has become depressingly commonplace. Consider a film titled *Hell's Angel,* sponsored a few years ago at the Baltimore Museum of Art in association with Johns Hopkins University, depicting Mother Teresa as an opportunistic "ghoul." It was written and narrated by Christopher Hitchens, whose book on Mother Teresa describes her as a "cunning and single-minded" fanatic who exploited the "simple and the humble." The rationale for the film was as spurious as its content: It was part of a series devoted to religious "extremism."

The situation is hardly better in the other arts. "In painting and sculpture," observes John Leo of *U.S. News & World Report*, "the bashing of Christian symbols is so mainstream that it's barely noticed." His litany of examples includes "satirical versions of the Last Supper" and a veritable parade of vile representations of the mother of Jesus: "Mary coming out of a vagina, Mary encased in a condom, Mary in pink panties with breasts partially exposed, an Annunciation scene with the Archangel Gabriel giving Mary a coat hanger for an abortion, Mary pierced with a phallic pipe. . . ." In such a toxic stream, the Brooklyn Museum of Art's notorious "Sensation" exhibit in 1999, featuring a portrait of Mary adorned with elephant dung, seems quite tame.

The critics' response to these assaults on religion has been predictably indulgent. Commenting on the "Sensation" exhibit, the *New York Times* opined that "cultural experimentation and transgression are not threats to civility but part of the texture and meaning of daily life." Early in 2001, the *Times* again leaped to the defense of the Brooklyn Museum, placidly dismissing public indignation over a photographic depiction of Jesus at the Last Supper as a nude black woman. When a gallery in Seattle featured obscene art involving Jesus and the pope, local art critics let it pass without objection.

A similarly tone-deaf approach to religious sensibilities can be found throughout the media. *The Nation* magazine sneeringly referred to Communion hosts as "crackers." National Public Radio calmly aired a musical satirist whose featured song mocked Catholic teachings. On the *Tonight Show*, Jay Leno presided over a skit in which actors dressed as the pope and four bishops twirled huge rosaries while singing verses that mocked Catholic beliefs about the Eucharist. People of deep religious conviction are depicted in the most unflattering light. Eric Siegel of the *Boston Globe*, for instance, declared that "When we do hear someone talking about the living presence of God, it's usually a fathead football player, a Gantryesque evangelist, or a reformed rapper or drug addict."

The influence of religion in politics is regarded as entirely detrimental. Columnist and TV commentator Bonnie Erbe was alarmed by a 1999 poll that found "46 percent of women say politicians should be guided by religious values, up from a much lower 32 percent six years earlier." Why was this frightening? "Women's equality under the law is the first thing to be tossed overboard when religion overtakes government." *Time* magazine's Lance Morrow foresees genuine equality arriving only "when the civilization pivots, at last, decisively—perhaps for the first time since the advent of Christian patriarchy two millenniums ago—toward Woman." When Ireland moved to ease its ban on divorce, CBS reporter Cinny Kennard welcomed this as a liberation from Christian repression. "It's been like an awakening," she exulted. "Ireland, long positioned on the world's stage as a church-dominated backwater, has reinvented itself as a new and energized Emerald Isle. A more open, a more tolerant place." In the same vein, syndicated columnist Robyn Blumner of the *St. Petersburg Times* insisted that "Only when we are unshackled from the institutions that have traditionally tried to control our lives—government and religion—are men and women free to follow their instincts for reason, inquiry and progress."

Prime-time television is a trove of antireligious sentiment. A report released in 1998 by the Parents' Television Council revealed that in the course of 1,800 hours of original prime-time programming, there were ten negative portrayals of religiously devout laypeople for every positive one, and nearly as many negative as positive portrayals of clergy. The genuinely faith-friendly series of recent years, such as *Touched by an Angel* and *Promised Land,* are certainly noteworthy—but partly for being so unusual.

"A change of fundamental importance has occurred in this country, and we have yet to come to grips with it," contends Stanley Kurtz of the Hudson Institute. "Religion itself—at least organized traditional religion—has become controversial in a way that it has never been throughout the whole of American history. With all their concern that no single religion be established by the state, the Founders never imagined a situation in which organized religion as such would be feared or repudiated by large numbers of citizens as a source of oppression."[4]

■ ■ ■

What explains this drumbeat of accusation and derision? One possibility is that the cultural elite sees religious faith as a superstitious worldview with which it cannot respectfully coexist. There is certainly evidence to suggest that America's major opinion shapers value religion much less than the rest of the populace. A significant percentage of journalists, entertainers, artists and intellectuals still identify themselves as Christians, but this proportion is far lower than in the general public.

In a 1996 survey of newspaper journalists by the American Society of Newspaper Editors, just 57 percent described their religious affiliation as Protestant or Catholic. Another study, examining five metropolitan areas around the nation, found major differences between the religious practices of journalists and those of the citizens they cover. The most recent effort to survey all types of journalists (with a sample of 1,037) was conducted in 1992 by Professors David Weaver and Cleveland Wilhoit of Indiana University, who found that although 84 percent of the journalists had been brought up in a Christian faith, only 37.5 percent agreed with the proposition that "religion or religious beliefs" were "very important" to them. By contrast, 61 percent of the general public asked the identical question in a Gallup poll that year answered in the affirmative. And while religious affiliation among journalists apparently rose during the 1990s, according to a survey of the major media by the Center for Media and Public Affairs, it still remained well below that of the overall populace.

The contrast between Hollywood and the rest of the country is even more striking. A 1995 survey by the Center for Media and Public Affairs found that nearly a third of those in the television and movie industry professed no religious affiliation whatsoever, 43 percent said they never attended religious services, and fewer than one in four identified themselves as either Protestant or Catholic.

Politics undoubtedly also contributes to antireligious bigotry. It is no secret that professors and journalists—to say nothing of entertainers and artists—generally tilt toward the political Left. Indeed, the American Society of Newspaper Editors' own 1996 survey identified more than five times as many liberals as conservatives in the nation's larger newsrooms. Religious activism once was largely the province of liberalism, from the time of abolitionism through the 1960s. Since 1973, however, when the Supreme Court declared abortion a constitutional right, religious activism has instead been dominated by political conservatives. Thus the cultural elite tends to identify religious commitment with incorrect politics.

In effect, the stigmatizing of the activist Christian Right has provided an excuse for a generalized antireligious rhetoric, and even for demands that people motivated by faith withdraw from the public square. Still, the hostility is plainly selective, in that other major religions have not been subjected to the same degree of ridicule. A public mocking of Judaism or Islam, such as pro basketball player Charlie Ward's public slam against Jews, typically prompts a stern rebuke by opinion leaders dedicated to preserving civic amity and respect. And rightly so. But why is this not true for mockery of Christians? When a major league pitcher (John Rocker) who indulges in inflammatory ethnic and sexual stereotypes draws nearly universal disapproval and official punishment, why can Ted Turner, the owner of the team that employs the pitcher, mock the pope in one public appearance (John Paul II should "get with it—welcome to the twentieth century") and Christians in another ("losers"), and encounter barely a hint of censure?

Is it possible that Christians themselves essentially permit this? That they don't particularly mind when their beliefs are ridiculed? The historian Thomas Reeves argues that "Christianity in modern America . . . tends to be easy, upbeat, convenient, and compatible. . . . The faith has been overwhelmed by the culture, producing what is rightly called cultural Christianity."[5] He is no doubt correct, but only to a degree. There remain a good many Christians who take their faith very seriously. And there is, we suspect, a point at which most of them do in fact mind, very much, the untruthful trashing of their faith, no matter how it is explained. And they almost certainly have noticed a bitter irony: in attempting to marginalize the Christian faith, America's anti-Christian bigots are committing the very offense they most commonly attribute to Christians themselves—the sin of aggressive intolerance.

■ ■ ■

In discussing the role of Christianity in history, this book plays no favorites. Our definition of Christianity is broad, and our story concentrates on figures and eras that are relevant to our analysis. If Roman Catholic priests once were prominent defenders of Native American human rights, our story will linger over their part in that story. If evangelical Christians dominated the leadership of the antislavery movement in the eighteenth and nineteenth centuries, we will give them their due. If a sect like the Darbyites was unusually active in sheltering Jews in southern France during the Holocaust, we must not forget it.

We realize that irreconcilable differences separate many Christian denominations and sects; but that is a sign of their health. As Roger Finke and Rodney Stark point out in *The Churching of America, 1776–1990*, pluralism is "the natural condition of any unregulated religious economy."[6] Yet there is risk in discussing the achievements of such a wide variety of Christians in a single book. Some readers may ask how a Roman Catholic can be expected to identify with the admirable legacy of Puritan covenant theology, given the anti-Papist violence of the English Civil War. Or how Protestants can appreciate the Dominican defense of indigenous peoples' rights, when that same order of priests helped man the institution that stamped out any chance of a Spanish Reformation.

At this late date, such historical resentments are blindingly self-destructive. The most potent hostility these days to every branch of Christianity emanates not from a rival limb of the faith, but from an aggressive secularism that seeks to confine all religion to a darkened sanctuary. This secularism applauded when the U.S. Sixth Circuit Court of Appeals, in 2000, told the state of Ohio to get rid of its motto, "With God, all things are possible"; when the National Park Service, in the same year, pledged to remove a war memorial in the shape of a cross that had stood in the Mojave Desert for more than half a century; and when successive class valedictorians at Oroville High School in California were barred from mentioning their faith in their commencement addresses. To the militant secularist, religion is a meddlesome, divisive enterprise (aren't its devotees, as Governor Ventura says, always sticking "their noses in other people's business"?), which should be strictly privatized—root, branch and leaf. Religion generally, and Christianity especially, must be neither seen nor heard, except as the butt of an amusing gibe.

This book does not stipulate or assume the truth of the Christian faith. It is written about Christians, but not necessarily for them. For that reason, the vast majority of the authorities cited are historians rather than theologians. If some are rather generously quoted, it is in part to demonstrate that we have not misrepresented their views.

The story of Christianity has sometimes been turbulent and tragic, blood-spattered and cruel, but that is far from the sum total of its legacy. It also boasts magnificent, redeeming achievements—shining moments when civilizing values have seized the upper hand. These too must be remembered.

CHAPTER ONE

CHRISTIANITY
AND THE FOUNDATION
OF THE WEST

Christians, we are often told, are easy to locate. They are the people marooned on the wrong side of history. Again and again, century after dispiriting century, they have dug in their heels against progress. In politics, the critics charge, a Christian's instinctive allegiance has been with despots and oppressors rather than democrats and liberators, with inquisitors and book burners as opposed to probing minds and pamphleteers. Christians have buttressed hierarchy against equality, patriarchy against women's rights, absolutism against individualism, and small-minded tradition against broad-minded tolerance. The most popular version of this indictment sees the whole of Western history since the fall of Rome as a difficult but increasingly successful struggle to wrest the human spirit from the fetters of the Christian church.

"It's not hard to be hostile to the church," Jane Fonda confided to Oprah. After all, "you can go through history, the Crusades and the inquisitions, and the formal church has a lot to apologize for." Fonda's view of the Christian past is not an uncommon one.

The indictment of Christianity as a reactionary faith usually spares the message of Jesus himself, but turns on the earliest church leaders including Paul, on the church fathers of Late Antiquity, and on the clerics of the Middle Ages. Augustine, the most influential of the patristic writers, is frequently seen as a grim prototype of Torquemada, encouraging church absolutism and the persecution of heretical ideas. The medieval church to which he contributed so much is portrayed as a kind of institutional incubus, sucking liberty and creativity out of Europe for hundreds of years. Every presumed sin of Christianity is seen in distilled form in the medieval West.

This is the viewpoint adopted by high school textbooks, as Paul Gagnon confirmed in his study of the five most-read books. "The Middle Ages, when they are mentioned at all," he concludes, "are dark and stagnant, their people without ideas or curiosity, and interested only in life after the grave." Popular historians and critics echo this attitude. For example, in his review of David Fromkin's sweeping survey of world history, *The Way of the World: From the Dawn of Civilization to the Eve of the Twenty-first Century,* Richard Bernstein of the *New York Times* praised the author for dealing "in about half a page with Galileo, Francis Bacon, Rene Descartes and Michel de Montaigne, saying that they were all men of 'skepticism in thought and moderation in action' who helped draw Europe out of 'the long sleep of feudalism.' That is correct, and to be correct is an achievement." The implication is that moving forward required retreating from the medieval faith.

Yet there is a quite different possibility: that the Middle Ages were the incubator for some of our most cherished modern values and institutions, and that the origins of those values and institutions may often be found in an earlier age of the church.

■ ■ ■

"Both slave and free must equally philosophize, whether male or female in sex ... whether barbarian, Greek, slave, whether an old man, or a boy, or a woman.... And we must admit that the same nature exists in every race, and the same virtue." These remarks by Clement of Alexandria (c. 200) cannot be confused with the views of most educated citizens of the Roman Empire in the third century. The sentiments they express would have been equally unusual, or more so, in the other great civilizations of the time: the various empires stretching across Asia, as well as those in the Americas and in Africa south of the Sahara. Clement spoke with the distinctively universalist tone of a Christian. "I would ask you," he declared, "does it not seem to you monstrous that you—human beings who are God's own handiwork—should be subjected to another master, and, even worse, serve a tyrant instead of God, the true king?"

This was explosive stuff, and its force rested in its premise: If human beings are all God's own handiwork—and if, moreover, they are made in God's image, as Christians from the early days believed—then it follows that they must be moral equals. And once they are moral equals, the progress associated with Western civilization cannot be far behind. Without belief in moral equality, there would have been little hope for the rise of the Western legal tradition, with its distinctive feature of equality before the law. The recognition of individual rights would scarcely have been possible. Without moral equality, democracy in the modern sense is not even a serf's fugitive dream.

Of course, it was many centuries after the first appearance of Christian communities before practical political philosophers would write, with self-conscious gravity—and a sense that they were expressing the will of God—"we hold these truths to be self-evident, that all men are created equal," and then found a nation committed to that principle. It took so long, in part, because it had to be *made* self-evident that all men are created equal, and that was the work of centuries. Someone could write such a statement in 1776 and expect his readers not to laugh out loud only because of a common culture steeped in the belief that mankind was "endowed by their Creator with certain unalienable Rights." That culture was a legacy of Western Christendom.

It is not that Christians were the first or only people to insist on the fraternity of mankind and the intrinsic value of each human being. Stoics such as Marcus Aurelius, the second-century Roman emperor, also held that all individuals are equals. Yet there was a grim and cheerless quality about the Stoics, who believed in the suppression of all passions, not just the bad ones, and who touted virtue while denying it had any positive effect. The Stoics never tapped the popular longing for a sense of moral equality in the way Christians did.

Jews of the ancient world put unusual value on human life, and as Elaine Pagels remarks, "Hebrew tradition sometimes reveals a sense of universalism where one might least expect it. Even God's election of Abraham and his progeny includes the promise of a blessing to extend through them to all people, for that famous passage concludes with the words, 'in you all the families of the earth shall be blessed.'"[1] For a time, Judaism appeared a candidate to become a world religion, as converts scurried toward its

3

impressive ethics and clear-headed monotheism. Yet in the end, the tribal legacy of Judaism presented obstacles too great for many pagans to overcome—circumcision being only the most obvious. It was Christianity that proved the more powerful lure. Up and down the social ladder, the doctrine of moral equality was to find an ever-expanding home.

How Christian Ethics Transformed the Pagan World

More than two hundred years after the death of Jesus, midway into the third century, Christians were still a small minority in the Roman Empire—no more than 5 percent of the multiethnic throng by the highest estimates, and probably less than half that much. "They were mostly concentrated in the bigger cities, but they were prominent in towns of varying rank and degree," Robin Lane Fox concludes in *Pagans and Christians*. "Their center of gravity lay with the humbler free classes, not with the slaves, whom they did little to evangelize.... Women of all ranks were conspicuous and there was a notable presence in some churches of women of high status."[2]

What was it that accounted for this particular social profile, if not Christianity's insistence on the equal value of every soul in God's sight? The apostle Paul had said, "there is neither Jew nor Greek, there is neither slave nor free, there is neither male nor female, for you are all one in Christ Jesus," and his words still resonate two thousand years later. How much more potent they must have seemed in an empire in which social class—from emperor down to slave—was so much more confining, and in which the portion of the population that could be bought and sold like oxen seemed to swell with Rome's stupendous military reach.

How much more inspiring, in particular, the early Christian message must have been to women. To put it plainly, women enjoyed higher status and more autonomy among Christians than among pagans, and could expect better treatment from their husbands. Pagan Roman women were "three times as likely as Christians to have married before age 13," according to the sociologist Rodney Stark.[3] Christian women also exercised far more choice in whom they wed, and were less likely to be forced into an abortion (a frequent cause of death for women of the time). The church expected men to remain faithful to their wives, a principle that cut sharply against the Roman norm. If widowed, Christian women enjoyed more freedom to choose for themselves whether to remarry, secure in the knowledge that their congregation would look after them if they elected to remain alone. "It is . . . an established fact, taken from simple evidence, that everywhere progress in free choice of a spouse accompanied progress in the spread of Christianity," declares Regine Pernoud.[4]

Women's status in the church itself was unusually favorable for the times. Wayne Meeks notes that "Both in terms of their position in the larger society and in terms of their participation in the Christian communities . . . a number of women broke through the expectations of female roles."[5] Paul is often rebuked these days for his offhand acceptance of the fact of slavery and for his allegedly regressive views on the status of women. But in fact what distinguished Paul from his non-Christian contemporaries was not the patriarchal views he sometimes expressed, especially in the admonition "Wives, be subject to your husbands as to the Lord," but rather his repeated emphasis on the obligations of husbands to wives. Thomas Cahill writes that in Paul we find "the only clarion affirmation of sexual equality in the whole of the Bible—and the first one ever to be made in any of the many literatures of our planet."[6] A. N. Wilson makes the same point: "In those days, you would have been hard put to find anyone who believed in 'sexual equality' in the modern sense, and the person who comes closest to it is, strangely enough, Paul."[7]

Paul also demanded that converts of Gentile background enjoy the same status as their brethren of Jewish origin, perhaps thereby sparing the Jesus movement a narrow future as another Jewish sect. This accomplishment is more extraordinary than it might now seem. It meant that the competition between paganism and Christianity, as Robert L. Wilken explains in *The Christians as the Romans Saw Them,* was something quite unusual: "a debate about a new concept of religion. . . . The ancients took for granted that religion was indissolubly linked to a particular city or people. Indeed, there was no term for religion in the sense we now use it to refer to . . . a voluntary association divorced from ethnic or national identity."[8] With Paul leading the way, Christianity would shatter this insular outlook for all time.

The crucial difference between pagans and Christians was not, as is commonly supposed, a belief in many gods versus a belief in one. By the first and second centuries, many pagans had begun to conceive of the major Roman gods as aspects of a unified divinity. This "striving after monotheism," in Henry Chadwick's phrase, also took the form of sun worship and an openness to spiritual imports from the East. But Chadwick points out that "Even after the cults of Isis and the Oriental mystery religions had spread from their original homes, there was curiously little sense of universality about their worship."[9] It wasn't the number of their gods that prevented the vast majority of pagans from developing an outlook that transcended town, region, class and sometimes even gender. It was, at least in part, the confining nature of the religious message itself.

To be sure, most early Christians did not hope to transform society to mirror their belief in moral equality. It made as much sense to advocate manned flight as to propose equality before the law in an empire utterly dependent on slaves, with rulers who functioned as a law unto themselves. How could there be moral equality when the emperor was believed to possess something akin to divine powers? Yet even in those early centuries, Christian morality worked like a great shock absorber on everyday life, softening the blows of a frequently pitiless existence and gentling the private realm.

For exhilarating cruelty, few spectacles in human history have surpassed the gladiatorial games. Crowds that included the very best citizens exulted as scores of men, and sometimes many hundreds, slaughtered one another for fleeting fame and honor. Not that they always had much choice in the matter. Elaine Pagels describes the action at the Roman amphitheater in the second century: "The spectators cheered the men who recklessly courted death, and thrilled to the moment of the death blow. The crowd would go wild when a defeated gladiator defiantly thrust out his neck to his antagonist's sword, and they jeered and hooted when a loser bolted in panic."[10] Major imperial shows could deploy thousands of pairs of combatants, not to mention all manner of animals and wild beasts—hounds, lions, bears, bulls—battling one another, or humans, to the death.

Christians deplored this entertainment, and not merely because there was always the chance that they might themselves someday wind up as prey. Rather, they were repulsed by the way this spectacle debased human life. When the Emperor Constantine outlawed gladiator games in the fourth century (or attempted to; they flourished for decades afterward), he did so as an affirmation of Christian values.

Even Edward Gibbon—the great eighteenth-century historian whose *Decline and Fall of the Roman Empire* so provoked pious Christians of his day—had to concede the impressive ethical standards of early Christians. He listed their "pure and austere morals" as the fourth of five reasons for Christianity's remarkable growth before Constantine.[11] Yet this is grudging tribute. It hardly does justice to a morality that rejected the casual practice of infanticide and the abandonment of unwanted babies, opposed the exploitation of children for erotic pleasure, elevated the status of women, accepted and broadened the Jewish tradition of concern for the poor (as Ramsay MacMullen tartly observes, "who outside that tradition in the ancient world would have been recorded on his tombstone as a 'lover of the poor'?"),[12] exalted humility, and tirelessly preached the gifts of charity and love. "Austere" is scant praise indeed for such bedrock beliefs. "Life-affirming" is more like it.

If the amphitheater was the gaudiest manifestation of pagan cruelty, the killing of infants, often by abandoning them on the local dung heap, was the saddest. Boys were disposed of when they were deformed; girls when they were inconvenient. The result was a society—not just in Italy but in the eastern Mediterranean and North Africa—in which males outnumbered females by 30 percent or more. Most families simply refused to raise a second girl. Consider the instructions written by a man named Hilarion to his pregnant wife around the year Jesus was born: "If you are delivered of a child, if it is a boy keep it, if a girl discard it." Such orders were so ordinary, so unexceptional, that they didn't require a single word of justification. Christians, on the other hand, had a starkly different attitude: female infants were to be cherished equally with males as gifts from God.

True, there was great variety among early Christians, such that it is sometimes difficult, in Wayne Meeks's words, "to draw firm boundaries" around their moral beliefs. Yet there is little doubt that within this diversity there existed "a family resemblance of moral traits."[13] Moreover, the contrast between pagan and Christian ethics is not only apparent retrospectively to historians; it was emphasized by early converts like Justin Martyr, who rejoiced at the "innumerable multitude who have reformed intemperate habits." And it was noted repeatedly by anti-Christian pagans of the time.

The Emperor Julian ("the Apostate"), whose last-ditch effort to reverse the Christian tide in 360–63 expired at the point of a Persian arrow, admitted that "It is generosity toward non-members, care for the graves of the dead, and pretended holiness of life that have specially fostered the growth of atheism" (a common term for Christianity at the time). Ammianus Marcellinus, the fourth-century historian who attributed Roman military setbacks to a failure to satisfy pagan gods, nevertheless described Christianity as a "just and gentle" religion. The satirist Lucian of Samosata (c. 170) knew "that the Christians were unbelievably generous with their money and preferred to be open-handed rather than inquire too closely into the recipients." Even the provincial governor Pliny the Younger, who executed Christians for no reason other than their stubborn profession of faith, acknowledged in a letter to the Emperor Trajan that their behavior appeared above reproach, except of course for their regrettable "superstition."

"During the plague in Alexandria," writes Robin Lane Fox, Christians "tended their own sufferers, while the pagans were said to abandon their sick at the first sign of disease; during the siege of the same year, the two Christian leaders contrived to save many old and weak people, Christians first, then pagans, too, later."[14] Moreover, "Whereas the corn doles of pagan cities had been confined to citizens, usually to those who were quite well-off, the Christians' charity claimed to be for those who were most in need."[15]

There is no doubt that Christian charity (about which more later) exercised a powerful pull on converts, and that Christian dedication to the poor, ill, disabled, imprisoned, elderly, widowed and exploited was notable from the outset. Early bishops, for example, were expected to eat one meal a day with the poor. In the larger cities, the church founded orphanages and the forerunners of hospitals. As the Roman Empire spiraled into chaos, the church expanded its philanthropic role until it was virtually the sole recourse of the poor. "St. Gregory is said to have taken his responsibilities so seriously," recounts Christopher Dawson, "that when a single poor man was found dead of hunger in Rome, he abstained from saying Mass as though he were guilty of his death."[16]

It is not that Christian ethics were entirely original; they were substantially Jewish in derivation, although with distinctive accents such as the command to love one's enemies. And it is possible to exaggerate the moral differences between pagans and Christians; for leading pagan citizens were capable of great acts of giving, if not often to the direct benefit of the poor, then at least to the local community and to their gods. Much of Christian ethics can be found articulated by pagan philosophers.

"Hence the paradox of the rise of Christianity as a moral force in the pagan world," observes Peter Brown.

> The rise of Christianity altered profoundly the moral texture of the late Roman world. Yet in moral matters the Christian leaders made almost no innovations. What they did was more crucial. They created a new group, whose exceptional emphasis on solidarity in the face of its own inner tensions ensured that its members would practice what pagan and Jewish moralists had already begun to preach.[17]

The result was that the ethical differences in practice between the pagan and Christian worlds could be stark. The concepts of mercy and humility were not just unappreciated in pagan culture, they were ridiculed by men of the highest learning. The idea that God put us on earth to love one another—that the duty of charity demolished family and community boundaries—was radically offensive to many wellborn pagans.

Gibbon believed that paganism had lost its religious vigor by the time of Jesus, becoming little more than a façade for vacant materialism. Some modern historians disagree. To Robert Wilken, for example, "the debate between paganism and Christianity in antiquity was at bottom a conflict between two religious visions. The Romans were not less religious than the Christians."[18] Yet even if the pagan and Christian outlooks overlapped at points, there was no reconciling the differences. "The Christian principle, 'Love your enemies,' is good," quipped Bertrand Russell, "but the Stoic principle, 'Be indifferent to your friends,' is bad. And the Christian principle does not inculcate calm, but an ardent love even towards the worst of men. There is nothing to be said against it except that it is too difficult for most of us to practice sincerely."[19]

But beginning in the first century, a swelling parade of men and women announced that they would try.

How Church/State Rivalry Prevented
the Total Domination of Either

When Theodosius the Great allowed the Visigoths, in the year 382, to settle within the Roman Empire in return for their promise to fight as allies, he committed one of those slow-moving blunders that take years to ripen into full catastrophe. The emperor had chosen a policy of coexistence rather than confrontation, believing that the barbarians could be contained, neutralized, exploited. Instead, by slow degrees, they and future invaders seized ever larger pieces of the empire, culminating first in the Sack of Rome in 410 and finally in the collapse of the Western Empire in 476.

Yet much as he sought to avoid a showdown with barbarians squatting on his territory, Theodosius was no pacifist. Like his predecessors, he countered challenges to imperial authority with a mailed fist. It was just such an incident that produced one of the defining moments in all of Christian, and indeed Western, history.

The spark was lit in 390 by a mob in Thessalonica that murdered an officer of the garrison. When Theodosius heard of it, he reacted with fury, ordering a wholesale reprisal. Roman troops set upon a large crowd assembled in the circus, and in a breathtaking massacre, slaughtered upwards of seven thousand. In an earlier age, the incident would have ended there. An emperor who wades through the blood of innocents need never glance back—unless, that is, he happens to be a nominal Christian and is called to account by the likes of Bishop Ambrose of Milan.

Ambrose had counseled Theodosius against his butchery, and now he threw down the gauntlet: The emperor must repent or the Holy Eucharist would be withheld from him. In his letter of condemnation, Ambrose declared, "There was that done in the city of the Thessalonians of which no similar record exists, which I was not able to prevent happening; which, indeed, I had before said would be most atrocious when I so often petitioned against it." Pointedly noting the biblical example of David's repentance, the bishop then wheeled out his heavy cannon: "I dare not offer the sacrifice if you intend to be present. Is that which is not allowed after shedding the blood of one innocent person, allowed after shedding the blood of many? I do not think so."

It was an act of magnificent valor, but even more memorable for the principle it enshrined: No ruler was above God's law, and no churchman might trample on that law in the service of his sovereign. The church's moral authority flowed from God, not the state.

Of course there is no particular reason why even a Christian emperor like Theodosius would necessarily flinch at such a high-handed challenge. There must have been a close moment or two as a result. Yet in the end, Theodosius consented to public penance at the cathedral in Milan. Ambrose had risked everything to assert ecclesiastical preeminence in moral judgment. In so doing, he provided an example that would echo through the centuries.

Ambrose and the other stiff-necked clerics who followed would help to check secular authorities in the Christian world from seizing the kind of suffocating, unimpeded power that rulers elsewhere usually enjoyed. They didn't do this because they endorsed a separation of powers in the modern sense. Medieval popes sometimes asserted not only independence but even supremacy over secular lords, and were often willing to exercise civil power when it fell their way. Yet the practical effect of their confrontations with temporal powers would be deeply important for the growth of freedom and the carving out of separate spheres of influence.

This was not Ambrose's first gamble on behalf of church prerogatives. A few years before, during the ascendancy of Valentinian II in the west, Ambrose had defied a direct order by the Empress Justina that he turn over a church to those who professed the Arian creed; he and throngs of supporters held out even after Gothic soldiers were dispatched to seize the basilica. "The counts and tribunes came and urged me to cause the basilica to be quickly surrendered, saying that the Emperor was exercising his rights since everything was under his power," Ambrose explained in a letter. "I answered that if he asked of me what was mine, that is, my land, my money, or whatever of this kind was my own, I would not refuse it, although all that I have belonged to the poor, but that those things which are God's are not subject to the imperial power."

Fortunately for Ambrose, the Goths—who might just as easily pillage as parley—were in no mood for a massacre. The bishop prevailed. Even if he were not a father of the Christian church, he would surely be remembered as one of very few unarmed men in all of Roman history to succeed in forcing more than one emperor to blink.

Although Ambrose lived decades after Constantine's Edict of Milan (A.D. 313), which ended the era of Christian persecution, he proved that church leaders (at least in the west) were not about to forget their past. Three hundred years of anxious, sometimes furtive, existence had molded a psychology of defiance and even contempt for the lordly pretensions of secular powers. This psychology was braced by what Richard Fletcher describes as the "rich Judaic literature of exile which was developed by early Christian writers,"[20] and by a Gospel that demanded Christians to distinguish between what they owed Caesar and what they owed God. Church leaders and philosophers who had risked martyrdom before the fourth century—and it was they who mainly had been targeted, not average communicants—were followed by men like Ambrose who maintained the same unchained spirit. "In matters of faith," Ambrose declared, "bishops are wont to be the judges of Christian emperors, not emperors of bishops."

Ambrose was not the most impudent of fourth-century churchmen. Christopher Dawson recounts how when the Emperor Constantius II attempted to meddle in ecclesiastical issues, he was "met with vehement opposition from two quarters: from Athanasius, the great bishop of Alexandria, and from the West, where the doctrine of the independence of the Church was uncompromisingly maintained, above all by St. Hilary and Hosius, the famous bishop of Cordova."[21] Hosius let Constantius have it without a speck of reserve:

> Remember that you are a mortal man. Fear the day of judgment.... Do not interfere in ecclesiastical affairs, or dictate anything about them to us, but rather learn from us what you ought to believe concerning them. God has given to you the government of the Empire and to us that of the Church. Whosoever dares to impugn your authority, sets himself against the order of God. Take care lest you likewise render yourself guilty of a great crime by usurping the authority of the Church. We are commanded to give unto Caesar the things that are Caesar's and to God the things that are God's. It is not lawful for us to arrogate to ourselves the imperial authority. You also have no power in the ministry of holy things.

As bold as such language was, it lacked a certain intellectual heft. That would be supplied in due course by Augustine (354–429), the great North African bishop of Hippo and, after Paul, the most important Christian philosopher of the first millennium. He wrote *The City of God* after the Sack of Rome in 410 had staggered the empire's self-confidence, and pagans were interpreting it as the vengeance of their now-neglected gods. Augustine countered with the long view: Empires rise and fall in the natural order of things, but the church's mission stands apart from any passing secular institution. Because the true church endures, it is government's duty to take instruction from religion, not the other way around. This view could reinforce arrogance and absolutism in the church, and eventually it did. Yet Augustine's political theory also provided a basis for ideals of human freedom and individual rights.

Augustine saw that the state often became a ravenous predator, in need of restraint. "Without justice, what then are kingdoms but great robberies?" he asked. "For what are robberies themselves but little kingdoms?" Still, he was not propounding an antigovernment theory. Because of man's fallen nature, he regarded the state as a necessary instrument for maintaining order. "Sinful man hates the equality of all men under God," he explained, "and, as though he were God, loves to impose his own sovereignty upon his fellow men." The state could at least keep these predators at bay—an essential but hardly exalted function.

In effect, Fletcher writes, Augustine "detached the state—any state, but in particular, of course, the Roman state—from the Christian community. Under his hands the Roman empire became theologically neutral."[22] By clearly delimiting the role of secular powers, Augustine helped set Western Christendom on a course in which the believer's duties to God (however interpreted) might trump his obligations to the state. It is impossible to understand the West's unique tradition of the dissenting conscience without granting Augustine his due.

The ancients tended to equate an individual's well-being with that of society. It is no wonder that "there seems to be scarcely any discussion of individual liberty as a conscious political ideal (as opposed to its actual existence) in the ancient world," as Isaiah Berlin once noted.[23] Yet the concept of the individual is embedded in the biblical emphasis on the sanctity of each life, which reaches its summit in Jesus' final commandment to his apostles that they "love one another as I have loved you." Augustine helped develop the concept of the individual by introducing to Western thought what Charles Taylor calls the "first-person standpoint."

13

Indeed, in his *Confessions,* a highly personal memoir, Augustine became "the first to make the first-person standpoint fundamental to our search for the truth."[24] It is no accident that when the discussion of individual liberty finally breaks into view, it is a gift of Christendom—in no small part because of the bishop of Hippo.

To be sure, Augustine is often burdened with precisely the opposite legacy. As Elaine Pagels observes, "Later in his life Augustine came to endorse, for the church as well as the state, the whole arsenal of secular government that [John] Chrysostom had repudiated—commands, threats, coercion, penalties, and even physical force."[25] Thomas Cahill goes so far as to dub Augustine the "father of the Inquisition" for applauding the persecution of the Donatist heresy in North Africa and then writing "the first Catholic justification for state persecution of those in error: error has no rights; to disbelieve in forced conversions is to deny the power of God; and God must whip the son he receives. . . . Augustine, the last great man of Roman antiquity, is going over the edge."[26]

Hardly. There is no doubt that Augustine sowed a number of minefields for later Christians to pick their way through: his somewhat sour attitude toward sex (which in fact was not uncommon among pagan intellectuals of late antiquity), his belief in every individual's predestined fate, his doctrine of original sin with its unnerving implications for those who remained unbaptized through no fault of their own—and his eventual enthusiasm for coercion. But critics who dress him in jack boots do so only by plucking him from his time. While the Roman Empire did tolerate, within limits, a variety of religions, it never embraced religious liberty in the modern sense. The imperial state was, Chadwick remarks, a place "where personal freedom counted for little . . . where the secret police . . . seemed ubiquitous, and where the screams of those under judicial torture and the gibbets of arbitrary executions were common sounds and sights."[27] Christians who lived under pagan emperors had meanwhile nurtured a remarkable commitment to nonviolence. There is apparently no record of their initiating attacks against pagan neighbors. A few, such as Tertullian, actually seemed to have broken through to a deeper conception of religious freedom. "It should be considered absurd," he concluded, "for one person to compel another to honor the gods."

By comparison, Augustine may sound brutal—but he also sounds like a man of his time. "There was religious intolerance all around," Garry Wills notes in his biography of the bishop. "It was not an aberration but the norm. Augustine, however, supplied something that was new—a theory of suppression. It is a sign of the general acceptance of religious intolerance that no one had felt the need to justify it." What is more, Augustine "formed his theory as a matter of conscience, trying to reconcile his own acts with his own values. In the process he mitigated what were harsher measures, gave a didactic restriction to repression, and opposed torture or execution."[28]

When the Vandals burst into North Africa from Spain in 429, they did not require lessons from Augustine or anyone else in the fine art of repression. Catholic and Donatist alike was tortured and put to the sword. Augustine might have fled, but stayed instead with his flock to face the siege and the inevitable slaughter. He died before Hippo fell, a firsthand witness to the uncertain prospects for the City of Man.

Thanks in part to Augustine, neither church nor state in the West would ever have an easy time absorbing the other. "It is not that the church or the state directly advocated religious freedom or any other freedom," writes Paul Marshall, a professor of philosophy and a senior fellow at Freedom House.

> They did not, and often inquisitions were defended. But people in both realms always believed that there should be boundaries, and they struggled over centuries to define them. This meant that the church, whatever its lust for civil control, had always to acknowledge that there were forms of political power which it could and should not exercise. And the state, whatever its drive to dominate, had to acknowledge that there were areas of human life that were beyond its reach.[29]

David Landes spells out the implications: "Earthly rulers were not free to do as they pleased, and even the Church, God's surrogate on earth, could not flout rights and take at will. . . . All of this made Europe very different from [other] civilizations around."[30]

How Christianity Preserved Civilization and Then Extended It

What does a man contemplate on the road up from Rome to parley with Attila, king of the Huns? Does he dwell on the fate of Milan, Verona or Pavia, all of which were brutalized by the Hun army to the point of civic and economic collapse? Or does he ponder the obliteration of Aquileia, which could hardly be found when Attila was through with it? Aquileia had virtually disappeared—razed, burnt, eliminated.

The road to Rome was open to Attila. What humanitarian arguments could one marshal to persuade a great and pitiless warrior that he should spare an ancient city from fire and sword? We don't know precisely what Pope Leo said to Attila when he appeared before him at Mantua in 452, but whatever the plea was, it seemed to work. Attila pulled back. Or perhaps his timely change of heart had something to do with the plague racing through his army, his imperiled supply lines, or the shortage of food. Whatever the cause of Attila's retreat, he and Pope Leo had set a pattern that would endure for more than five hundred years. Time after time, on their own initiative, the best and bravest of Christian clerics would gamble their lives in attempts to tame the barbarian heart.

Leo himself tried again three years later, when he met the Vandal Gaiseric at the gates of Rome in the hope of deflecting him from wanton destruction. Gaiseric complied, in a manner of speaking. He pillaged Rome with the artful control of a second-story man, while leaving the looted city more or less intact.

In the centuries to come, the contrast between Christian peacemaker and barbarian brute would not always be so stark, of course. Sometimes the peacemaker and the brute were kinsmen, even brothers, nominally of the same faith, living side by side in the same kingdom. And sometimes the brute was the Christian leader himself, particularly when coercion offered a shortcut to the otherwise painstaking labor of conversion.

In the waning years of the fourth century, mobs of Christian enthusiasts, aided by recent laws or simply indulged by imperial troops, smashed pagan shrines and closed their temples—as if determined to pay back three hundred years of intermittent repression in the space of a lifetime or two. Long after Constantine, vast reaches of countryside were Christian in little more than name, and the tenacity of primitive folk cults was a recurring scandal. The measures employed by some church messengers, like Martin of Tours in the later fourth century, were hardly more sophisticated than the cults they opposed. Realizing that abstract argument had no chance to win the day, ancient evangelists often resorted to raw proofs of the power of their God. "Miracles, wonders, exorcism, temple-torching and shrine-smashing were in themselves acts of evangelization," explains Fletcher.[31]

Christian heroism took new forms as the empire collapsed, to be parceled out among various hordes of barbarians, some of the Arian creed (like the Visigoths) and others heathen (Huns, Franks, Angles, Saxons and others who poured into northern and central Europe). As Chadwick recounts, "the task of organizing local resistance often fell in the main to the bishops. One Hun attack on a town in Thrace was resisted only by the energy of the local bishop who placed a huge ballista [a catapult for hurling stones] under the patronage of St. Thomas and then fired it himself to such purpose that he scored a direct hit on the barbarian chief."[32] Not every bishop remained at his post, but enough did to ensure that the fate of classical culture in the West soon rested solely in the church's hands, where it would remain for hundreds of years.

In the ninth and tenth centuries, Western Christendom was pounded from all sides, with Vikings slamming from the north and west, Muslims from the south, and Magyars from the east. Even during this turmoil, lives of peaceful example were never in short supply. It is difficult to exaggerate the significance of ascetic monks, an import from Asian/African Christianity, on the course of European history. Thomas Cahill has told the best-selling tale of how Irish monks "saved civilization"—a grand claim, yet one surely merited by the facts. Not only did these monks salvage Latin literature from impending oblivion, they scattered across Europe scores of monasteries that restored learning and books to their rightful place. They also reinvigorated the literary spirit and offered to pagan peasants a compelling example of the power of the Christian message.

Cahill disdains the rival Benedictine tradition as "a monasticism of disciplined uniformity, enforced—through floggings, if necessary—by an autocratic abbot."[33] This is like scorning a Marine because he failed to enroll at Julliard. What the Benedictines may have lacked in playful irreverence and intellectual audacity (but only in comparison with the Irish monks) they more than made up for in sheer dedication and patient scholarship. "St. Benedict found the world, physical and social, in ruins," John Henry Newman wrote memorably more than a hundred years ago, and his mission was to restore it in the way not of science, but of nature, not as if setting about to do it, not professing to do it by any set time, or by any rare specific, or by any series of strokes, but so quietly, patiently, gradually, that often till the work was done, it was not known to be doing. It was a restoration rather than visitation, correction or conversion. The new work which he helped to create was a growth rather than a structure. Silent men were observed about the country, or discovered in the forest, digging, clearing and building; and other silent men, not seen, were sitting in the cold cloister, tiring their eyes and keeping their attention on the stretch, while they painfully copied and recopied the manuscripts which they had saved. There was no one who contended or cried out, or drew attention to what was going on, but by degrees the woody swamp became a hermitage, a religious house, a farm, an abbey, a village, a seminary, a school of learning and a city.[34]

These painstaking efforts of draining, clearing, planting and building came to be—at least in west, north and central Europe— "the prime economic facts of the entire Dark Ages," writes Paul Johnson. "In a sense they determined the whole future history of Europe: they were the foundation of its world primacy. The operation was so huge, and took place over so long a period—nearly a millennium—that no one element in society can claim exclusive credit: it was a collective effort. But it was the monasteries that led the movement and long sustained it."[35] It was monasteries, too, that helped give birth to Europe's unrivaled tradition of mechanical and technical invention, from clocks to brewing, from mining to waterpower. Books were only one of many legacies of the monastic movement, if no doubt the most consequential.

Even in early times, to be sure, a few monasteries resembled privileged fraternities more than barracks for the devout. Some bishops, for that matter, luxuriated in feasting, fine clothes and the hunt. "The gap between precept and practice is as old as human moral teaching," Fletcher observes. "It is not, therefore, a difficult matter to assemble evidence for clerical behavior which fell short of the ideal enunciated by rigorists."[36] But an ideal may still be important even where it is widely flouted. If nothing else, Christian ideals and ethics functioned like a gravitational force, slowly pulling into their orbit those who repeatedly heard them.

The virtues of charity, patience, humility and love for those outside one's immediate circle are difficult enough to practice even after they have been absorbed into the cultural lifeblood through generations of ethical teaching. Their chances are slimmer still in a world dominated by the warrior spirit and memories of heroic combat, as was still the case throughout the Dark Ages. Indeed, on the northern fringes of what had been the Roman Empire, the religions displaced by Christianity sometimes still involved human sacrifice, and almost always paid homage to a god of war. "Through-out the heathen period in northern Europe there was clear need of a god of war," explains H. R. Ellis Davidson in *Gods and Myths of Northern Europe*. "The story of the Germanic peoples and the Vikings is one in which local battles, feuds, invasions, and wars on a national scale are the order of the day."[37] This is the world, so alien to us today, that Christianity gradually absorbed and transformed.

How Christianity Set the Stage for the Rule of Law
The Middle Ages have become an embarrassment to many Christians, in no small part because of descriptions like this one by Cambridge professor Patrick Collinson:

> It is with the twelfth century that we come to the greatest challenge confronting the historically naive Christian who may fondly suppose that his religion has been consistently faithful to the boundless philanthropy of its founder. For it is at this point in history ... that the Christian West, that is to say the Church itself, became what Professor Robert Moore has called a "persecuting society," the exact inversion of a martyr society. That society, often regarded in retrospect as Christianity in a state of religious and social perfection, now became a gross and habitual violator of human rights.[38]

It is difficult to say who, in this age of apology, might be those naive Christians who still have no inkling of the depressing persecutions of Jews and heretics during the Middle Ages, or the monstrous bloodletting of the Crusades. After all, there are regular reminders of these in mainstream news stories. In 1999, for example, on the 900th anniversary of the crusaders' conquest of Jerusalem, hundreds of Christians were on hand in that ancient city, fresh from a Reconciliation Walk begun in Germany, to apologize to one and all for their ancestors' frightful behavior. If there is ignorance among the faithful, it pertains to dark episodes from other eras, like Charlemagne's merciless conversion of the Saxons in the eighth century, a campaign so brutal that the Nazis would resurrect its memory twelve centuries later in order to justify their anti-Christian policies. But what historically naive Christians mainly fail to appreciate about medieval Christendom are not its moral lapses, but its extraordinary achievements.

They are unlikely to know, for example, that the Middle Ages were the incubator for representative and constitutional government, based on the principle that power must have clearly defined limits. They would perhaps be surprised to discover in this era the growth of enforceable property rights and taxation by consent. They are unlikely to have learned that the diffusion of the Bible's skeptical view of secular power—I Samuel 8 was an especially popular citation—helped to check the ambitions of would-be tyrants. They are probably unaware that the same popes who, to their everlasting shame, introduced the Inquisition also helped throttle feudal lawlessness and humbled more than one monarch angling for absolute power.

The church's resistance to secular bullies was not merely a means of protecting its own power. Its humanitarian and civilizing mission was meant to benefit directly the mass of peasants as well. The barbarian challenge had largely been thrown back by the end of the tenth century, but habits of lawless pillage and private warfare endured. As David Landes writes, "The tenth and eleventh centuries were filled with baronial brigandage, eventually mitigated by popular, Church supported revulsion and outrage that found expression in mass 'peace' assemblies; and from the top down, subdued by stronger central government allied with urban interests."[39] These peace assemblies, which in some respects resembled modern mass demonstrations, were instigated in south and central France by local bishops, and they quickly spread. In every locale they were led by clergy. Bishop Fulbert of Chartres declared in his lyrical verses: "The spear is made into a pruning hook and the sword into a plowshare; peace enriches the lowly and impoverishes the proud. Hail, Holy Father, and grant salvation to all who love the quiet of peace."

The church's efforts to rein in the lingering warrior spirit even helped create the code of chivalry. Christopher Dawson explains, "The ancient barbarian motive of personal loyalty to the war leader was reinforced by higher religious motives, so that the knight finally becomes a consecrated person, pledged not only to be faithful to his lord, but to be the defender of the Church, the widow and the orphan.... In this way the knight was detached from his barbarian and pagan background and integrated into the social structure of Christian culture."[40]

The church also put checks on the greater powers. Medieval popes and bishops of a reformist bent, beginning with Gregory VII in 1073, never stopped badgering princely rulers with reminders of their duties to those who served them. Medieval kings did not usually possess the absolute powers that later monarchs would seize. And since kings were consecrated, it was believed, by God, they were expected to keep their oaths, meet their legal obligations, and recognize the prerogatives of the church. Gregory VII was adamant about this, and his hectoring was vital to what Paul Johnson describes as "the most important political development of the second millennium," the rule of law.[41]

The church had long been carrying the Roman tradition of law into barbarian backwaters, at first simply by writing down and organizing the customary rules of these illiterate tribes. But even the legalistic civilization of Rome, which guarded private property more successfully than most rival nations, fell far short of the rule of law in the modern sense. For one thing, not everyone was equally subject to the law. The emperor answered to no one. Most residents of the empire were not even citizens, and a huge number were slaves. Although descending from Roman tradition, church canon law under Gregory operated with a different purpose. As Johnson describes it, canon law provided a "refuge for the physically weak and oppressed—not just the clergy themselves but women, children, the poor and the sick—against the rule of force and fear in an age when the armored knight dispensed what law there was. Gregory won some battles, lost others.... But his successors carried on the struggle until churches and monasteries, nunneries and all consecrated ground, at least, were free from arbitrary sword."[42]

Thomas à Becket (1118–70) for a time even persuaded his fellow English bishops to qualify their traditional oath of obedience to the "ancient customs" of the kingdom. His murder in Canterbury Cathedral so shocked the Christian world that Henry II, in a replay of Theodosius' humiliation, was forced into public penance. Unlike ancient and modern despots, medieval monarchs lacked either a divine or a legal right to do whatever they pleased.

And while this was by no means solely the church's doing—diffusion of power in western Europe resulted from many factors, including a tough and militant nobility who resisted royal encroachments with their swords—the church clearly played a leading role.

Roots of Capitalism and Popular Consent

The medieval groping toward legal equality was far from complete, but its ultimate significance extended well beyond the treatment of the individual to the shape of the economy itself. Market economies depend upon the secure ownership of property, and property is secure only when the law treats everyone alike. In *The Noblest Triumph,* Tom Bethell's history of property rights, the author contends that the medieval world was still too highly regulated—thanks in part to the church—to nurture a thriving market economy. But he acknowledges that "something about the Christian teaching was essential to the emergence of the market order; in particular, belief in the underlying equality of human nature."[43] Bethell explains, "Just as all were equal in the eyes of God, so it began to be recognized that all should be equal before the law. . . . The feature of law that is most conducive to the modern market system is equality before the law."[44]

In fact, a great deal more of Christian teaching undoubtedly came into play. A market economy thrives in a culture of invention and creativity. This too was a distinctive gift of the Christian West, which flowered in its first full glory during the medieval era. The Judeo-Christian belief in the dignity of manual labor also played a role. And although Christian culture has had its share of sybarites and showoffs, Christianity itself has always honored humility and modesty—something that cannot be said for either the pagan culture of imperial Rome or the barbarians who engulfed it. Finally, the "emergence of the market order" required a belief in progress and a sense of linear time, both of which achieved their fullest expression in a Christian context. At its core, the idea of progress is an expression of optimism, an embrace of human possibility.

It is no wonder that the first true renaissance in western Europe occurred not in the sixteenth century but in the twelfth, soon after the consolidation of Christian civilization. It was then that scholastic philosophers began their wholesale effort to retrieve and reinterpret the treasures of ancient learning, culminating in the brilliant work of Thomas Aquinas in the thirteenth century. "One of the curious things about the Middle Ages is that they were original and creative without knowing it," Bertrand Russell once noted. "The scholastics, however they might revere Aristotle, showed more originality than any of the Arabs—more, indeed, than any one since Plotinus, or at any rate since Augustine. In politics as in thought, there was the same distinguished originality."[45]

In the thirteenth century, representative assemblies become a common feature of civil government. "This probably owed something to the example of the church," concludes Professor Antony Black, "since representative church councils were the obvious and, indeed, the only precedent."[46] Any association between Christianity and early republicanism may seem surprising, given the church's history of alliances with various monarchical thrones. But early Christianity had embraced election of bishops and participatory decision making on a wide scale, even generating "the entirely new idea of a general consensus achievable by representatives of all peoples in an ecumenical council of bishops." If these republican habits had withered during the early Middle Ages, they had not been discarded. The medieval church continued to rely upon representative councils, while religious orders such as the Franciscans held elections and practiced a form of self-governance that required cooperative consent. Thomas Aquinas himself was no friend of either absolute secular power or papal theocracy, actually arguing, according to Black, that "divine law prescribed election."[47]

Far from being a dead or stagnant time, the Middle Ages must go down as an unusually fertile, creative and even liberating era, on a variety of fronts. And despite periods of almost stupefying turmoil, and leaders of sometimes stunning greed and cynicism, the Middle Ages could and did produce Christians of such unequaled moral example as St. Francis of Assisi, whose boundless love and high spirits made sure that even pigeons were not excluded from his sermons.

CHAPTER TWO

CHRISTIANITY
AND SLAVERY

Despite being a religion supposedly dedicated to the downtrodden, it is said, Christianity offered a justification for slavery right from the outset, in the approving words of Paul, and its embrace of human bondage only strengthened over time. Church leaders during the Roman Empire counseled submission of slave to master, reinforcing the brutal exploitation of the time. By the Middle Ages, a militant church deployed slavery as a weapon, authorizing its use against the infidel—an ominous sign of things to come. As Europe expanded behind its great explorers, Christian leaders refined theories that lent aid and comfort to conquest—and, by the nineteenth century, to some of the most brutal slaveholding systems the world had ever known. By the time of slavery's demise, black bondsmen were being told that their condition was divinely ordained, the result of the Biblical curse of Ham.

"Christianity as an organized religion has to redeem itself on many fronts," declares Bill Maxwell, a *St. Petersburg Times* columnist.

> Sure, I trust certain individual Christians, care for them and admire them, but I keep a wary eye on this thing called Christianity. Growing up, I witnessed many atrocities committed by Southern Baptists and some Methodists. I know of white preachers who stood in their pulpits and delivered racist sermons. The Southern Baptist Convention, in fact, was founded before the Civil War by whites who saw no ethical conflict between worshiping Christ, owning slaves and going to heaven no less.

24

Maxwell's viewpoint is common among those who denounce Christianity for having supported slavery at one time or another. While the sins of the faithful are rehearsed at length, the grand redemption orchestrated by Christian abolitionists is neglected. David Brewster takes much the same tack in a column for Scripps Howard News Service. "The slavery of America's antebellum South found support in the theology of many of men's churches," he writes, "until the nation ran red with blood and the righteousness of reason prevailed." Brewster's entire column contrasts "reason," "science" and "justice" with what he takes to be the backward follies of organized religion. In the *New York Times,* William McDonald meanwhile wonders "how an institution that spread a message of love . . . could also engage in brutality and persecution and turn a blind eye to slavery."

Hollywood appears equally reluctant to give religious abolitionists their due, even in a story where the abolitionist cause was absolutely central. Steven Spielberg's *Amistad,* recounting the true story of fifty-three Africans who mutinied on a slave ship in 1839, discounts the critical role played by white evangelical abolitionists, and even presents them as feckless hypocrites. The one great abolitionist depicted in the film, Lewis Tappan, is portrayed as brutally indifferent toward the Africans whose lives are at stake.

Granted, it is not news that one-dimensional portrayals of Christianity's attitude toward slavery emanate from Hollywood or from such organizations as the Council for Secular Humanism. (According to a document on the council's website, "The official position of Christian clergy was approval and support of participation in slave trading despite the horrendous suffering it produced. Slavery was a close companion of Christianity and was not thought to conflict with religious doctrines.") What is surprising is for a similarly dim view of religion to be expressed by a mainstream historian like Arthur M. Schlesinger Jr., who in a speech at Brown University in 1989 deplored religion's "enthusiastic justifications" for slavery, persecution, torture and genocide.

Nor do the critics stop at downplaying or ignoring Christian opposition to slavery. As John H. Bunzel documented in the *Public Interest* a few years ago, some Afrocentric scholars characterize Christianity as a "white supremacy religion" while deriding abolitionists as hypocrites whose motives had little to do with genuine concern for slaves. No less striking is the claim of a leading

25

high school history textbook of the 1990s, *Rise of the American Nation* (Harcourt, Brace, Jovanovich): that slavery was unknown in North America until introduced by Europeans. Perhaps the most single-minded portrayal to date (at least by a serious historian) of Christianity as an inherently oppressive, racist religion is *The Arrogance of Faith: Christianity and Race in America from the Colonial Era to the Twentieth Century.* In that 1990 work, Forrest Wood argues that "Christianity has been fundamentally racist in its theology, organization and practice." Indeed, according to Professor Wood, "English North-Americans embraced slavery because they were Christians, not in spite of it."

■ ■ ■

Christianity was born into a world teeming with slaves and quickly came to terms with the ancient institution. Yet there were tremors of discontent among the faithful virtually from the inception of the new religion. Early Christians like Justin Martyr deplored the buying and selling of children for prostitution. Others railed against the trade in gladiators. In the early fifth century, St. Patrick rejected all forms of slavery, apparently the first public person in history to adopt such a categorical stand.

The attitude of Patrick's more influential contemporary, Augustine, was more complex. On the one hand, Augustine wrote that "slavery has been imposed by the just sentence upon the sinner." Yet while the church might teach "slaves to be loyal to their masters," it would also teach that masters be "more inclined to persuade than to punish." In *The City of God,* moreover, Augustine even suggested that God "did not intend that His rational creature, who was made in His image, should have dominion over anything but the irrational creation—not man over man, but man over the beasts." Slavery was "an inconceivable horror" in this view, "introduced by sin and not by nature."

As Paul Johnson writes, Christianity has been "the one great religion which had always declared the diminution, if not the final elimination, of slavery to be meritorious."[1] It would be Christians who eventually pulled themselves free from the historic status quo and organized the movement that ended slavery everywhere they held sway. The speed of this accomplishment was breathtaking. Robert William Fogel observes, "It is remarkable how rapidly, by historical standards, the institution of slavery gave way before the abolitionist onslaught, once the ideological campaign gained momentum." Like many others, Fogel sets the beginning of this onslaught in 1787, "the year a handful of English Friends and evangelicals launched a public campaign against the slave trade," and its conclusion in 1888, with the emancipation of slaves in Brazil. Thus, "within the span of a little more than a century, a system that had stood above criticism for 3,000 years was outlawed everywhere in the Western world."[2]

In this respect, declares James Walvin, "The impact of Christianity was seismic."[3] No other human rights campaign compares to the ending of slavery. The fact that its heroes are largely unknown in our day represents an intellectual scandal of the first order.

From Saint Paul to Sojourner Truth

When Christianity was emerging in the ancient world, slavery was not considered a "peculiar institution." It was accepted as part of life. "No one escaped some contact with slavery, and no Greek seriously questioned the need for the practice," writes Milton Meltzer.[4]

Plato, though much ahead of his time regarding women's rights, welcomed slavery into his ideal Republic. Aristotle insisted in his *Politics* that "From the hour of their birth some are marked out for subjection, others for rule." Slavery, he explained, was good for all parties: "the master gained a worker, and the slave came under the guidance of a superior, reasonable being." This argument would have many adherents, and was still popular more than two thousand years later among some of the most socially refined residents of the American South.

It was certainly the reigning belief in the Roman Empire. Edward Gibbon estimated that slaves equaled the number of free men by the time of Claudius (A.D. 41–54), and the eminent historian may not have been far off. Given their numbers, slaves naturally could be found in an astonishing variety of occupations, as J. P. V. D. Baldson describes:

> for sex (pretty boys for homosexuals, prostitutes for the brothels), for public entertainment (gladiatorial trainees), for administration (imperial and municipal slaves), for the internal and external needs of the city-dwelling family (household servants and employees in

family business and trading interests), for work on the farms and for hard labor (the mines and quarries). Different purchasers were in search of different qualities: good looks, intelligence, physical strength, previous experience of one sort or another.[5]

Slavery was so much a way of life, indeed, that it is perhaps not surprising that most of Christianity's early leaders failed to mention its existence, let alone advocate its abolition. Paul's views on the question are by far the best known, and thus worth a closer look.

A full reading of his views lends little support to the belief that he was in any principled sense a friend of human bondage. In Ephesians 6:5, the most familiar passage, he advises, "Slaves, obey your earthly masters with respect, and fear, and with sincerity of heart, just as you would obey Christ." Readers who venture a bit further, however, discover that Paul has stern words for the slave-owners, too: "And masters, treat your slaves in the same way. Do not threaten them, since you know that he who is both their Master and yours is in heaven, and there is no favoritism with him."

Paul certainly acknowledged slavery as an inescapable reality. He could hardly do otherwise, considering that, as Wayne Meeks points out, "a typical Pauline congregation would include both slave owners and slaves."[6] Yet Paul insisted on reciprocity in a relationship where none existed in law and little or none occurred in practice. Christian salvation—to believers, the faith's greatest gift—is equally available to all, he also insisted, regardless of economic or social status. Indeed, salvation is the ultimate leveling experience. "For we were all Baptized by one Spirit into one body—whether Jews or Greeks, slave or free—and we were all given the one Spirit to drink," Paul writes in his first epistle to the church at Corinth (12:13). "There is neither Jew nor Greek, slave nor free, male nor female, for you are all one in Christ Jesus," he reiterates in Galatians (3:28). No worldly impediment can stand between a believer and the love of God, he writes in his epistle to the Romans (8:38).

Paul would no doubt have been surprised by subsequent developments in his faith. The movement championing the meek and the poor in spirit became the official religion of imperial power, blurring the distinction between that which is Caesar's and that which is God's, often to the advantage of the former. Not only did slavery remain very much part of the human enterprise, but some Christian leaders saw merit in it. Ecclesiastical estates at times employed hundreds or even thousands of slaves, and Pope Gregory I (590–604) took the extraordinary step of barring slaves from marrying free Christians. As late as the fourteenth century, Pope Gregory XI would sometimes follow excommunication with an order of enslavement. Meanwhile, creative theologians argued that Christian doctrine, supported by various biblical citations, had no inherent conflict with slavery, and indeed supported it.

Yet this interpretation failed in the end to inspire nearly as much moral energy as that inspired by slavery's Christian opponents. As Regine Pernoud points out, slavery was progressively choked off from the fourth century on, until by the High Middle Ages it had virtually vanished in much of northern Europe.[7] It was revived on a colossal scale in Europe's sixteenth-century colonies, of course, but not without protest from religious quarters. In 1537, Pope Paul III memorably declared that no Indian should be "given into servitude," and in the seventeenth century, Pope Innocent XI ruled that it was not permitted to buy or sell Africans who had been seized against their will. The papacy condemned slavery or the slave trade in 1462, 1741, 1815 and 1839. Needless to say, slaveholders in the New World paid little attention to any of these pronouncements, except occasionally to issue ringing protests.

Paul Johnson believes that "no real case for slavery could be constructed, in good faith, from Christian scriptures,"[8] although a number of Christians certainly tried. But whether Johnson is right, the essential point is surely this: Not only did a majority of the most motivated Christians decisively choose abolition over tradition when push came to shove, but they forced the issue onto the agenda of secular governments in the first place.

While we focus on the struggles over slavery in portions of the Christian West, we must not leave the impression that this institution was in any way less entrenched elsewhere. Not only was slavery endemic in the Greco-Roman culture in which Christianity first appeared, but it thrived around the world, too. Slavery in fact is one of the true universal institutions of human society, found at one time or another in every continent and among every race and people. Every great ancient civilization—from Mesopotamia to China, from the Indus Valley up to Crete—was defined by the ubiquitous presence of slaves.

It is true that these civilizations relied on slavery to varying degrees. The Egyptian pharaohs, for example, seemed to find nearly enough cheap, servile agricultural labor among the native peasantry without resorting to predatory efforts to import legions of chattel slaves. Yet the pharaoh himself owned a host of slaves, and in Egypt as in other ancient civilizations human bondage was considered a natural state of affairs.

Elsewhere in Africa, slaves were captured, traded and sold as part of the endless spectacle of war and commerce. Indeed, an estimated four million African slaves were exported to Islamic countries before the New World was even discovered. Muslims were known to enslave Christians, too. Tunis is estimated to have harbored more than thirty thousand Christian slaves, Meltzer says, and slaving continued to flourish after the Nile was closed as a slave route in the nineteenth century. (One estimate has it that over four hundred thousand slaves were harvested from the Sudan between 1869 and 1876 and marketed in Egypt and Turkey.) Indeed, the trade in African slaves, both within Africa and between Africa and some Arab nations, continues in our day.

Such was the world that the antislavery cause would confront. Its partisans were taking on not only history and custom, but also powerful economic interests. James Boswell, the eighteenth-century British man of letters and bon vivant, touched all those buttons in his defense of slavery: "To abolish a status which in all ages God has sanctioned ... would not only be robbery to an innumerable class of our fellow subjects, but it would be extreme cruelty to the African savages, a portion of which it saves from massacre or intolerable bondage in their own country; and introduces into a much happier state of life."

Two other points should be emphasized. The pious activists who lit the antislavery movement's fuse and sustained it after it moved into the political realm undertook their crusade on behalf of people who not only were outside of their religion (at least initially), but were considered so vastly different as perhaps to be inferior beings. While overt displays of racism, in the United States at any rate, are now largely confined to poorly educated people, the antislavery crusade unfolded at a time when the best minds took the inferiority of some races for granted. Consider this appraisal of blacks:

Vices the most notorious seem to be the portion of this unhappy race: idleness, treachery, revenge, cruelty, impudence, stealing, lying, profanity, debauchery, nastiness and intemperance, are said to have extinguished the principles of natural law, and to have silenced the reproofs of conscience. They are strangers to every sentiment of compassion, and are an awful example of the corruption of man when left to himself.

This description was taken not from the pages of a South Carolina newspaper, but from the 1797 *Encyclopedia Britannica*.

The philosopher David Hume (1711–76) was a leader in arguing that blacks were "naturally inferior to whites," and once commented that a Jamaican black who had gained a reputation for intelligence was "admired for very slender accomplishments, like a parrot, who speaks a few words plainly." Inferiority was assumed by Thomas Jefferson, Voltaire and even John Locke, who, as Fogel reminds us, made a great name for himself by promoting the "inalienable rights of man" yet did not hesitate to defend slavery in his draft of the Fundamental Constitution of Carolina. Indeed, Locke did more than invest his literary skills in this dreadful enterprise. He also sank some of his money into the Royal Africa Company, the preeminent British slaving enterprise. It is ironic indeed—at least for those today who advance the notion that religion is a hindrance to tolerant attitudes—that the most advanced secular thinkers of that day, men like Hume in Britain and Jefferson in the United States, tended to be those most likely to flirt with pseudo-scientific racism, while Christian abolitionists served as their most uncompromising critics.

The antislavery forces thought of themselves as cultural combatants. To their mind, the battle lines were drawn between differing worldviews. David Brion Davis notes that the racist language of intellectuals such as Hume "enabled orthodox Christians to make defense of the Africans a defense of religion itself. John Wesley, for example, called Hume 'the most insolent despiser of truth and virtue who ever appeared in the world.'" Other antislavery leaders, such as James Ramsay and Granville Sharp, "repeatedly identified the theory of racial inferiority with Hume, Voltaire, and materialistic philosophy in general; they explicitly presented their attacks on slavery as a vindication of Christianity, moral accountability, and the unity of mankind."[9] Sharp, a lawyer who specialized in filing suits on behalf of slaves, denounced the "open declarations of Deists, Arians, Socinians, and others, who deny the Divinity of Christ, and the Holy Ghost." In modern terms, Sharp was a man who saw value in "polarizing" a debate.

While Hume compared black Africans to parrots, Methodist founder John Wesley, in his *Thoughts upon Slavery* (1774), posed a rhetorical question to the captains of slave ships: "Do you never feel another's pain? Have you no sympathy?... When you saw the flowing eyes, the heaving breasts, or the bleeding sides or tortured limbs of your fellow beings, were you a stone or a brute?" Methodist preacher George Whitefield went so far as to ask whites to consider the children of slaves as equal to their own. "Think your children are in any way better by nature than the poor Negroes? No! In no wise! Blacks are just as much, and no more, conceived and born in sin, as white men are; and both, if born and bred up here, I am persuaded, are naturally capable of the same improvement." As the editors of the *Columbia History of the World* put it, the opposition of the Quakers, who began the public antislavery campaign, "resulted from their interpretation of the New Testament. 'Christ died for all,' declaimed the great Quaker George Fox, 'for the Taiwanese and for the blacks as for you that are called whites.' "[10]

Eventually, no one made this point so well as the black abolitionists themselves. In 1851, Sojourner Truth laid the credentials of her humanity before a convention in Akron, Ohio, in a stirring passage of antislavery oratory that drew its strength from her reliance on her faith:

> Look at me! Look at my arm! I have plowed and planted, and gathered into barns, and no man could head me—and aren't I a woman? I could work as much and eat as much as a man (when I could get it), and bear de lash as well—and ar'n't I a woman? I have borne thirteen children and seen em mos' all sold off into slavery, and when I cried out with a mother's grief, none but Jesus heard—and ar'n't I a woman?

Sojourner Truth was speaking to a convention also concerned with women's rights, a cause that had its first major American flowering during the antislavery campaign. But before we more fully consider the crusade against American slavery, a closer look at the British campaign is in order, for in some ways it served as a guide.

How an Improbable Movement Prevailed

The movement that brought down the British slave trade began very small, but not lukewarm in conviction. Among its initial concerns was slavery within England itself. A seminal group organized in 1756, the Anti-Slavery Society, worked along with a small band of legal and philosophical compatriots to promote an intellectual environment in which right-thinking Englishmen would consider slavery unacceptable, at least within their national boundaries. This attitude was reflected in a 1772 legal decision resulting from the travails of a West Indian slave named James Somerset. Brought to England by his master, Somerset had escaped and been captured, and then faced export to Jamaica, where he would be put on the block. After a long trial, Somerset was freed, with the court ruling there was no provision supporting slavery in English law. While this was hardly an emancipation proclamation, it did reinforce the growing antislavery animus (slavery is "odious," the court allowed). The last public sale of a black slave in England took place in Liverpool in 1779.

Yet opposing slavery within England was a good deal different from opposing the business of slaving abroad. Declaring that the slave trade must end, a trade in which some powerful Englishmen reaped immense profits, was a provocation of the first order. It was one thing to denounce intellectuals like Hume for racist viewpoints, and quite another to take on slavers themselves. The latter had real money and political power with which to back their position. Emancipation was the ultimate goal of antislavery activists, of course, but they recognized that first they would have to end the trade. This step would, among other things, inspire masters to treat their slaves better, for once those slaves were gone, they could not be replaced.

A great deal of human property was at stake. In 1770, slaves comprised 22 percent of the population of Britain's thirteen American colonies, concludes historian Hugh Thomas in *The Slave Trade,* and a remarkable 90 percent in the East and West Indies. Supplying workers to the plantations was a massive business, and would remain so throughout much of the antislavery campaign. While some historians have argued that slavery was outlawed only when it lost its economic viability, Thomas, among others, notes that between 1791 and 1800, some four hundred thousand slaves were sent to market, making these among the trade's most vibrant years.

As the antislavery campaign picked up steam, so did slavery's contribution to the Colonies' economy.

"The British economy," Thomas asserts, "appeared even more to depend either on slavery or on slave-produced goods in the first years of the nineteenth century than when the movement for abolition had been launched. In 1803, for instance, less than 8 percent of the cotton used in Britain derived from free areas such as Turkey."[11] Thus he concludes that "Moral conviction was the determining element in the unusual chapter of British parliamentary history about to begin."[12]

Defeating a huge and historic industry closely tied to economic stability is never an easy assignment. In this case, it was not only the financial well-being of fellow citizens that would be wrecked, but also, some argued, Britain's standing in the world. One member of Parliament said that banning the trade would both destroy the "essential nursery of seamen and give up the dominion of the sea in a single stroke." These were serious arguments to overcome.

The Quakers, who had refused to participate in slavery from the 1680s on, were among the first to the barricades. At their 1783 London Yearly Meeting they named a committee to draft a petition calling on the House of Commons to forbid the slave trade. In 1787 a small group began plotting the actual public campaign. James Walvin remarks that few if any of the original Quaker organizers had the least suspicion they were unleashing a campaign that would actually succeed within their lifetime.[13]

With a rise in literacy and the increasing availability of the printing press, the antislavery campaign became a showcase for Christian tract writers. The Africans and West Indians had no greater ally than the black ink that told their story to Great Britain's citizens. Tracts and appeals on behalf of slaves issued forth in blizzards.

Among the more popular was a study of the slave trade by the Reverend John Newton, formerly captain of a slave ship who is best known today as the author of the hymn "Amazing Grace." John Wesley's *Thoughts upon Slavery* brought the Methodists fully into the campaign, a huge boost because of their growing numbers and reliable fervor. Once aroused, British citizens signed antislavery petitions in droves. This aspect of the campaign reached its peak in 1791–92, when 519 abolitionist petitions arrived at Parliament. Some 400,000 persons signed these petitions—one out of every eleven adults. The saturation record may have been established in Manchester, Fogel says, where 20,000 adults signed petitions out of a total adult population of around 30,000.[14]

The religious inspiration of the campaign was never far from center stage, even after the antislavery cause moved fully into the political arena. As David Brion Davis reminds us, "this political dimension should not obscure the crucial points: from the 1770s onward, devout Quakers were always the backbone of active antislavery organization and communication.... Religion was the central concern of all the British abolitionist leaders; the grassroots support, especially after 1823, came overwhelmingly from Baptist, Methodist, and Presbyterian Dissenters."[15] Adds Thomas: "It must be doubtful whether abolition would have carried the day when it did had it not been for the Quaker movement's capacity for organizing first their members and then others."[16]

The chief crusaders within government were themselves men of very deep religious faith, none more so than William Wilberforce, "as religious in temperament as he was socially successful."[17] Wilberforce was most certainly a driven man. After a conversion experience in his twenties, he joined forces with William Pitt, later the great prime minister, to oppose the trade in slaves. While Pitt was more measured in his ways, Wilberforce believed his mission had been sanctioned at the highest level. "Almighty God has set before me two great objectives," he wrote in his journal. "The abolition of the slave trade and the reformation of manners." Wilberforce was convinced that if fellow citizens became aware of the brutalities inherent in slaving, most would oppose it with a fervor matching his own.

In this educational endeavor he was aided by Thomas Clarkson, a man of similarly deep faith whose name now graces the building that houses Anti-Slavery International in London. Clarkson was the son of an Anglican curate and was headed for a pulpit himself before the slavery issue intervened. His religious temperament is well summed up in his belief that "to Christianity alone are we indebted for the new and sublime spectacle of seeing men going beyond the bounds of individual usefulness to each other—of seeing them carry their charity, as a united Brotherhood, into distant lands."

Clarkson was a heroic and tireless chronicler of the misery and horror that befell victims of the slave trade, traveling to British slaving ports to interview whichever captains and crewmen would talk to him. His investigations also took him several times to Africa. In one instance, he is said to have searched 317 ships in order to find a willing witness. Among Clarkson's more influential contributions was an artistic rendering purporting to show how slaves were tightly packed during the nights of their Atlantic crossing. It was a depiction that caused a British politician to observe, "In the passage of the Negroes from the coast of Africa, there is a greater portion of human misery condensed within a smaller place than has ever yet been found in any other place on the face of this globe."

Clarkson's painstaking work was countered by a storm of sophistry. According to slaving advocates, Clarkson did not understand that slavery was an altogether benevolent institution, rescuing the poor Africans from a much worse existence, one that might well end at a banquet with the African as the main course. Charges of misuse of slaves, they insisted, were terribly exaggerated. One slavery sympathizer, for instance, announced that contrary to assertions that transported slaves lived and sometimes perished in their own filth, the holds of slave ships were actually "redolent with frankincense."

Wilberforce, who was elected to Parliament in 1780, began his series of antislavery bills in 1788. The first gained little support. In 1791, a bill against the trade was brought to a vote but lost by a measure of nearly two to one. Bills rose and fell in fairly quick succession in 1795, 1796, 1797, 1798, 1799 and 1802. No vote garnered even as much as 15 percent of Commons support.

For his troubles, Wilberforce not only suffered continuous defeat but endured savage ridicule, though apparently with equanimity. A contemporary observer noted that "All the filthy channels of the dictionary were turned upon Wilberforce, and they fell like water upon the back of a swan." Some of this disparagement was directed at his religious beliefs; Lord Melbourne sneered that "Things have come to a pretty pass when religion is allowed to invade public life." (Wilberforce meanwhile foresaw a "fast approaching" time "when Christianity will be almost as openly disavowed in the language, as in fact it is already supposed to have disappeared from the conduct of men; when infidelity will be held to be the necessary appendage of a man of fashion, and to believe will be deemed the indication of a feeble mind.")

Wilberforce was so incapacitated by health troubles in 1788 that his death was expected at any moment. His condition inspired some degree of revelry in the opposing camp, but the celebrations were short-lived. Wilberforce managed to pull himself back to work and press on, sustained by both his personal faith and the faith that fellow believers had in their mutual cause. Encouragement came from the nameless and the great, including John Wesley, who assured Wilberforce that he was an agent of higher powers than the slave industry could muster against him:

> My dear Sir:
> Unless the Divine power has raised you up to be an *Athanasius contra mundum,* I see not how you can go through your glorious enterprise in opposing that execrable villainy, which is the scandal of religion, of England, and of human nature. Unless God has raised you up for this very thing, you will be worn out by the opposition of men and devils, but if God be for you who can be against you? Are all of them together stronger than God? Oh, be not weary of well-doing. Go on in the name of God, and in the power of His might, till even American slavery, the vilest that ever saw the sun, shall vanish away before it. That He that has guided you from your youth up may continue to strengthen in this and all things, is the prayer of,
> Your affectionate servant,
> John Wesley

Wilberforce did not in fact weary of well-doing, and his speeches in Parliament provide compelling proof. They could be magisterial and quite long, sometimes upwards of four hours. They were also rich in reminders that the debate concerned, at its heart, whether slaves were children of God and thus worthy of the great birthright of freedom. The opposition was equally firm in its views. At one point Wilberforce felt obliged to denounce a historian's statement that "An orang-outang husband would by no means disgrace a Negro woman." An insight of similar quality was offered in debate by one John Fuller, MP for Sussex and himself a planter in Jamaica, who said he "had never heard the Africans deny their mental inferiority."

Wilberforce was not the only antislavery member of Parliament, and not always the most eloquent. There was also, for instance, Henry Peter Brougham, who said:

Tell me not of the property of the planter in his slaves. I deny the right.... I acknowledge not the property.... In vain you tell me of laws which sanction such a claim. There is a law above all the enactments of human codes—the same throughout the world, the same at all times—it is the law written by the finger of God on the heart of man; and by that law, unchangeable and eternal, while men despise fraud, and loath rapine, and abhor blood, they will reject with indignation the wild and guilty phantasy that man can hold property in man!

In 1805, Wilberforce asked Prime Minister Pitt to end the selling of slaves to Dutch Guinea and a group of French islands. In a decree, Pitt complied. The back of the beast was cracking, and was soon to give way. Thanks in part to the relentless efforts of James Stephen, an ardent evangelical who rose to influential positions in the government, Parliament outlawed the trade effective May 1, 1807, inspiring the Duke of Norfolk to hail the vote as an unprecedented "humane and merciful Act." And no accident, he added, since it had occurred during Passion Week, a time of observing "that stupendous instance of Mercy towards Mankind, the redemption of the world by his Death upon the Cross."

Nor were the British abolitionists through. Upon Wilberforce's retirement, the antislavery leadership passed to Thomas Fowell Buxton, another Christian reformer. Buxton's labors were instrumental in the abolition act of 1833, freeing slaves throughout the British Empire. Britain would eventually emancipate 780,000 colonial slaves, at a cost of two million pounds in payment to their owners. That nation also turned with force against the Atlantic trade. Between 1820 and 1870 the British navy captured nearly 1,600 slave ships and freed over 150,000 slaves, reports James Walvin. British ships, adds Fogel, may have reduced the traffic off some parts of the African coast by 75 percent. Brazil and Cuba were eventually convinced to end their participation in the trade. India, with as many as sixteen million people enslaved, was also targeted; it became illegal to own a slave in British India in 1862, the same year President Abraham Lincoln announced the Emancipation Proclamation.

As slavery's advocates promised, ending the trade was an expensive undertaking. All told, says Fogel, the direct and indirect costs, "including lost profits from slaves and manufacturers in African markets, higher sugar prices at home, and red tape, equaled England's entire expenditure on poor relief during the first seven years of Queen Victoria's reign."[18]

Christianity's central role in this drama, not only at its origins but throughout the drive for legislative relief for the slaves, was symbolized by an action of the British and Foreign Bible Society on West Indian Jubilee Day, August 1, 1834. The society said it would present a Christmas copy of the New Testament and Psalms to any freed slave—which was no minor promise, as there were some 800,000 possible recipients. By this time, the missionary roots in the West Indies were fairly deep. Indeed, "the missionary work of dissenting churches among West Indian slaves, especially the work of the Methodists and Baptists, may have been the most important stimulus to the popular campaign for emancipation which began in 1823," says Fogel.[19] The slaves knew who their friends were—not the sneering Lord Melbournes, but men like Wilberforce, who was celebrated in a popular island song:

> Oh me good friend, Mr. Wilberforce, make me free!
> God Almighty thank ye! God Almighty thank ye!

After the parliamentary vote abolishing the slave trade, Wilberforce had turned his attention to emancipation. He retired in 1825, saw the Bill for the Abolition of Slavery pass its second reading on July 29, 1833, and died three days later. Among his last words: "Thank God that I should have lived to witness a day in which England was willing to give twenty millions sterling for the abolition of slavery."

Hugh Thomas believes "Wilberforce's achievement is one of the most remarkable examples of the triumph of an individual statesman on a major philanthropic issue, and at the same time one more reminder that individuals can make history."[20] John Stuart Mill held a similar, if not more expansive, view, arguing that the British antislavery campaign offered proof that "one person with a belief is a social power equal to ninety-nine who have only interests," and further noting that "It was not by any change in the distribution of material interests, but by the spread of moral convictions, that Negro slavery has been put an end to in the British Empire and elsewhere." Alexis de Tocqueville agreed, saying there was no denying "the philanthropic and especially Christian conscience that produced British emancipation."[21]

How Faith Spurred Abolitionism in the United States

Once prodded into action by its more pious and humanitarian citizens, Great Britain made relatively quick work of the ancient institution of slavery. But what of the United States? When it came to democracy and the rights of man, the colonials had no peers— or so America's revolutionaries believed. Yet Dr. Samuel Johnson, departing from his slavery-praising acolyte Boswell, posed a deflating question: "How is it that we hear the loudest yelps for liberty among the drivers of Negroes?"

This was a sure-footed indictment. Slavery was commonplace in America, and not only in the South. In 1703, 42 percent of New York households owned slaves. In those early years of the eighteenth century, adds Robert William Fogel, "the slave share of the population in New York and New Jersey was larger than in North Carolina and only a little less than in Maryland."[22] Five of America's first seven presidents were slaveholders, including the author of the Declaration of Independence. Innumerable other prominent Americans were associated with the trade. Samuel Phillips Savage, whom history places at Boston's Old South Church at the time patriots called the tea tax an intolerable burden on American freedom, was an insurer of slave ships. John Paul Jones, the naval hero, served on slaving vessels early in his career. Even Benjamin Franklin, one of the more enlightened of all Americans, allowed the buying and selling of slaves to be advertised in his paper, though he himself opposed the trade.

The American struggle to reconcile slavery with Christianity began only a few decades after the peculiar institution was established in Virginia in 1619. As Herbert S. Klein explains,

> Coming from the Spanish West Indies and therefore being Christians, the majority of these first Negroes were treated in the matter of labor and rights much as their fellow white servants, some receiving an education, and most being granted their freedom dues after their period of labor. But with the beginning of direct heavy African importations after 1640, the colored population of Virginia began to be increasingly divided between servants and slaves, with the majority who came after the fourth decade being immediately reduced by the planters who bought them to servitude "for life."[23]

Even then the religion of the slave was a thorny problem, since most Christians in the Colonies believed they must not enslave others of the same faith, or even keep in bondage those who converted. Several slaves in these early American decades actually gained their freedom by proving they had been baptized. By the eighteenth century, however, this principle was repudiated in law; conversion would have no legal consequences for slaves. "Slowly it came to be accepted that their color, their race, not their non-Christian status, was the chief rationale for the enslavement of Africans," explains John B. Boles.[24]

Some men who owned slaves argued, and very possibly believed, that slavery was wrong. Others were profoundly uneasy about their role as slave-owners, but considered the institution a necessary evil. Some even freed their slaves, though at times only posthumously. Ending slavery altogether was, however, the consuming passion of a small group of religious believers.

Boston judge Samuel Sewall, an early critic, wrote an antislavery salvo entitled *The Selling of Joseph* (1700), which many of his contemporaries found jarring in its explicitness and urgency. There is no disputing that Judge Sewall, a Presbyterian, took his moral principles seriously: in 1692 he had been among the judges of the unfortunate Salem witches. This time around he chose a better cause. It was soon taken up by the Quakers, who had quickly come to the fight in Great Britain and were especially well suited as social insurgents given their refusal to take oaths, bear arms or remove their hats to supposed superiors (an affront that in their early years brought considerable persecution upon them). At their yearly meeting in 1758, Quakers banned anyone who participated in the slave trade from church membership. In 1776 they went further, asking all slaveholding members to resign from their community.

And so America's break with its slave-filled past began, a break that also reflected the growing belief that Christianity should take a more active role in public life. "A growing number of mainstream Protestants swung into opposition with the eighteenth-century development of the idea of 'progressive revelation' and 'benign Providence,' which increasingly identified Christian action with reform," notes Paul Johnson.[25] Congregationalists, Presbyterians, Unitarians and Methodists flocked to the antislavery barricades, the latter becoming the first church in America to exhort its preachers to teach the gospel of Christ to slaves. That in turn helped produce the first black denomination: the African Methodist

Episcopal Church. Once activated, the Methodists would deliver some of the loudest cries for liberty.

After the Revolution, antislavery agitation found fertile ground in many parts of the North. Pennsylvania abolished slavery in 1780, and gradual or qualified emancipation soon followed in Massachusetts, New Hampshire, New York, New Jersey and Rhode Island. Nor was the religious inspiration behind these victories overlooked by the pro-slavery forces. A Maryland congressman, echoing Lord Melbourne, complained in 1790 of the "disposition of religious sects to imagine that they understood the rights of human nature better than all the world besides."

The revivalism of the Second Great Awakening and the explosive growth of insurgent denominations like the Methodists and Baptists changed the South, too. For one thing, a growing number of slave-owners were persuaded of their duty to support the religious instruction and churchgoing of their slaves. No less important, in Walvin's words, the revival movement "allowed conversion by the experience of God's saving grace. . . . Slaves could forge their own relationship with God; they did not need the intercession of a third party."[26]

Yet in the end, southern whites could not bring themselves into a full embrace of the truly egalitarian implications of Christianity. Reaction set in, eventually splitting several Protestant sects along regional lines. While more than 80 percent of Baptist clergy in Maine declared themselves "decided abolitionists" during an 1835 church conference, Baptists in the South, along with Presbyterians and Methodists, sought justification for slavery through a rigorous application of certain biblical passages (including Leviticus 25:44–46, I Corinthians 7:20–24, Ephesians 6:5–8 and I Peter 2:18–21). If slavery was good enough for Abraham, how could it not be part of God's plan? If St. Paul could urge slaves to "be obedient to those who are your earthly masters," by what logic did abolitionists denounce slaveholders for giving the orders that Paul insisted must be obeyed? "Pro-slavery Christians had no patience with the notion that the Bible merely tolerated slavery rather than advocated it," observes Rebecca Merrill Groothuis. Indeed, they "grounded the practice of slavery in the order of creation, or the God-ordained order of things. African people were viewed as designed by God for poverty, hard labor, and subservience."[27]

(The Catholic hierarchy in the United States, cultural outsiders united in loyalty to the Vatican, tended to sit out the raging controversy over the institution of slavery and a Christian's duty with regard to it, although the ranks of bishops included both ardent abolitionists such as Cincinnati's John Purcell and slaveholders such as Peter Kenrick of St. Louis. Anxious to avoid inciting nativist reaction, church leaders in the South generally threw in their lot with the slaveholding class.)

The tragic transformation of an evangelical tradition that had once looked upon slavery as an affront to Christian principles is summed up by John G. West: "As early as 1822 South Carolina Baptists had accepted ... scriptural justifications of slavery, and many more would embrace such arguments as time went on. Nevertheless, the notion of slavery as a positive good would not wipe away all evangelical scruples on the subject for several years.... On the whole, however, southern evangelicals acquiesced— and then supported the social system in which they found themselves."[28]

Supporting the social system did not necessarily mean applauding every dehumanizing aspect of it. A number of evangelicals recognized slave marriages, for example, even though secular law did not. In a study of religion in antebellum Amite County, Mississippi, Randy Sparks discovered evidence of white ministers marrying slaves. He also recounts how, in 1822, an indignant evangelical community prompted the state legislature to revise a law it had passed restricting blacks' religious freedom and curtailing the rights of black preachers. Indeed, Sparks maintains that the churches continued right through 1865 "to prick the consciences of slave-owners and thereby won better treatment of slaves."[29]

Professor Clarence L. Mohr reports a similar phenomenon in Georgia. "In the generation before the Civil War," he writes, "Georgia clergymen became leading advocates of protecting slave marital and family arrangements," while some devout whites "taught slaves to read the Bible in open defiance of state law."[30] Once the war was under way, reform-minded clergymen openly began to advocate more sweeping changes, including the legalization of black education.

For American abolitionists, meanwhile, slave importation was not the major hurdle it had been during the initial stages of the campaign in Britain. In 1807, the same year Britain outlawed the trade, Congress passed a bill stating that from January 1, 1808, it would be illegal to introduce any "Negro, mulatto, or person of colour, as a slave." And although no American was executed for illegally importing slaves until 1862, the large internal slave traffic was primarily sustained by births among slaves themselves. About forty thousand slaves were exchanged in 1836 alone, with a single slave bringing around $360 in the Virginia marketplace.

It was obvious enough to abolitionists that slavery was not about to wither and die on its own. By 1838, the American Anti-Slavery Society had 1,346 auxiliaries with about 100,000 members, thus matching the British movement at its greatest moment. The American abolitionists, like the British, were dependent on the printing press. In one notable project they collected stories of slave mistreatment from southern newspapers to create a massive indictment: a multitude of facts "that would thrill the land with horror," as one abolitionist leader characterized the project. "Shall such facts lie hushed any longer, when from one end of heaven to the other, myriad voices are crying 'O Earth, Earth, cover not their blood.'" The campaign may have pioneered the mass mailings that are so much a part of contemporary political life. An 1835 mailing of 175,000 pieces of antislavery propaganda to southern addresses caused no lack of uproar on the receiving end, though southerners were not alone in their hostility to those who would extend equality to blacks.

In Cincinnati, the board of trustees of Lane Theological Seminary, which Lyman Beecher had founded in 1832 with a color-blind admissions policy, was so unnerved by the abolitionist bent of the students that it soon banished antislavery activities altogether. Not that this stopped the students. Fifty-three of them simply moved their activities to Oberlin College. "The Lane rebels eventually covered a tremendous territory in the Middle West," writes historian Stanley Elkins, "holding revivals and making thousands of converts. They were easily the most effective of any single group working in the cause."[31]

The importance of such revivals as inspiration for the abolitionist impulse can scarcely be overstated. James M. McPherson explains that the "evangelical enthusiasm" of the Second Great Awakening "generated a host of moral and cultural reforms.

The most dynamic and divisive of them was abolitionism. Heirs of the Puritan notion of collective accountability that made every man his brother's keeper, these Yankee reformers . . . preached the availability of redemption to anyone who truly sought it, urged converts to abjure sin, and worked for the elimination of sin from society. The most heinous social sin was slavery. All people were equal in God's sight; the souls of black folks were as valuable as those of whites; for one of God's children to enslave another was a violation of the Highest Law, even if it was sanctioned by the Constitution.[32]

Many abolitionists would need that moral enthusiasm just to buoy them through trying times. Indeed, the students expelled from Lane got off lightly compared with some abolitionists. Consider the experience of Arthur and Lewis Tappan, wealthy merchants in New York and Boston associated with the First Free Church who bankrolled a number of reform projects including college education for blacks. "We owe it to the cause of humanity, to our country and our God," declared Lewis Tappan, whose money established the American Anti-Slavery Society in 1834. "The motives which should induce the Christian and all the friends of humanity to make untiring efforts to . . . raise them from the depths of their degradation and misery are irresistible." Yet such humane sentiments were a provocation to many, and the Tappan brothers "faced nationwide denunciation, death threats (including a bounty on their heads), and mob violence for their antislavery activities," recounts Warren Goldstein. Abolitionist editor William Lloyd Garrison was actually dragged on a rope through the street in 1835 by a Boston mob chanting "Lynch him!" (Garrison survived this terrifying ordeal.) In 1837, Elijah Lovejoy, editor of an abolitionist paper in Alton, Illinois, was murdered by opponents, while Theodore Dwight Weld, a prominent antislavery orator, survived numerous attacks—so many, in fact, that his heroic life is worth a closer look.

"I have seen in no man such a rare combination of great intellectual powers with Christian simplicity," wrote James G. Birney, a Kentuckian who also took up the antislavery cause. He added that Weld was "the most simple hearted and earnest follower of Christ that I have known." A diary entry itemizing his speaking schedule makes clear the profound nature of Weld's commitment:

"In most places I have lectured from six to twelve times, sixteen, twenty and twenty-five, and once thirty times." The length of his typical address ranged from two to five hours, and he evidently had little trouble holding an audience's attention. "It may seem extravagant," one listener wrote, "but I have seen crowds of bearded men held spell-bound by his power for hours together and for twenty evenings in succession."

Others were not so taken with Weld's talents, or at least his message. Critics, often armed with eggs and stones, were common, and sometimes made their way into the buildings, usually churches, where Weld delivered his message of brotherhood and hope. A witness quoted Weld's reaction to being struck in the face with an egg. "I beg the audience will be composed," he remarked, then produced a handkerchief and "wiped it away calmly ... and proceeded as deliberately as if he had paused to take a draught of water." On another occasion an assailant threw a stone through a church window, an incident described by Weld himself in his journal. The stone was "so well aimed that it struck me on the head and for a moment stunned me. Paused for a few moments till the dizziness had ceased, and then went on and completed my lecture. Meanwhile some of the gentlemen had hung their cloaks up at the window so that my head could not be so easily used as a target. The injury was not serious, though for a few days I had frequent turns of dizziness." Weld and his fellow activists, it should be remembered, had set themselves to this task on behalf of people who were widely held to be inferior, and who had nothing to offer in return.

Some antislavery enthusiasts broke with their families and their region over the issue. These included James Thome, a southern convert whose address to a meeting of the American Anti-Slavery Society was entitled "The Southern Slave Kitchen, the Sodom of the Nation." Thome was not the only southerner who saw the abolitionist light. Probably no converts to the cause generated more interest and controversy than the sisters Sarah and Angelina Grimke, members of a Charleston, South Carolina, slave-owning family, whose brother was also a major backer of the abolitionist cause. Angelina traced her conversion to reading an antislavery tract in 1835. A letter to her sister explaining the change was reprinted in a pamphlet entitled "An Appeal to the Christian Women of the South."

Other devout women likewise involved themselves in the abolitionist cause. As in Great Britain, women motivated by faith played a crucial role throughout the American antislavery campaign, a role sometimes overlooked because the movement's principal leaders, with rare exceptions, were men. It was a woman, however, who produced the single most influential attack on slavery ever penned. Harriet Beecher Stowe, daughter of a Presbyterian minister and wife of a Congregationalist Old Testament professor, was herself a lay theologian who, in McPherson's words, had "breathed the doctrinal air of sin, guilt, atonement, and salvation since childhood." Her *Uncle Tom's Cabin* "rebuked the whole nation for the sin of slavery. She aimed the novel at the evangelical conscience of the North. And she hit her mark."[33]

The mixing of religious belief and public commitment was common at all levels of the antislavery campaign. Robert William Fogel observes that even "the principal architects of the secular appeal—including John Quincy Adams, Joshua R. Giddings, and Salmon P. Chase—were deeply religious men" who also realized that "the evangelical movement was a major political constituency that could not be won to the antislavery banner by purely secular appeals."[34]

Indeed, Christianity's importance to abolitionists may have been equaled only by its importance to slaves themselves, who were sustained by its message of hope and its assurance of a liberty that transcended their current bondage.

How Slaves Embraced and Transformed Christianity

Christianity could be a great moral leveler, and no one knew this better than many of the slaveholders. In the West Indies, Walvin observes, planters "were, from the first, reluctant to see their slaves converted and baptized. They held fundamental objections to the prospect of black Christianity; it would come between them and their slaves, would serve to undermine their authority and perhaps persuade the slaves to get above themselves. In addition, they worried about the connection between conversion and freedom; did baptism emancipate a slave?" For that matter, did not moral equality imply political equality? Adds Walvin: "The simple message of the brotherhood of Christ, of the equality of all believers and the fraternity of the life-hereafter sent a fizz through the slave quarters—and a cold chill through the slave-owning community."[35]

Planters were justified in fearing a link between religion and slaves' sense of their own self-worth, but historians hotly debate to what degree the churches themselves blunted slavery's sharper edges. In the 1950s and 1960s, historians such as Stanley Elkins argued that the existence of a strong institutional church in Latin America had been a bulwark against brutality—that the Catholic Church was able to shield slaves there from some of the most dehumanizing aspects of slavery that existed in the American South. In Brazil, for example, slaves were married in church and could not be separated by sale; they could accumulate property, sell their labor on their days off and save toward the price of their own freedom. For that matter, the law was supposed to avenge them if they were the victims of wanton brutality or murder at the hand of a sadistic master. "It may be asserted that the church, functioning in its capacity as guardian of morals, was responsible for whatever human rights were conserved for the slave within the grim system," Elkins explains.[36]

The Catholic Church reached an accommodation with slavery, but never closed its eyes to the system's intrinsic evil. "In effect," says Elkins, "the church with one hand condemned slavery and with the other came to an understanding with it as a labor system. Its doctrine asserted in general that the practice of slavery and the slave trade was fraught with perils for those of the faithful who engaged in it and that they stood, at innumerable points, in danger of mortal sin."[37]

Yet whether the juridical difference between Latin America and the southern United States really mattered in the everyday treatment of slaves remains in doubt. Many historians are extremely suspicious of the idea, with David Brion Davis, for example, arguing that "laws intended to protect slaves from assault, cruelty, and injustice were seldom enforced."[38] Also, access to religious instruction and ritual for slaves varied from place to place, and could be tightly circumscribed by apprehensive slave-owners. The West Indian colonies were notoriously indifferent to religion well into the nineteenth century. Even so, as early as the 1790s the black Baptist evangelist George Leile is said to have preached before audiences of eight hundred Jamaican slaves. "Like nonconformists in Britain," notes Walvin, "Leile's most effective ploy was to preach from horseback." As some planters feared, the slaves eventually did get above themselves. "When a new chapel was opened on Hampden estate in Jamaica, slaves thronged the pews and refused to make space for local whites, who were forced to stand in the aisles; slaves sat and masters stood."[39]

Evangelization took hold more widely in the South. The most determined outreach by southern churches to blacks didn't commence until the 1840s, though slaveholder efforts to Christianize their bondspeople had begun in the mid-eighteenth century. The level of religious practice available to slaves varied dramatically depending on the interest of the planter. Boles elaborates:

> Slaves worshipped apart from whites on some occasions, often with the knowledge of their owners and often without the white supervision the law called for. Some black churches were adjuncts to white churches, and completely independent and autonomous black churches existed in southern cities. Blacks worshiped privately and often secretly in their cabins and in the fields. . . . But such practices should not lead us to forget that the normative worship experience of blacks in the antebellum South was in a biracial church.[40]

Eugene Genovese adds, "Whatever the religion of the masters, the slaves, when given a choice, overwhelmingly preferred the Baptists and secondarily the Methodists."[41] Yet they did not merely copy the Christianity of whites. For one thing, African folk beliefs often survived side by side with Christianity in the same households. Also, black faith quickly became a tool of survival. Slaves "fashioned their own kind of Christianity, which they turned to for strength in the constant times of need," Julius Lester observes. "In the Old Testament story of the enslavement of the Hebrews by the Egyptians, they found their own story. In the figure of Jesus Christ, they found someone who had suffered as they suffered, someone who understood, someone who offered them rest from their suffering."[42]

However much white preachers might care about the welfare of slaves, for black audiences they tended to emphasize a biblical message of obedience—or, in slavery's final decades, even to suggest that slavery could be explained by the biblical curse on Ham. Black preachers never accepted this theory, preferring biblical passages with a more comforting and hopeful message. In time, Genovese writes, these black preachers transformed Christianity into "a religion of resistance—not often of revolutionary defiance, but of a spiritual resistance that accepted the limits of the politically possible."[43] The liberating belief that God was on their side was reflected in a popular slave song:

We will be slaves no more
Since Christ has made us free,
Has nailed our tyrants to the cross
And bought our liberty.

This pattern held true beyond the large estates. "Blacks in the cities took charge of their own churches—organized, planned, and administered them for slave and free alike," says Milton Meltzer. "They ran Sunday schools for the children and Bible classes for adults. They prayed for the sick and buried the dead. Their very independence and separation made the whites worry about them as 'nurseries of self government.'" Which indeed they were. From the churches "emerged great preachers, editors, educators, orators, and organizers. These talents were best revealed where it mattered most—in the antislavery movement."[44]

According to William Loren Katz, "Christianity inspired Harriet Tubman, hero of the Underground Railroad and liberator of three hundred slaves, who said, 'I must go down, like Moses into Egypt, to lead them out.'"[45] Colonel Thomas Wentworth Higginson, who commanded black troops during the Civil War, noted the "flower of poetry" and religious nature of their songs, observing that "Behind the gentle words in praise of God lurked the spiritual armor of people long at war with oppression."

This same spirit has survived to the present day, not only fueling the civil rights movement of the mid-twentieth century, but also acting as a buffer against continuing assertions of black inferiority. Says Orlando Patterson, "For the majority of lower-class, poorly educated Afro-Americans the Christian creed has been the only escape from the twin grip of racist biologic determinism and liberal environmental determinism." Religion also "offered the only meaningful nationwide organizational base for Afro-Americans at a time when such a base was desperately needed."[46]

American slavery would not end without a bloody civil war—a war which, Paul Johnson maintains, "can be described as the most characteristic religious episode in the whole of American history, since its roots and causes were not economic or political but religious and moral."[47] Religious spirit had not dried up after the Second Great Awakening, despite what revivalists such as Charles G. Finney feared at the time. Not only was church membership on the eve of the Civil War significantly higher than it had been in 1776, but many churches would soon be as active in their politicking as their predecessors had been in the previous century.

Moreover, when the prosecution of the war itself was on the line in Lincoln's bid for reelection in 1864, only the full-bodied intervention of abolitionist Protestants saved the day. In *Religion and the Radical Republican Movement,* Victor B. Howard describes in considerable detail how antislavery churches rallied their congregations to Lincoln's cause, so that "Republicans carried almost all of the evangelical votes."[48] Contemporaries were well aware of this evangelical preference. As the *Elmira Advertiser* observed, "If McClellan is elected he must breast and overcome almost the entire ecclesiastical and ministerial force of the land." And the abolitionist *Christian Advocate and Journal* declared, with some justification, "There probably never was an election in all our history into which the religion element entered so largely, and nearly all on one side." Antislavery Christians ensured that the election became, in effect, a referendum on whether to abolish slavery for good.

How Christians Lead Antislavery Efforts to This Day
Slavery was not extinguished in the nineteenth century, despite widespread expectation that its final chapter was unfolding. This was due in part to a development no one quite foresaw: revolutionary, often explicitly antireligious governments would revive the ancient practice of human bondage to an unparalleled degree in the Soviet Union, Nazi Germany, China, imperial Japan, Cambodia and elsewhere. The total number of slaves in forced labor camps during Stalin's regime alone (1927–53) ranged up to twenty-five million, with the death rate at some camps estimated at 30 percent a year.

In some places, slavery survives to this day. The American Anti-Slavery Group estimated at the dawn of the twenty-first century that millions of slaves or near-slaves were laboring in numerous countries around the world. Tens of thousands were children weaving rugs for export from South Asia, the so-called "carpet slaves." They toiled at looms from dawn to nightfall, their childhood stolen, their spirits obliterated. Tens of thousands more children in the same region labored in stone quarries, in brick kilns or in fields. Many others—mostly girls but also some boys—had been abducted, or sometimes sold by desperately indebted parents, into the Southeast Asian sex trade. Some were confined to guarded compounds to prevent their escape, while forced to service a parade of clients, many of them sex predators from abroad.

Incredibly, even whip-and-chain slavery of the most brutal sort persisted in at least two nations: Mauritania and Sudan. By the 1990s, Mauritania almost certainly held more slaves on a per capita basis than any other nation on Earth, typically blacks owned by North African Arabs. For sheer horror, however, probably nothing exceeds the recent experience in Sudan. In early 2000, Christian Solidarity International estimated that the number of Sudanese slaves topped a hundred thousand. Most were Christian and animist black Africans from the Dinka tribe, captured and transported to northern Sudan. (There is some irony in the fact that Christians broke the back of slavery in the nineteenth and twentieth centuries, only to wind up among slavery's major victims in the twenty-first.) Charles Jacobs, president of the American Anti-Slavery Group, described their enslavement in the *Boston Globe:* "Slave-raiding is the terror weapon of choice. Arab militias storm African villages, kill the men, and take women and children. Escaped and redeemed slaves tell of being ripped from their homes, roped by the neck, and force-marched in columns north where they are raped, branded, bred, and forcibly converted."[49]

Christian Solidarity International, whose primary objective is "worldwide respect for the God-given right of every human being to choose his or her faith and to practice it," freed nearly twenty-one thousand Sudanese slaves between 1995 and 2000 through its redemption program, purchasing slaves and releasing them. It also did its utmost to goad the civilized world into action against the government of Khartoum. Meanwhile, the greatest champions of the black Sudanese from within their own ranks were two bishops, one Roman Catholic and the other Episcopalian.

As the involvement of Christian Solidarity International in Sudan suggests, the tradition established by Wilberforce, the Grimke sisters, Thomas Clarkson, Harriet Beecher Stowe, Harriet Tubman, and a legion of fellow believers continues to this day. Even at the opening of the twenty-first century, the antislavery movement finds itself still buoyed by the Christian ethic of moral equality, the single greatest enemy of human bondage during the past two thousand years.

CHAPTER THREE

CHRISTIANITY
AND SCIENCE

The reason we live in a scientific age, we are told, is that enlightened free-thinkers shook off the suffocating dogma of Christianity after the Middle Ages and began to examine the material world as it really exists. Virtually every scientific theory that has altered our understanding of how humans fit into the cosmos—the sun-centered solar system, the age of the earth and the evolution of species, to cite three examples—has been resisted by Christians as a threat to their faith and advanced against the grain of Christian orthodoxy. The friction between Christian theology and secular intellectual inquiry is no accident. Indeed, the two are naturally in conflict because religion relies on doctrine and faith—in other words, irrationality—for its justification; it stifles curiosity and creativity. Science and other modes of modern thought depend on fact; they cultivate a dispassionate search for truth.

"In 1992, 359 years after condemning Galileo as a heretic, the Vatican apologized and admitted the astronomer had a point." So begins an article published in the *New York Times* in February 2000—242 years after Pope Benedict XIV lifted sanctions against books teaching that the earth revolves around the sun, thus admitting, in 1758, that Galileo had a point. But never mind the discrepancy. The *Times* understood that it would get no correction from its readers, who by and large share the assumption, breezily reinforced in the article, that Christian faith and intellectual progress are mutually exclusive.

A belief in Christianity's oppressive effects on learning has a long and illustrious pedigree, going back at least to the time of Voltaire and the other *philosophes* of the Enlightenment. They regarded Christianity as reactionary and authoritarian, and were particularly keen to indict the Middle Ages as a boorish era top-heavy with clergy and dogma, and thus hostile toward practical knowledge or creative pursuits. This notion is crystallized in Condorcet's claim that "the triumph of Christianity was the signal for the complete decadence of philosophy and the sciences." In time, such views would prevail, to the point that the very word "medieval" is now most frequently deployed as an insult, a term of rank disdain.

Even some historians who presumably have looked at the evidence—Daniel Boorstin in *The Discoverers,* for example—present the Middle Ages as an era of intellectual slumber. "A Europe-wide phenomenon of scholarly amnesia . . . afflicted the continent from A.D. 300 to at least 1300," Boorstin asserts. Indeed, Europe's creative energies and inventiveness are acknowledged only from the dawn of the "scientific revolution" in the sixteenth and seventeenth centuries. It was also during this period—1633, to be precise—that the Holy Office and Pope Urban VIII bequeathed to all future enemies of Christianity one of their greatest propaganda clubs: the persecution of Galileo Galilei.

It was not until the nineteenth century, however, that the notion of an eternal conflict between religion and science hardened into secular doctrine. To Karl Marx, religion was "the opiate of the people" and his scientific socialism a bracing alternative to false consciousness based in faith. Friedrich Nietzsche galloped still farther down this road, mocking religion's intellectual impotence and famously declaring that "God is dead." Other figures were at least as influential. In *The Conflict between Science and Religion,* John William Draper accused the Catholic Church, for which he harbored special bile, of "ferociously suppressing by the stake and the sword every attempt at progress." Draper popularized the belief that the church had rejected and crushed the idea of a spherical earth, a thesis reinforced by Andrew Dickson White, probably the greatest chronicler ever of the "warfare of science with theology." White's judgment was contained in a two-volume compendium that seemingly gathered together every anti-intellectual utterance by a religious figure in the history of Christendom.

The publication of James Frazer's *The Golden Bough* in 1890 represented another bomb tossed into the collapsing fortress of Christian respectability. Frazer was an anthropologist who considered religion an adolescent phase that mankind would pass through in a journey toward "the sunlight of science and rationality." Sigmund Freud reinforced this notion, arguing that monotheism emerged in human society because "in primeval times there was a single person who was bound to appear huge at that time and who afterwards returned in men's memory elevated to divinity.... An idea such as this has a compulsive character: It *must* be believed."

Variations of this theme still persist, solidified by a century and a half of sniping over the Darwinian theory of evolution. Modern indictments of Christianity's baleful influence on scientific pursuits range from the grandly sweeping (for example, Professor Edwin A. Locke's contention that scientific and technological progress became possible only "once man's mind was freed from the tyranny of religious dogma") to the narrowly damning (Richard S. Westfall's claim that after the church's persecution of Galileo, Copernican astronomy became "a forbidden topic among faithful Catholics for ... two centuries"), to condemnations somewhere in between (Nathan Myhrvold's essay in the online publication *Slate* claiming that the astronomical insights of the scientific revolution threatened "the religious dictatorships" of that time).

To some modern intellectuals, Christian faith and intellectual backwardness are so naturally linked that the relationship is not even argued; the connection is asserted as established fact. When historian of science William Provine quipped that people have to "check their brains at the door" of church, he was being crueler than most critics, but no more condescending.

■ ■ ■

Those who argue that Christianity has slowed intellectual progress find no shortage of examples to draw upon. There is no denying, for instance, that Christian theology stymied the advance of mapmaking and geography for several centuries; no question that the system of Copernicus was condemned by the Catholic Church in 1616 as dangerous to faith, setting Galileo up for his later fall; no disputing that Protestants were even quicker to condemn Copernicus than was Rome, with Lutherans leading the way; no ducking the fact that the Roman church put the work of Descartes on its Index of Prohibited Books in 1663. It is undeniable that a long caravan of Christian theologians and clergy, particularly in the nineteenth century but also before and since, have issued astonishingly foolish statements regarding geological time, fossils and the origins of man.

For that matter, it is a sorry truth that even many clear-cut findings of biblical scholars have been resisted or rejected in some Christian quarters. The "Anti-Modernist Oath" devised in 1910 and imposed by Pope Pius X on every Catholic cleric stifled scholarship in the Roman church for decades to come.

Yet such anecdotes—and there are plenty more to stockpile for the connoisseur—are not the whole story of Christian influence on the history of knowledge and intellectual discovery. They are not even half of it. Far from being an eternally heavy weight on intellectual progress, Christianity has frequently been its inspiration and spur. After all, if Christianity is so irredeemably hostile to intellectual inquiry, how is it that modern science sprang from the one civilization on earth grounded in the Christian worldview and habits of mind? One possible answer is that Christianity equipped its followers with a mindset uniquely disposed to pursue rather than retreat from the scientific adventure. The critical ingredients, in the words of Stanley Jaki, a Benedictine priest with a doctorate in physics, were "confidence in the rationality of the universe, trust in progress, and appreciation of the quantitative method."[1] Inquiry into the natural world, Christians believed, would help them gain a clearer glimpse of their Creator. This willingness to look closely at the physical world was not new with Christianity, of course, but it did assume a distinctive place in the Christian consciousness.

How Christianity Rejected a World of Fate and Cycles
It would be misleading to draw too sharp a distinction between the Christian outlook and the pagan worldview. Early Christians lived in the same world as pagans and shared common influences. And there wasn't a monolithic pagan (or Christian) perspective in the first place; the Roman Empire was a far-flung, polyglot enterprise with vast regional and ethnic differences, and within which a variety of beliefs and philosophies claimed their separate followers.

Early Christian thinkers were often steeped in classical learning, and quite deliberately brought aspects of pagan thought into their ethics and politics. The classical heritage remained an important component of Western thought even before the major rediscoveries of the High Middle Ages. Theology may have triumphed over classical philosophy, but "the victory was by no means as one-sided as the spokesmen for Christian doctrine claimed it was," observes Jaroslav Pelikan.[2]

Indeed, one of the last great scholars in the classical tradition, Boethius (c. 475–525), was also a Christian theologian who wrote several influential treatises on church doctrine. Yet his most celebrated work is *The Consolation of Philosophy,* which contains not a single reference either to the Bible or to any specific tenet of the Christian faith despite the fact that it was written from the desperate straits of a prison cell. The highest ranks of the clergy could be well versed in classical learning. Gregory I, whose papacy (590–604) is often linked with the consolidation of Catholic orthodoxy, was "second in erudition to none of his contemporaries," according to Edward Gibbon.[3]

Even so, it is still fair to make general distinctions between Christian and pagan thinking. Christians refused to "melt . . . into the syncretistic hodge-podge of the Roman Empire," as Pelikan puts it,[4] and their outlook therefore tended to differ from a large swath of pagan opinion in several respects important to the birth of science. Broadly speaking, Christians rejected the notion of an implacable fate that determined an individual's prospects; they believed, on the other hand, that history had a direction and a purpose, and renounced the idea of recurring cycles; they banished the supernatural from the material world (or at least redefined and limited its place); and they worshiped a rational God who took a personal interest in human affairs.

To most residents of the Greco-Roman world, the supernatural knew few boundaries. The gods mingled with men, and sometimes men became gods. Paul Johnson notes that the Roman Senate "usually voted the deification of an emperor, provided he had been successful and admired; a witness would swear he had seen the dead man's soul wing to heaven from the funeral pyre."[5] Shirley Jackson Case painted a more expansive portrait in his classic *History of Christian Supernaturalism:*

The sky hung low in the ancient world. Traffic was heavy on the highway between heaven and earth. Gods and spirits thickly populated the upper air, where they stood in readiness to intervene at any moment in the affairs of mortals. And demonic powers, emerging from the lower world or resident in remote corners of the earth, were a constant menace to human welfare. All nature was alive— alive with supernatural forces.... The common man lived his life under the constant danger of interference by arbitrary supernatural powers.[6]

Christians did not completely depart from this portrait of a spirit-charged world, but their view of it gave them unusual leverage (in their minds) in the daily struggle to control their destiny. The Christian God was not just another supernatural being. He was separate from all others, such as angels and demons; indeed, He had created them along with the material world. And because Christians (like Jews) believed that God had made them in His image, and had a personal interest in their welfare, the growing Christian community carried with it a confidence that their fate was not at the mercy of arbitrary whim. God's will might be inscrutable at times to mere humans, but it was nonetheless accepted as just.

There were many in the ancient world who believed that man's fate was simply written in the stars. This idea was so controlling, reports the fourth-century historian Ammianus Marcellinus, that "There are many who do not presume either to bathe, or to dine, or to appear in public, till they have diligently consulted, according to the rules of astrology, the situation of Mercury and the aspect of the moon. It is singular enough that this vain credulity may often be discovered among the profane skeptics, who impiously doubt or deny the existence of a celestial power."[7] If the stars imposed destiny on human beings, then humans could not possibly be masters of their fate. One pagan commentary explained, "Fate has decreed as a law for each person the unalterable consequences of his horoscope." Plato held that "even God could not oppose necessity." Pelikan observes, "Even the emperor Tiberius stopped paying homage to the gods because everything was already written in the stars."[8]

From its early days, Christian doctrine sought to usher humanity out of this intellectual cellblock. "With very few exceptions," notes Pelikan, "the apologists for the gospel against Greek and

Roman thought made responsibility rather than inevitability the burden of their message.... The only unavoidable fate was the rule that reward was based on the actions of a man's free will, whether good or evil."[9]

Early Christians also rejected belief in cyclical time, the conviction that history replays itself in great, ineluctably recurring phases. The philosopher Seneca (c. 3 B.C.–A.D. 65) was quite specific about the cyclic destruction and creation of the world. "There will be no Adriatic any longer," he predicted, "no strait in the Sicilian Sea, no Charybdis, no Scylla.... All these names will be obliterated.... All distinctions will disappear. All will be mixed up which nature has now arranged in its several parts." Worse, "a single day will see the burial of all mankind ... all will descend into the one abyss, will be overthrown in one hour." At that point, Seneca believed, the cycle would begin anew. "Every living creature will be created afresh," before they too go the way of all before them.

The musings of the second-century emperor Marcus Aurelius reveal a similar mindset, although with a perhaps slightly more somber hue. "These two things, then, must needs be remembered," he wrote in his *Meditations,* "the one, that all things from time everlasting have been cast in the same mold and repeated cycle after cycle, and so it makes no difference whether a man see the same things recur through a hundred years or two hundred, or through eternity: the other, that the longest liver and he whose time to die comes soonest part with no more the one than the other."

Not all Greeks and Romans believed in a cyclical theory of history, let alone were infected with its dispiriting undertones. Some Romans considered their empire a potential exception to the rule of inevitable fall. But the decisive emergence of a linear view of time surely helped to nurture optimism, curiosity and initiative, and—no less important—a trust in the lasting significance of the human saga.

The concept of progress was familiar to the Judeo-Greco-Roman world long before Christianity. As Robert Nisbet has pointed out, Christian philosophers in part merely adopted Jewish views on the sacred nature of history and Greek attitudes on the growth of knowledge and understanding. And yet, Nisbet explains,

> The Christian philosophers, starting with Eusebius and Tertullian
> and reaching masterful and lasting expression in St. Augustine,
> endowed the idea of progress with new attributes which were bound
> to give it a spiritual force unknown to their pagan predecessors. I
> refer to such attributes as the vision of the unity of all mankind,
> the role of historical necessity, the image of progress as the unfold-
> ing through long ages of a design present from the very beginning
> of man's history, and far from least, a confidence in the future that
> would become steadily greater.[10]

Christians worshiped a personal, rational, loving God; they
believed that history had purpose and direction, centering on the
narrative of salvation. It was inconceivable to them that "Jesus
will come again to visit this life and will do the same things that
he has done, not just once but an infinite number of times according to the cycles," as the third-century Christian philosopher Origen of Alexandria put it. There was but one redemption.

It is Augustine who, in *The City of God,* provided the crowning
expression of Christian historical confidence. Never mind that Rome
had been sacked, that the empire was reeling before a barbarian
onslaught, that the classical heritage was at risk of being buried in
rubble and ruin. The universe had been created just once, Augustine confirmed. Moreover, that creation was fundamentally good.
Empires might wash away, but the human drama retained its meaning and its promise of fulfillment. "For once Christ died for our sins;
and, rising from the dead, He dieth no more. 'Death hath no more
dominion over him,' and we ourselves after the resurrection shall
be 'ever with the Lord.'" The notion of recurring cycles was utterly
incompatible with such a vision. "Let us therefore keep to the straight
path, which is Christ," declared Augustine, "and, with Him as our
Guide and Saviour, let us turn away in heart and in mind from the
unreal and futile cycles of the godless." Nisbet observes, "In Augustine, especially in his *The City of God,* all of the really essential elements of the Western idea of progress are present."[11]

Finally, because the Christian God is distinct from creation,
the spread of Christianity undermined the host of animistic taboos
that characterized virtually all ancient cultures, and which could
represent a psychological obstacle to examination of the natural
world. Christians might treasure a magnificent tree, for example,
but they would not consider it sacred. It could be an object of
scrutiny by those with a practical turn of mind.

It is true that varieties of animism persisted in the Christian era, in traditional or altered form. Protestant reformers later suppressed the veneration of saints and angels partly on the grounds that it was a vestige of a pagan past. Francis of Assisi may have seemed to flirt with nature worship in his lyrical references to "Brother Sun," "Sister Moon" and "Sister Earth, our mother" in his "Canticle of the Sun." Yet he left no doubt who alone is owed reverence:

> Most high, all-powerful, all good, Lord!
> All praise is yours, all glory, all honor
> And all blessing.
> To you alone, Most High, do they belong.

Did these changes in religious outlook make a practical difference? Did mental machinery oiled and buffed by a thousand years of Christian influence really stimulate the culture of invention and investigative science that bubbled up within Europe in the second millennium? Did the rejection of cyclical time, the separation of the supernatural from the material world, the suppression of determinism, the embrace of progress and historical destiny, and the belief in a God who takes a personal interest in human affairs truly give Christendom an edge over other civilizations in the pursuit of knowledge? Religion cannot be completely isolated from other factors, and some historians recoil at conceding so much to religious ideas, but others invite precisely such an explanation for the triumph of the West.

Certainly *something* must account for Christian Europe's pioneering breakthroughs. Historian of science Lynn White notes that "The attitudes, motivations and most of the basic skills of modern technology before the electronics revolution originated not in Mediterranean antiquity but during the 'barbarian' Middle Ages."[12] The act of invention, says Arnold Pacey, "depends on the exercise of imagination. Idealism is important in the history of technology partly because ideals are often a more effective trigger to the imagination than are economic incentives."[13] Religion surely contributed to those attitudes, ideals and motivations. David Landes, a self-identified non-Christian, cites the "sharp departure from widespread animistic beliefs," the triumph of linear time and "the Judeo-Christian respect for manual labor" as reasons for "this peculiarly European ... cultivation of invention."[14] Historian of science D. S. L. Cardwell credits the "boldness" and "lack of inhibition about both the medieval approach to nature and medieval technics" to "the universal religion of Europe. Christianity ... provided the right spiritual armour for a man confronting nature in the raw."[15] Such was "the precocity, diversity and importance of medieval technics," he says, "that one is inclined to believe that a mutation, philosophical or spiritual, had occurred, so that medieval civilization was sharply and basically different from all those that had preceded it."[16]

Every other great civilization indulged in scientific reflection, often with impressive results. But everywhere except Europe, the effort stagnated or got lost in an intellectual cul de sac. By the High Middle Ages, around 1100, there were essentially three possible cradles for the birth of a scientific revolution: the Islamic realms, China and Western Europe—probably in that order of likelihood. Within three or four centuries, the issue was settled. Europe was sprinting into technological supremacy and scientific inquiry was becoming a self-sustaining enterprise that would never again lose its momentum.

The stillbirth of Chinese science is sometimes explained by reference to the intellectual conservatism of its mandarin class, or to the fact that China (and the Muslim world, too) was rocked by such demoralizing disasters as the Mongol onslaught. Alternatively, historians note that Europe's political fragmentation led to competing centers of creativity, and that friction between church and state often kept the two at arm's length. All of which is true, and yet insufficient as explanation.

After all, Western Christendom itself had faced the possibility of extinction as recently as the ninth and tenth centuries, under invasion by Vikings, Magyars and Saracens. As for demoralizing influences, few exceed the Black Death of the fourteenth century, which swept away a fourth of the continent's population and which Frederick F. Cartwright has called "probably the greatest European catastrophe in history."[17] Civilizations such as China and Egypt had enjoyed many more centuries of relative tranquility than ever were granted to Western Europe.

Nor does Europe's political fragmentation begin to account for the thrill generated by the recovery of classical scholarship from Islamic sources, an exuberance altogether lacking in China. As Jaki observes, "the centuries-long presence of Muslim astronomers in medieval China made no dent on it. This was in sharp contrast with the excitement and ferment created in medieval Europe by news about Arabic science."[18] Europe not only borrowed from other cultures—the fiddle bow from Java, the spinning wheel from India or China—it frequently exploited and transformed these novelties in ways not even imagined by their creators.

"It is a feature of Chinese technology," observes Jean Gimpel, "that its great inventions—printing, gunpowder, the compass—never played a major evolutionary role in Chinese history."[19] By the time the Jesuit missionary Matteo Ricci received permission to enter the capital of the Middle Kingdom in 1600, the Chinese had fallen far behind the West. No less shocking to Ricci than China's relative backwardness was the complacency of the Chinese intellectual elite. "If China was the entire world," he wrote, "I could undoubtedly call myself the principal mathematician and philosopher of nature, because it is ridiculously and astonishingly little what they know; they all are preoccupied with moral philosophy, and with elegance of discourse, or to say more properly, of style."

A preoccupation with elegance and style is a dream-state. If the Chinese missed their chance to launch the scientific revolution, it was because they didn't really seek it. Western Europeans did. And the decisive difference was cultural. Albert Einstein—hardly a Christian apologist—once wrote, "I have never found a better expression than the expression 'religious' for this trust in the rational nature of reality and of its peculiar accessibility to the human mind. Where this trust is lacking science degenerates into an uninspired procedure. Let the devil care if the priests make capital out of this. There is no remedy for that."[20]

The Astonishing Creativity of the Middle Ages

Islamic crusaders of the seventh century cut Western scholars off from the main repositories of Greek learning, an isolation lasting several hundred years. Hence the particular importance of the founding of Monte Cassino by Saint Benedict in 529.

Benedict is not a household name these days, yet he was indispensable to the advance of Western learning. "The Latin culture of medieval Europe could hardly have prospered without the enthusiasm, the passion, and the good sense of Saint Benedict of Nursia," remarks Daniel Boorstin. "The father of Christian monasticism in Europe, he was also the godfather of libraries. The preservation of the literary treasures of antiquity and of Christianity through the Middle Ages was a Benedictine achievement."[21]

In addition, as we have noted, monasteries took a leading role in the painstaking efforts of "clearing, planting and building" that were to be so critical to Europe's future economic supremacy. No less critical was a revolution in farming methods from the sixth to the ninth centuries. Innovations included the labor-saving heavy plow, the three-field system of crop rotation, and the use of iron to an extent unprecedented in any previous rural society. "The Age of Iron really only began with the Middle Ages," writes Gimpel. "Roman times still depended heavily on bronze, while in the Middle Ages bronze was of only minor importance."[22] It was in the early Middle Ages that the legendary village smithy strode onto the historical stage.

The result was a huge boost in productivity and nutrition, and therefore in population, with the meanest peasant markedly better off than his predecessor who had toiled on the Roman estates. Lynn White marvels at the "new exuberance of spirits which enlivened that age. In the full sense of the vernacular, the Middle Ages, from the tenth century onward, were full of beans."[23]

Monasteries, which accumulated immense amounts of land, embraced and extended this agricultural revolution. The monastic spiritualization of manual labor provided a diligent work force for the task of cultivation. Yet Christian monks were no mere drones. Monasteries also became fountains of new technologies, especially when the Cistercians appeared in the twelfth century.

These white-robed ascetics, pledged to poverty and supporting themselves chiefly by farming, founded monasteries with the dynamism of a modern franchising corporation—530 abbeys by the close of the thirteenth century. The order's rapid growth was not the only modern characteristic of the White Monks. Gimpel judges their monasteries to have been perhaps the most efficient economic enterprises that "had ever existed in Europe, and perhaps in the world, before that time."[24]

Not only did the Cistercians introduce a number of improvements to farming, they soon bolted to the forefront in wool production in England and iron making in both England and France. Their creativity in these areas was unrivaled, and they helped popularize the use of waterwheels in the smelting of iron. Arnold Pacey notes that "one of the first forges with a water-powered trip hammer was at Fontenay Abbey. It is certainly significant that nearly all the information we have about hammer forges operating before 1200 comes from documents written by Cistercian monks."[25] Their zeal to harness waterpower prompted the Cistercians to hire large numbers of lay brothers, becoming the first monastic order to resort to such a full-scale division of labor.

"All of this gave rise on monastic estates to remarkable assemblages of powered machinery," observes Landes, "complex sequences designed to make the most of the waterpower available and distribute it through a series of industrial operations."[26] Waterpower drove grinding, crushing and fulling mills, while it mechanized forge hammers and tanneries. But let an anonymous monk of that era speak for himself, as he puckishly describes the Abbey of Clairvaux:

> Once the river is let inside the abbey through a sluice, it first rushes against the flour mill, where it is very solicitous and occupies itself in many tasks, both in grinding the grain and in separating the flour from the bran. . . . But the river is far from being through with its work. It is invited by the fullers who labor next to the flour mills and who rightly demand that just as the river was busy in the mills so that the brethren may be fed, it should also assist the fullers so that the brethren may also be clothed. The river does not decline any work the fullers demand from it.

In modern eyes, medieval man is usually imagined as a hapless beast of burden. Yet if medieval economic production was grim enough by our standards, the headlong pursuit of labor-saving mechanical devices was already, in Pacey's view, the "most outstanding feature of the European scene." Indeed, he maintains, "if we see the use of non-human energy as crucial to technological development, Europe in 1150 was the equal of the Islamic and Chinese civilizations."[27] As Gimpel concludes, "The Middle Ages introduced machinery into Europe on a scale no civilization had previously known."[28]

No medieval invention was more important than the clock, the ancestor of all modern scientific devices and the first complex machine built entirely of metal. The main importance of clocks, however, lay in their revolutionary effects on human psychology and habits. In Lewis Mumford's famous phrase, they "dissociated time from human events." Human attention to clocks led to standards of punctuality and productivity, to an acute awareness of even the uneventful passage of time. It led, in other words, to a civilization much more like our own.

Who would want such an intrusive device? Above all, monks, who had a strict prayer schedule to meet. Under the Rule of Saint Benedict, prayer gave structure to every day. A monk's duty included six (later seven) daytime prayer breaks and one very inconvenient one at night ("are you sleeping, Brother John?"). "The very word clock," Boorstin explains,

> bears the mark of its monastic origins. The Middle English *Clok* came from the Middle Dutch word for bell and is a cognate of the German *Glocke,* which means bell. Strictly speaking, in the beginning a timepiece was not considered to be a clock unless it rang a bell.... Monks needed to know the time for their appointed prayers. In Europe the first mechanical clocks were designed not to show the time but to sound it. The first true clocks were alarms.[29]

These early clocks, which ran for hours, should have satisfied practical medieval needs, but the tinkerers wouldn't stop. They became obsessed with a desire to mimic the heavens in continuous, steady, predictable motion. It was a quest for perfection—invention driven by idealism and not any economic or practical need. By 1271, Robert the Englishman reported that clockmakers were sparing no effort "trying to make a wheel, or disc, which will move exactly as the equinoctial circle does; but they can't quite manage the job." They managed this by the early fourteenth century, when weight-driven mechanical clocks replaced water-driven models. By then, something akin to recent excitement over the Internet was sweeping Europe. Clocks were seen as mechanical wonders, confirming a sense of riding in the vanguard of progress. Astoundingly intricate clocks everywhere became symbols of civic achievement.

Monks also led the way in the study of medicine. "Medicine was studied in the earliest Benedictine monasteries," reports A. C. Crombie, "and the long series of medical works written during the Middle Ages, and continuing without a break into the 16th century and modern times, is one of the best examples of a tradition in which empirical observations were increasingly combined with attempts at rational and theoretical explanation, with the result that definite medical and surgical problems were solved."[30]

The scientific interest in medicine complemented—and may have been partly inspired by—another Christian gift to civilization: hospitals for the poor. The Emperor Constantine was said to have established the first of these facilities. Eventually, many monasteries would be outfitted with infirmaries and, finally, hospitals dedicated to the care of lepers. To be sure, medicine until the dawn of the twentieth century was a rough-and-ready affair that could kill as readily as it cured. But we should not underestimate the healing power of charitable attention, especially when it could mean that desperately ill patients received such basics as food and drink. And what may seem like haphazard treatment had elements of the trial and error that would later blossom into scientific method.

"Taken as a whole," Crombie concludes, "medieval medicine is a remarkable product of that empirical intelligence seen in Western technology generally in the Middle Ages." It was not the result of necessity, he adds—there is no compelling need to treat the sicknesses of the impotent poor—but of a theological vision. The Christian belief that individuals were eternal beings of boundless worth "placed a value upon the care of each immortal soul and therefore upon the charitable relief of physical suffering, and gave dignity to labor and a motive for innovation. The inventiveness that resulted produced the practical skill and flexibility of mind in dealing with technical problems to which modern science is the heir."[31]

That technical creativity expressed itself in a host of breakthroughs. In the twelfth century, inventors perfected the horizontal-axle windmill, which seized the popular imagination as yet another labor-saving boon. Windmills sprouted across Europe literally in a matter of a decade or two. The blast furnace, once attributed to China, was probably invented independently in Europe, also. Medieval technicians who strove to harness steam power refined a steam-driven bellows to stoke reluctant fires—the ancestor of the steam turbine. They imported the spinning wheel from Asia and quickly added improvements. They layered sand below paving stones to prevent the fracturing that had plagued Roman engineers. They were the first people to mechanize the manufacture of paper. They introduced improvements to printing that set the table for Gutenberg. They mined more stone in France in just two centuries than the total quarried by the ancient Egyptians.

They developed musical notation, including the system of sylla-bles—*ut, re, mi, fa, so, la*—still used today. They built pipe organs of daunting complexity. They invented crude eyeglasses, thanks in part, it seems, to the labors of two Dominican friars. They con-ceived the world's first crankshafts—rotary motion being absolutely essential to the mechanical age. By the late Middle Ages, they would exploit gunpowder and rockets (most obviously by the invention of guns) in ways apparently not imagined by other cul-tures possessing the same knowledge of explosives. They would quickly refine the compass once it had been imported from abroad. They were, in fact, "power-conscious to the point of fantasy," White reports. "But without such fantasy, such soaring imagina-tion, the power technology of the Western world would not have been developed."[32]

Such fantasizing could prod medieval dreamers into astound-ing stunts. A thousand years ago, a monk at Malmesbury Abbey flew a glider he had built several hundred feet. It crashed, but the exploratory imagination of medieval Europe remained intact. Roger Bacon, the great Franciscan scientist and philosopher of the thirteenth century, would prattle on about "flying machines" as if he'd stood with the Wright brothers at Kitty Hawk. "It is the intention of philosophy," the learned friar wrote, "to work out the natures and properties of things." For Bacon, the empirical route—real-world verification through controlled experiments and observation—was the only reasonable way to proceed.

Some clerics, such as the Dominican friar Giovanni de San Gimignano (d. 1323), actually encouraged sermonizing on tech-nical topics. He included in his encyclopedia for preachers a descrip-tion of everything from windmills to fortifications, to glass making. For that matter, observes Gimpel, "the greatest homage the Mid-dle Ages offered the architect-engineer was to represent the Almighty, in thirteenth and fourteenth century miniatures, as an architect-engineer Himself, measuring the universe with a large compass. It is as if today, in film on the Almighty, God were to be represented programming a computer."[33]

It would be misleading, of course, to suggest that medieval soci-ety was wedded solely to rational methods. Far from it; no soci-ety ever is. Even the highly educated men who would play central roles in the development of science often endorsed beliefs that look silly from the comfort of today's armchairs.

Despite Roger Bacon's empiricism, for example, he was prone to fanciful turns of thought that abandoned all factual foundation—for instance, blaming the great comet of 1264 for an outbreak of jaundice as well as armed combat. "Well down into the 16th century the connection between magic and one side of experimentation was close," notes Crombie. "In the 17th century Bishop Wilkins, one of the founders of the Royal Society, was to include, in a book on mechanics called Mathematicall Magick, being borne through the air by birds and by witches among recognized methods of human transport."[34] Alchemists in particular wed magic to serious experimentation, and while they never succeeded in turning base metals into gold, their quest did give birth to modern chemistry. It was astrology and the occult, however, that exercised the most powerful pull toward fatalism on the medieval mind. Their influence at royal courts is legendary, and astrology was so prevalent even at the University of Paris that Bishop Etienne Tempier felt obliged to include the influence of stars in a list of 219 propositions he condemned in 1277. (Tempier's targets were so sweeping, unfortunately, that his action was more of a hindrance than a help to scientific inquiry.)

Still, such distractions never reached the point of sapping the medieval world's intellectual vitality—a vitality that can be sensed to this day through a visit to any one of the many cathedrals that remain its most magnificent legacy.

The cathedrals were not technological innovations in the same sense as the weight-driven clock; they did not open new mechanical vistas or transform the psychology of everyday life. Still, their construction required the same sort of exploratory courage, as well as the same ability to master, through trial and error if necessary, a host of complicated innovations such as flying buttresses and rib vaults. Cathedral building also stimulated a competitive civic pride, with merchants and other townsfolk joining the clergy in a collective effort to make their aesthetic mark. It is in this sense that historians speak of the "cathedral crusade"—the peaceful counterpart to the armed expeditions to the Holy Land—whose high tide of innovation began about 1140 and subsided within 150 years. Pacey remarks:

> Although it cannot be claimed that the townsmen were conscious of technical progress as distinct from changes in architectural style

and aesthetics, we can say that they were deliberately and successfully promoting change in an art that had a strong component of engineering and mechanical skill. Thus, possibly for the first time in history, a society was consciously committed to systematic and deliberate change in a wide range of practical arts. In this restricted sense, the cathedral crusade can be taken as the beginning of the modern phase in the history of technology.[35]

How Christian Universities Classified Knowledge

One more enduring institution from this era, the university, must be credited to the Christian church. Universities were often established by ecclesiastics or grew out of cathedral schools, and some of the great ones—at Paris, for example—specialized in the study of theology. Dominican and Franciscan friars in particular were instrumental in the universities' early growth.

Theology had become a knotty field in the twelfth century, owing to the translation into Latin of the later works of Aristotle along with a host of other philosophical and scientific treatises. This knowledge was both exciting and unsettling—exciting because it exposed previously unknown vistas of systematic thought; unsettling because it was grounded in a radically non-Christian outlook. Yet the medieval world was too curious to simply censor challenging thought, and too self-confident to be demoralized by it. Instead, the scholastic philosophers studied it, debated it—and Christianized it.

The scholastic method, which began to take shape decades before the systematic recovery of the Aristotelian corpus, was above all a commitment to the use of reason to elucidate faith and provide it with rational content. The eleventh-century thinker Anselm of Canterbury, for instance, insisted that reason and investigation were crucial to verifying Christian teaching. Anselm, writes Williston Walker, was "persuaded that dialectical explanation could but support the doctrines of the church. His bold confidence in reason was an outgrowth of his firm trust in reason's Creator and in the inherent rationality of the creation."[36] Study creation, Anselm believed, and one would learn about its Creator.

Such beliefs led to ambitious attempts to order and classify knowledge, most notably by Thomas Aquinas (d. 1274), the great synthesizer of Christian and Aristotelian thought. But Aquinas's teacher, Albertus Magnus, was nearly as important himself. A

Dominican like Aquinas, Albert devoted his life to the promotion of Aristotle's scientific methods as well as to encyclopedic research of his own, especially in botany and metals. "Albert's intrepid faith convinced him that nothing uncovered by research could prove detrimental to the Christian revelation, and he felt that the cause of the faith would ultimately be served better by honest recognition of difficulties than by fearful condemnations," remarks Thomas Bokenkotter.[37] Albert's motives are clear enough from his own testimony: "I am moved with spiritual sweetness towards the Creator and Ruler of this world, because I follow Him with greater veneration and reverence, when I behold the magnitude and beauty and permanence of His creation."

Some historians consider scholasticism the most remarkable product of the medieval mind, an architectonic achievement equivalent to the great cathedrals. Its importance to our story lies not only in its commitment to the marriage of faith and reason, but also in the methods that endured as the foundation for every important legal tradition in the West: canon law, civil law, common law and international law.

More than seventy-five years ago, the great mathematician and philosopher Alfred North Whitehead summed up the legacy of the scholastic tradition in a judgment that endures to this day. "The Middle Ages formed one long training of the intellect of Western Europe in the sense of order," Whitehead said. "There may have been some deficiency in respect to practice. But the idea never for a moment lost its grip. It was preeminently an epoch of orderly thought, rationalist through and through." As one of the more memorable stylists in the history of science, Whitehead is worth quoting at length:

> It needs but a sentence to point out how the habit of definite exact thought was implanted in the European mind by the long dominance of scholastic logic and scholastic divinity. . . . I do not think, however, that I have even yet brought out the greatest contribution of medievalism to the formation of the scientific movement. I mean the inexpungible belief that every detailed occurrence can be correlated with its antecedents in a perfectly definite manner, exemplifying general principles. Without this belief, the incredible labours of scientists would be without hope. It is this instinctive conviction, vividly poised before the imagination, which is the motive power of research: that there is a secret, a secret which can

be unveiled. How has this conviction been so vividly implanted on the European mind? When we compare this tone of thought in Europe with the attitude of other civilizations when left to themselves, there seems but one source for its origin. It must come from the medieval insistence on the rationality of God, conceived as with the personal energy of Jehovah and with the rationality of a Greek philosopher. Every detail was supervised and ordered: the search into nature could only result in the vindication of the faith in rationality.[38]

How Christians Helped Man the Scientific Vanguard

The intention of the Holy Ghost is to teach us how to go to heaven, not how heaven goes. —Cardinal Baronius

The overthrow of the old model of the heavens, with the earth at its center, is not a simple tale of conflict between religious belief and enlightened skepticism. Christian belief was in fact common to both sides of the struggle. Nicholas Copernicus, Johannes Kepler and Galileo Galilei—astronomy's peerless pathfinders during the Scientific Revolution—were all as sturdy in their faith as those who rejected their discoveries.

Copernicus (1473–1543) was a canon at the Catholic cathedral in Frauenburg, Prussia. While he may have entered this service for temporal reasons, attempts to recast him as a Renaissance skeptic founder before evidence that he took his spiritual duties seriously and was behind a book published in 1525 supporting the orthodox position against Luther. Kepler (1571–1630) was a Protestant mystic who wrote books on religion, fled his home in Austria rather than embrace the Catholic faith of Archduke Ferdinand, and repeatedly (if somewhat obscurely) compared the parts of the universe to the Father, Son and Holy Ghost. To Kepler, observes Marie Boas Hall, "his newly discovered mathematical harmonies were so many laws which revealed the wonder and order of the world of God."[39] And Galileo was a loyal Catholic who, as Francis X. Rocca notes, "considered taking monastic vows as a very young man, made a pilgrimage to the shrine at Loreto after recovering from a grave illness later in life and consoled himself with devotional literature after his daughter's death."[40]

Galileo considered the church officials who condemned him misguided, of course, but not because he was bent on destroying a pillar of their faith. He believed, along with many theologians of that time and before, that when an indisputable fact conflicts with a common interpretation of Scripture, then the interpretation—not the divine revelation itself—must be at fault. His condemnation by the Holy Office of the Inquisition contained only two statements he absolutely refused to sign; one was the allegation that he was not a good Catholic.

No one should imagine, either, that the conflict over the Copernican system, with the sun at the center of the cosmos, pitted rank ignorance against irresistible evidence. As Boas Hall reminds us, "knowing that Copernicus was right makes the opposing arguments seem trivial. We falsify both the achievement of Copernicus and the difficulties in his way if we do not realize that it was not so simple; he had reason to fear scorn because his position seemed at the time so untenable as to approach the ridiculous."[41]

Unfortunately, Copernicus lacked proof. Galileo's observations strengthened the heliocentric hypothesis, but it was still vulnerable to attack when he was summoned before the Holy Office in 1633 and forced to recant. Alfred North Whitehead explains: "At the date of Galileo's controversy with the Inquisition, Galileo's way of stating the facts was, beyond question, the fruitful procedure for the sake of scientific research. But in itself it was not more true than the formulation of the Inquisition. But at that time the modern concepts of relative motion were in nobody's mind; so that the statements were made in ignorance of the qualifications required for their more perfect truth."[42]

Significantly enough, Copernican ideas were in general circulation for more than sixty years before the Catholic Church turned on them. To the church, good astronomy offered a practical payoff: the ability to set the date of Easter far in advance. What was needed was a reliable prediction of the vernal equinox, yet good predictions were hard to obtain. By the fifteenth century, in fact, a crisis was at hand: Not only did the most learned forecasts conflict wildly with actual observations, but the errors were apparently getting worse. Why *not* give the Copernican model a chance?

By the early seventeenth century, however, second thoughts were setting in. The Congregation of the Index moved against Copernican writings in 1616, requiring that they be banned or corrected. (In the case of *De Revolutionibus,* however, the "corrections" amounted to little more than the insertion of reminders of its hypothetical nature.) Meanwhile, the Holy Office directly declared the heliocentric worldview "foolish and absurd in philosophy, and formally heretical, since it explicitly contradicts in many places the sense of Holy Scripture, according to the literal meaning of the words and according to the common understanding of the Holy Fathers and doctors of theology." For later church fathers, these stern words would become a banquet of crow.

Galileo, whose *Sidereal Messenger* had propelled him to fame in 1610, was personally warned by the Jesuit scholar Cardinal Robert Bellarmine to soften his noisy promotion of the Copernican view. Galileo being Galileo, this could not be. He was a controversialist, an intellectual who relished the parry and thrust of debate. He misjudged the value of his relationship with Pope Urban VIII and pushed the pontiff beyond his limit. With almost suicidal rashness, Galileo created the character of Simplicio in 1632 for his brilliant *Dialogue,* and then let the simpleton mouth the pope's own arguments. This was the insult that brought the great scientist down.

Church apologists are sometimes ridiculed for pointing out that papal authority itself was never invoked against Copernican ideas, as if this were mere hairsplitting. After all, Urban VIII actively supported the charge against Galileo and the disgraceful punishment of house arrest. But hairsplitting is precisely what helped save Catholic astronomy, as J. L. Heilbron explains in his groundbreaking 1999 work, *The Sun in the Church:*

> Galileo's heresy, according to the standard distinction used by the Holy Office, was "inquisitorial" rather than "theological." This distinction allowed it to proceed against people for disobeying orders or creating scandals, although neither offense violated an article of faith defined and promulgated by a pope or a general council.... Since, however, the church had never declared that the biblical passages implying a moving sun had to be interpreted in favor of a Ptolemaic universe as an article of faith, optimistic commentators ... could understand "formally heretical" to mean "provisionally not accepted."[43]

Galileo's great offense was disobedience, and this was not lost on his contemporaries. They "appreciated that the reference to heresy in connection with Galileo or Copernicus had no general or theological significance," writes Heilbron.[44]

If the heresy had no theological significance, why should it have decisive scientific significance? The answer is, it didn't—not even in astronomy. "Catholic scientists in France and elsewhere (outside Italy) cheerfully ignored the decree" of 1633, Boas Hall reports.[45] But the full truth is even more surprising. As Heilbron painstakingly relates, the church continued to support astronomical research actively in the seventeenth and eighteenth centuries, even in Italy, in the Papal States, in Rome, and even though the research inevitably reinforced the Copernican system. Cathedrals were transformed into the most sophisticated solar observatories in the world by strategic placement of a hole in the roof and the tracking of the resulting circle of sunlight as it inched across the church floor. Indeed, the church "gave more financial and social support to the study of astronomy for over six centuries, from the recovery of ancient learning during the late Middle Ages into the Enlightenment, than any other, and, probably, all other institutions," Heilbron maintains.[46]

His book is replete with stories of eminent Catholic scientists, many of them clerics, who counted as leading mathematicians and astronomers of the age. There was Pierre Gassendi, priest and professor, who observed the movement of Mercury across the sun's disk. There were the Jesuits Giambattista Riccioli and Francesco Maria Grimaldi, whose map of the moon was "the most detailed and accurate of its time, drawn from their own observations and their corrections of descriptions by others," and whose book *Almagestum novum* "no serious astronomer could afford to ignore."[47] There was the devout, Jesuit-trained Giovanni Domenico Cassini, who never took a stand on the debate over heliocentrism but nevertheless became one of Europe's leading astronomers (among his many accomplishments: calculating Jupiter's rate of rotation); and there were men like the learned Pietro Ottoboni, who first as a cardinal and then as Pope Alexander VIII would become a major patron of scientists. So eager was Ottoboni to promote research that upon his election as pope in 1689, he immediately summoned his friend Francesco Bianchini, who had constructed the observatory in the Church of Santa Maria degli Angeli in Rome, and declared: "I am the Pope! What do you want me to give you?"[48]

Urban VIII had stumbled badly by permitting the condemnation of Galileo, and many in the church knew it at once. After Riccioli published a major argument against heliocentrism in 1665, it was a cardinal, Leopold de Medici, who engineered the publication of the most formidable reply. Even the Jesuits, those great defenders of church authority, "were teaching heliocentrism before the end of the seventeenth century, using the convenient fiction that it was a convenient fiction," concludes Heilbron. "Those willing to call a theory a hypothesis could publish any astronomy they wanted."[49]

How Science Rocked Religious Respectability, Then Began to Restore It

As unlikely as it may seem today, the scientific revolution was a period when discoveries about the natural world were believed to strengthen arguments *against* atheism. Paul Johnson observes that "Robert Boyle and Isaac Newton agreed that nature showed God's order and beauty; and John Ray argued in the same manner from the evidence he found in the structure of plants and animals." Similarly, "all agreed that scientific knowledge was a powerful agent against atheism; Boyle, in fact, endowed a lectureship for the defense of Christian truth, and its first holder, Richard Bentley, used Newtonian physics to confute those who argued there was no God."[50]

Scientific experimentation was the tool with which the divine secrets would be pursued, and all discoveries would be chronicled in the most precise of languages. René Descartes (1596–1650), a Catholic whose contributions to mathematics included the Cartesian coordinates and analytical geometry, asserted that "all conceptions must be doubted until proved and that any adequate proof must have the certainty of mathematical demonstration." But Descartes had no doubt why such demonstrations were possible in the first place. "If we did not know that all that is in us of reality and truth proceeds from a perfect and infinite Being, however clear and distinct were our ideas, we should not have any reason to assure ourselves that they had the perfection of being true."

The faith of most of the era's leading scientists was indisputable. Isaac Newton (1642–1747), thought by many to be the greatest scientist who ever lived, was a believer whose output on biblical and theological topics, notes Daniel Boorstin, was 1.3 million words, much more than he devoted to scientific writings. These theological works "baffle Newtonian scholars," Boorstin adds, "who try to fit them into the rational frame of Newton's universe.

Without doubt, Newton took the Prophets seriously, exercising all his linguistic learning to seek a common meaning for the mystical terms used by John, Daniel, and Isaiah."[51]

Newton's writings also provide an insight into the spirit with which scientists of that era greeted their discoveries. "The usual reaction of these early scientists, most of whom were very religious men, was to marvel at the orderliness of God's creation and the intricate plan which science was revealing," observes John Habgood.[52] Boorstin puts it more poetically: "Newton proved so effective an apostle of the bright light of mathematics precisely because he was so acutely aware of the enshrouding darkness. Who but God could penetrate the innermost workings of the universe?"[53] Inadvertently, however, Newton may have done as much as anyone to undermine religious faith (indeed, he himself would eventually come to doubt the divinity of Jesus). His discoveries seemed to imply a clocklike universe governed by immutable laws and an impersonal God, and many people found this a demoralizing insight. Habgood (both a scientist and an Anglican priest) sums up the problem: "A God who works through natural laws feels much more remote than a God whose special acts of creation and whose interventions are obvious for all to see."[54] By the end of the eighteenth century, according to Jeffrey Burton Russell, "the methods of theology, philosophy, and natural science had diverged. Still it was accepted by most intellectual leaders that an accommodation between science and theology was both feasible and desirable."[55] Such optimism would not survive the next hundred years.

The 1800s were pivotal, and what happened then can be summarized by reference to two names: Charles Lyell and Charles Darwin, a geologist and a biologist. The one rattled theologians—or a great many of them, at any rate—with his insistence on the antiquity of the earth and of man. The other, even more, alarmed them with his description of the "origin of species."

"Charles Darwin ... presented us with natural selection as a patient process by which such marvels of 'design' could come about, without the intervening purpose of a Designer being at work to bring them into being. At a stroke, one of the most powerful and seemingly convincing arguments for belief in God had been found to be fatally flawed," explains John Polkinghorne, another Anglican priest who doubles as a scientist.[56] It is at this

point—the second half of the nineteenth century, and not before—
that science and religion appear to have fallen out entirely, with
the most militant on either side eager to declare a state of war.
Prominent ministers railed against evolution (although perhaps
none as colorfully as would early-twentieth-century evangelist
Billy Sunday, who denounced any preacher willing to consider
the merits of evolution as "a stinking skunk, a hypocrite and a
liar"). Meanwhile, Pope Pius IX threw down the gauntlet in 1864
with his Syllabus of Errors, a shocking document that repudiated
the idea that "the Roman Pontiff can and should reconcile himself with progress, liberalism, and recent civilization."

The "free thinkers" didn't merely return fire. Darwin had provided them with a banner under which to march, and they
launched a frontal assault on religious belief. The "parson-baiting"
biologist Thomas Henry Huxley jeered that "extinguished theologians lie about the cradle of every science as the strangled snakes
beside that of Hercules," and others echoed his truculence. More
insidiously, talented propagandists invented the myth of an ancient
and perpetual conflict between Christianity and science that influences the attitudes of educated people to this day.

J. B. Russell tells how this was accomplished in *Inventing the
Flat Earth: Columbus and Modern Historians,* a revealing and dis-
turbing history of ideas. Russell identifies two men as the chief
culprits, John W. Draper (1811–82) and Andrew Dickson White
(1832–1918), each the author of a work of profound and lasting
influence.

Draper struck first. His *History of the Conflict between Religion
and Science* "is of immense importance," Russell explains, "because
it was the first instance that an influential figure had explicitly
declared that science and religion were at war, and it succeeded
as few books ever do. It fixed in the educated mind the idea that
'science' stood for freedom and progress against the superstition
and repression of 'religion.' Its viewpoint became conventional
wisdom."[57] Draper reserved his most potent venom for the Catholic
Church, which he considered "absolutely incompatible" with science: "They cannot exist together; one must yield to the other;
mankind must make its choice—it cannot have both."

Draper concluded—and the facts be damned—that theologians throughout history had been so backward, so anti-intellectual,
so driven by fanatical hostility to learning and empirical proof

that they had even suppressed knowledge of the spherical shape of the earth. Here he borrowed from a fictitious scene in Washington Irving's *History of the Life and Voyages of Christopher Columbus,* an imaginative account published in 1837 in which the plucky mariner is portrayed as confronting a cabal of ignorant clerics spouting "citations from the Bible and the Testament: the book of Genesis, the psalms of David, the orations of the Prophets, the epistles of the Apostles, and the gospels of the Evangelists."

It was utter fiction, but the image stuck. Never mind that, according to Russell (and other careful historians of science), "All educated people throughout Europe knew the earth's spherical shape and its approximate circumference" in 1492.[58] Indeed, only "five writers seem to have denied the globe" during the entire Christian era.[59] Never mind, for that matter, that the actual argument between Columbus and his learned antagonists was over the probable length of his voyage, and that on this issue it was Columbus who was the ignorant fantasist. "Columbus's opponents, misinformed as they were, had more science and reason on their side than he did on his," Russell writes. "He had political ability, stubborn determination, and courage. They had a hazy, but fairly accurate, idea of the size of the globe."[60] Yet in Irving's and Draper's fictional accounts (repeated by White several decades later in his monumental *History of the Warfare of Science with Theology in Christendom*), the church's critics had found a club to beat it with, and they wasted no time.

By the late nineteenth century, the Flat Error had infiltrated school textbooks. There it would remain for many decades, despite repeated attempts by historians of science to dislodge it. Less careful chronicles, meanwhile, casually repeated the myth right through the twentieth century, so that even today many educated people believe that Columbus was forced to buck a church-supported belief in a flat earth.

Thanks to Draper, White and their many followers, educated Americans also absorbed the idea that religion and science could not coexist peacefully. And their prejudices seemed to be confirmed by such spectacles as the Scopes Trial in 1925, involving the teaching of evolution in Tennessee, and the clashes over that same issue that have bedeviled public education ever since.

Behind this image of conflict, however, lay a somewhat different reality. For one thing, the scientific enterprise itself was still populated with many people of serious religious outlook. Even priests, parsons and other religious figures were represented in the front ranks of mathematicians, astronomers and other scientists well into the nineteenth century—as attested, for example, by a review of the officers and fellows of the Royal Society of England (itself begun at a Christian college in London) and by the accomplishments of such pioneers as Gregor Mendel, an Augustinian monk. As Jaki points out, "The leading physicists and astronomers of the 19th century were conspicuous by their firm adherence to a Christian or at least to a theist interpretation of the universe."[61]

If Christianity by the end of the century was identified with "an outmoded, obsolete, medieval worldview," as Russell contends, a poll by sociologist James H. Leuba in 1916 nevertheless found 42 percent of scientists expressing belief in a "God to whom one might pray in expectation of receiving an answer." More remarkably, despite the general expectation that the percentage of believers in scientific ranks would dwindle to nothing over time, a Gallup poll near the end of the twentieth century found nearly the same proportion of scientists (40 percent) expressing an identical belief in a God responsive to individual prayer. Ironically, as Professor Laurence R. Iannaccone points out, today "irreligion is most pronounced in the humanities and the social sciences; faculty in the physical sciences and professional fields are much more likely to attend church, profess faith, and approve of religion."[62]

What had happened to nearly halt the hemorrhage of scientists out of religion? Polkinghorne cites two developments: "one is the realization in the late 1920s that the universe itself has had a history, and that notions of evolving complexity apply not only to life on earth, but to the whole physical cosmos. The other is the acknowledgement that when we take this cosmic history into our reckoning, evolution by itself is not sufficient to account for the fruitfulness of the world."[63] What he means is that a number of physicists believe the "interplay of chance" necessary to create a universe capable of nurturing conscious life is so wildly improbable as to raise questions about why it happened. "Most universes that we can imagine would prove boring and sterile in their development, however long their history," Polkinghorne explains.[64] Some scientists see the work of God in this remarkably fortunate (for us) history of the cosmos.

The science writer Gregg Easterbrook has put our good fortune in perspective.

> Researchers have calculated that, if the ratio of matter and energy to the volume of space, a value called "omega," had not been within about one-quadrillionth of one percent of ideal at the moment of the Big Bang, the incipient universe would have collapsed back on itself or suffered runaway relativity effects. Instead, our firmament is stable and geometrically normal: "smooth," in the argot of cosmology postdocs. Had gravity been only slightly stronger, stars would flame so fiercely they would burn out in a single year.... The universe would be a kingdom of cinders, devoid of life. Had the "strong" force that holds the interior of atoms together been only slightly weaker, subatomic particles would have attenuated into vapor: stars would not have shone in the first place.

On and on the remarkable breaks for carbon-based life extend, to the point that "the English physicist Roger Penrose once estimated the odds against a cosmos with this one's pleasantly anthropic physical laws as about one in ten to the three hundredth power, a figure far larger than the number of atomic particles believed to exist in the universe."[65]

Skeptics handle these so-called anthropic coincidences generally in one of three ways. The most common is to dismiss them as simple-minded tautologies. Look, they say, why all this fuss about the incredible odds against any universe unfolding exactly as ours did? We happen to be here, which means that the wildly improbable did occur, in the cosmic equivalent of a Powerball jackpot for all of conscious life. It only looks purposeful from the standpoint of the winners. Another response is to suggest that unfamiliar forms of life might evolve under entirely different physical laws—an argument that cannot be disproved or tested. The third response is to suggest that our universe is not alone, that many other parallel universes exist, even if we can't detect them, or that our "universe is a minuscule bubble embedded within a giant cauldron of energy that has been inflated by quantum fluctuations," as the *Chronicle of Higher Education* explained one popular theory.[66]

But here we have left the realm of testable hypothesis and entered metaphysics. The physicist Charles Townes remarks,

> Perhaps life and the universe are inclined toward anthropocentric features for reasons of structure we do not yet know. But I see a

strong possibility intelligent design is present. To get around the anthropocentric universe without invoking God may force you to extreme speculation about there being billions of universes. Positing that essential features of the natural world are explained by billions of variables that cannot be observed strikes me as much more free-wheeling than any of the church's claims.[67]

In any event, concludes Easterbrook, science "is trending away from dispirited views of a merciless cosmos toward a new vision of creation as poignantly favorable to life. That is more than enough to constitute news."[68]

Yet it is not enough, apparently, to prevent a number of scientists from aggressively suggesting, or even stating outright, that atheism is the only outlook compatible with modern knowledge. "Your joys and your sorrows, your memories and ambitions, your sense of personal identity and free will are in fact no more than the behavior of a vast assembly of nerve cells and their associated molecules," contends Nobel laureate Francis Crick.[69] Another Nobel winner, the biologist Jacques Monod, once wrote that "man knows at last that he is alone in the universe's unfeeling immensity, out of which he emerged only by chance."[70] This theme is also a perennial favorite of biologist Richard Dawkins, who insists we live in a universe of "blind physical forces and genetic replication, [in which] some people are going to get hurt, other people are going to get lucky, and you won't find any rhyme or reason in it, nor any justice."[71]

Yet expressions of the meaninglessness of life cannot be proved. They are *opinions* about what a body of scientific knowledge means, nothing more. Other scientists who embrace the same set of facts reach more hopeful conclusions. Even a few scientists skeptical of faith have tired of the hostility toward religion they hear from some of their colleagues. Niles Eldredge, a curator at the American Museum of Natural History and longtime warrior against creationism, recently deplored "the arrogant intolerance of the scientists who claim that their science—evolution in particular—demonstrates unequivocally that there is no God."[72] Biologist Stephen Jay Gould invoked the same theme in his *Rocks of Ages*, writing,

> I do get discouraged when some of my colleagues tout their private atheism (their right, of course, and in many ways my own suspi-

cion as well) as a panacea for human progress against an absurd caricature of "religion," erected as a straw man for rhetorical purposes. . . . If these colleagues wish to fight superstition, irrationalism,
philistinism, ignorance, dogma, and a host of other insults to the
human intellect (often politically converted into dangerous tools
of murder and repression as well), then God bless them—but don't
call this enemy "religion."[73]

Unfortunately Gould has difficulty practicing what he preaches;
elsewhere in the same volume, for example, he ridicules the
anthropic principle with unrelenting contempt. Yet his point about
the caricature of religion is clearly correct. And scientists who
indulge in the sort of antireligious polemics that Gould condemns
don't seem to realize the extent to which their rhetoric fuels doubts
about their own professional enterprise.

Alfred North Whitehead long ago saw the possibility of religion surviving, and even eventually rejuvenating, under the challenge of science.

The immediate reaction of human nature to the religious vision is
worship. Religion has emerged into human experience mixed with
the crudest fancies of barbaric imagination. Gradually, slowly, steadily
the vision recurs in history under nobler form and with clearer
expression. It is the one element in human experience which per-
sistently shows an upward trend. It fades and then recurs. But when
it renews its force, it recurs with an added richness and purity of
content.[74]

The late Sir John Eccles, a Noble laureate, neurobiologist and,
as it happens, devout Christian, always disputed the notion of a
science/religion divide. "Science and religion are very much alike,"
Eccles believed. "Both are imaginative and creative aspects of the
human mind. The appearance of conflict is a result of ignorance."[75]

At the very least, religion can infuse science with moral restraint
and humility. "Science searches for impersonal knowledge," Habgood explains.

Christianity insists that knowledge carries responsibilities, and that
we only know the world truly as we use it rightly for God. . . . Science gives us power; Christianity shows us the power of God in
action in a rejected man on a cross; it turns upside down our ideas
about the use of power. These contrasts do not exclude each other.
There is no need for science and Christianity to be in fundamental

conflict.... It is possible to be both an honest Christian and an honest scientist, and to find the two allegiances both illuminating and correcting one another.[76]

Polkinghorne's distinguished career in particle physics is a case in point. "Only in the media, and in popular and polemical scientific writing," he concludes, "does there persist the myth of the light of pure scientific truth confronting the darkness of obscurantist religious error. Indeed, when one reads writers like Richard Dawkins or Daniel Dennett, one sees that nowadays the danger of a facile triumphalism is very much a problem for the secular academy rather than the Christian Church."[77]

FOUR

CHRISTIANITY AND THE SLAUGHTER OF THE INNOCENTS

One of the most common charges against Christianity is that it stimulates believers to kill and torture in the name of their creed—either in order to spread Christianity to others or to keep coreligionists in line when they show signs of straying from the faith. Christians have been so sure that they and they alone possessed the truth, and so determined to "save" the rest of humanity, willing or not, that they have waded joyfully through pools of blood in their effort to proselytize. This violence commenced against pagans in the Roman Empire and achieved its greatest excess in such sanguinary exercises as the Crusades. Christianity is, in short, an inherently militant religion—a religion of war.

"Is World War III to be fought over religion?" Paul Harvey wondered during a 1998 broadcast. "Most wars are."

Harvey's view is commonplace—in the news media and popular culture, certainly, but even among scientists and scholars. "Religious fanatics are the worst fanatics," insists Garry Wills. "More people have been killed in the name of Jesus Christ than any other name in the history of the world," maintains Gore Vidal. "Violence is authorized by religion because religion is inherently absolutist in the type of authoritative claims it makes and in the all-encompassing nature of its demands upon its followers," argues Brian K. Smith in the *Journal of the American Academy of Religion*.

The biologist Richard Dawkins, author of *The Selfish Gene,* so firmly believes that "religion causes wars" that he ridicules belief in

God not merely as a superstition but as a dangerous delusion. Asked by an interviewer in 1995 to explain his contempt for religion, Dawkins turned immediately to the familiar thesis that it is a spawning ground for violence. "Certainly [belief in God] can be positively harmful in various ways," he replied, "obviously in causing wars, which has happened often enough in history . . . causing people to do ill to one another because they are so convinced that they know what is right. Because they feel it from inside—they've been told from within themselves what is right—anything goes—you can kill people because you know that they're wrong. That is certainly evil."

For such critics, examples of religion's deadly arrogance can be found virtually any place one cares to point on the map: from the Balkans to the Middle East, from Northern Ireland to the southern Philippines, and a hundred places in between. These conflicts pit Catholic against Protestant, Christian against Muslim, Muslim against Jew, Shiite against Sunni, and Hindu against Buddhist, to mention only some of the permutations.

As the farthest-flung religion—as a religion, moreover, both missionary and universalist from the start—Christianity is charged with a heavy burden of guilt. According to Harvard law professor Alan Dershowitz, Christians still owe the world a full accounting for the Crusades, "the prelude to the Holocaust." He charges that "Entire undefended communities—babies, pregnant mothers and the aged—were all slaughtered in the name of religious cleansing." And the same religious fanaticism that provoked the massacre of Muslims and Jews in the campaigns to capture the Holy Land would later set Christian upon heretic in the Inquisition, and then Christian against Christian in the terrible religious wars that followed the Reformation.

Even these blood-drenched episodes fail to rank as Christianity's most unforgivable crime in modern eyes. That took place in the New World, where marauding Christians committed "the greatest genocide in human history," according to Tzvetan Todorov, an influential literary theorist and author of *The Conquest of America*. His opinion is seconded by historian David Stannard, who believes "The road to Auschwitz led straight through the heart of the Americas." This great bloodletting, say Christianity's critics, occurred with churches as its accomplice and cheerleader.

Even some Christian organizations seem to accept this indictment. In a statement issued before the 500th anniversary of the first voyage of Columbus, the National Council of Churches not only deplored the legacy of that voyage for its "oppression, degradation, and genocide," while counseling "repentance," but it reserved a special condemnation for the Christian church. "With few exceptions," the council said, the church "accompanied and legitimized this conquest and exploitation. Theological justifications for destroying native religious beliefs while forcing conversion to European forms of Christianity demanded a submission from the newly converted that facilitated their total conquest and exploitation."

The themes of holocaust and genocide pervade the rhetoric of political activists, too. Russell Means of the American Indian Movement believes that "Columbus makes Hitler look like a juvenile delinquent," while Professor Glenn Morris, also of AIM, describes Columbus as "the architect of a policy of genocide that continues today." Its victims, these and other revisionists insist, often were not even familiar with organized violence until their brutal encounter with Europeans. This notion was seriously proposed some years ago by D'Arcy McNickle, who estimated that perhaps 70 percent of Indian tribes in pre-contact North America did not engage in warfare. A similar claim appears in Kirkpatrick Sale's 1990 book, *The Conquest of Paradise*. Sale contends, "what little we do know [of pre-Columbian conflict] suggests that where wars took place they were infrequent, short, and mild; in fact 'war' seems a misnomer for the kinds of engagements we imagine might have taken place." In the Caribbean, for example, the Tainos "seem, remarkably, to have been a society without war . . . and even without overt conflict." More remarkably, Sale insists, they "lived in general harmony and peace, without greed or covetousness or theft."

Like a number of other writers of the past twenty years, Sale adopts wholesale the thesis of anthropologist William Arens, who argued in *The Man-Eating Myth* that Indian cannibalism is largely an invention of fearful European imaginations. The Caribs, Sale explains, "were not, contrary to the persistent European image, either fierce or warlike—or cannibals."

Their Christian conquerors, while not literally cannibals, might as well have been; for when they had finished with the natives, according to critics, little but parched bones remained to tell the tale.

— — —

Those like Richard Dawkins who assert that "religion causes wars" have some truth on their side. But what they neglect to announce with equal fervor is that religion also prevents wars. The question is, which effect is greater? Is religion more or less dangerous than irreligion, and is Christianity more or less dangerous than its alternatives?

As it happens, Christianity was much less dangerous than its competitors for at least the first few centuries, and in many ways for the better part of a thousand years. Ambivalent about power, the new religion focused on the distinctive ideal of Christian love. As Roland H. Bainton points out in *Christian Attitudes toward War and Peace,* "martial valour" is essentially absent from the New Testament. "The apocalyptic doomsday of Judaism, when God would annihilate the enemies of Israel, became the day when wrath would be pronounced upon those who had not clothed the naked."[1] The first Christian legion in the Roman army appears only in the final decades of the second century; and Bainton notes that no writing of the time "countenanced Christian participation in warfare."[2]

This began to change in A.D. 312, when Constantine discerned a cross in the sky before the battle at Milvian Bridge, along with the legendary promise *in hoc signo vinces* ("by this sign you will conquer"). Having vanquished his rival Maxentius, Constantine converted, and from that day forward Christianity began its long and checkered embrace with secular power.

Yet even then Christians did not rush headlong to seize the sword and lance. Not until almost the end of the century—four hundred years after Jesus—would Ambrose and then Augustine begin to formulate Christian theories of just war. Not surprisingly, they turned out to be much like existing Roman theories: Even when war was justified, massacre, looting and other forms of uncontrolled and vengeful violence were not.

War was justified, Augustine explained, to check evil, defend against attack and right wrongs inflicted by others. His definition came to cover so much ground, however, that it was sometimes difficult to say when even a purely offensive campaign had breached the standard. In any case, the difference between just and unjust war was of precious little interest to the warrior tribes who were being brought into the fold. Their business *was* war, and they were not about to abandon it. And the church itself, in trying to convert the barbarian kings, often emphasized the worldly victories that awaited those who embraced the true faith. As Richard Fletcher notes in *The Barbarian Conversion: From Paganism to Christianity,* "The injunction to turn the other cheek would surely have fallen on deaf ears if addressed to Clovis"[3] (the Frankish king whose conversion to the Roman church in 496 is a watershed in Western history).

"The barbarians militarized Christianity," is Bainton's simple declaration, and his conclusion is hard to deny.[4]

Yet even a militarized Christianity seems to have had more reservations about slaughter than its pagan predecessors, with their pitiless gods of war. Consider Charlemagne's savage conquest and forcible conversion of the Saxons in the eighth century. It pleased some churchmen, to be sure, but by no means all. Alcuin, the Northumbrian monk who became one of the king's most influential advisers, repeatedly protested the policy. Secular and religious imperialism may have tied the knot, but one party could never quite get over its second thoughts. The pacifist tradition lingered too strongly in Christian memory, while the gospel's message of peace was too pervasive simply to ignore. Had not Jesus proclaimed, "Blessed are the peacemakers" (Matt. 5:9)? Had he not warned Peter, in the garden of Gethsemane, "Put your sword back into its place; for all who take the sword will perish by the sword" (Matt. 26:52)?

"The Christian acceptance of warfare was always somewhat conditional," observes James Turner Johnson. "The use of force was justified only if it was undertaken against evil, and the soldier was enjoined to hate the sin against which he was fighting, not the sinner. Through much of the Middle Ages, canon law required that soldiers do penance after battle as a precaution against having sinned by allowing themselves to be overcome by such wrong intentions as listed by Augustine."[5]

Those wrong intentions included emotions that only saints could have fully subdued. For Augustine had written that "the passion for inflicting harm, the cruel thirst for vengeance, an unpacific and relentless spirit, the fever of revolt, the lust of power, and such like things, all these are rightly condemned in war." Soldiers who succumbed to these weaknesses were forbidden to take the Holy Eucharist. After the Norman Conquest, men who weren't even sure whether they had killed anyone were told to do penance for forty days.

Priests and monks, meanwhile, were forbidden altogether to bear arms or shed blood. Not that they always obeyed this rule, and prelates such as Cardinal Pelagius in the Fourth Crusade could occasionally be found commanding troops. Yet the fact remains that the church frowned on military freelancing by the clergy and opposed aggressive war that was not conducted to punish some variety of evil. The God of the Christians honored peacemakers even when turbulence was the order of the day.

Yet Charlemagne's campaigns of conquest and conversion had been a portent. They foretold the style of campaigns waged in eastern Europe in centuries to come—against the Prussians, Wends and Lithuanians, militant pagans all—and in another theater of action, against the natives of the New World. Even so, however much the church might justify the occasional war, it did not actually inaugurate one itself—until the Crusades.

How Christianity Discovered Holy War
When all is said and done, the Crusades were a long-term catastrophe for Christianity, forever sealing in the minds of some an allegiance between the cross and the sword. There is no getting around the fact that Pope Urban II galvanized the church's first holy war with his speech at Clermont in 1095, or that the saintly Bernard of Clairvaux exhorted the faithful to join the Second Crusade a half-century later, or that popes such as Gregory VIII and Innocent III drummed up combatants for later campaigns. Never mind that the Crusades percolated with secular motives as well as religious—there were colonies to be seized by the Normans, expanded trade for Italian cities, plunder for nobles, footloose freedom for common soldiers. Never mind, for that matter, that the columns of enthusiasts trekking east were reacting to actual grievances involving Muslim persecution and imperialism, and that crusading Muslim warriors had overrun much of the Christian world centuries before. Even at a distance of nine hundred years, the Crusades still haunt Christianity with the spectacles that ensued.

"Doubtless there were among the Crusaders some righteous and high-minded men, such as Godfrey of Bouillon, the first Christian king of Jerusalem," acknowledges Stephen Neill. "But to the

majority of the Christian warriors Muslims were simply unbelievers, who had no right to existence, with whom no faith need
be kept, and who might be slaughtered without ruth or pity to
the glory of the Christian God."[6] Indeed, crusaders often reveled
in the bloodshed. "Piles of heads, hands, and feet were to be seen
in the streets of the city," wrote a triumphant Raymond of Agiles
after Jerusalem fell.

> It was necessary to pick one's way over the bodies of men and horses.
> But these were small matters compared to what happened at the
> temple of Solomon.... What happened there? If I tell the truth, it
> will exceed your powers of belief. So let it suffice to say this much
> at least, that in the temple and portico of Solomon, men rode in
> blood up to their knees and the bridle reins. Indeed, it was a just
> and splendid judgment of God, that this place should be filled with
> the blood of the unbelievers, when it had suffered so long from
> their blasphemies.

Such slaughter was not unique to Christian holy war, of course.
The same breathtaking cruelty could be found at that time—perhaps any time—wherever organized powers clashed. There is no
practical difference between the sack of Jerusalem by crusaders,
for example, and the sack of crusader-held Acre by Muslim
Mameluks in 1291, or the scorched-earth policies so beloved a
century later by Tamerlane, the Mongol conqueror who built pyr-
amids of human skulls after his victories. For that matter, the triumphant Raymond of Agiles and his contemporaries may have
exaggerated the gore. According to Jonathan Riley-Smith,

> Recent work on the sack of Jerusalem in July 1099 ... is leading
> some historians to look at the evidence again. We know it to be a
> myth that the crusaders targeted the Jewish community in Jerusalem.
> We also know that the figure for the Muslim dead, which used to
> range from ten to seventy thousand on the basis of accounts writ-
> ten long after the event, ought to be revised downward. A con-
> temporary Muslim source has been discovered that puts the number
> at three thousand. Three thousand men and women is still a lot of
> people, of course, but it is low enough to make one wonder why
> the Western eyewitnesses, who gloried in generalized descriptions
> of slaughter, felt the need to portray a bloodbath.[7]

Whatever the scale of violence, the church at least temporarily
lost the well-deserved claim it once held to a higher ethic regarding

the use of force. For the first time, it endorsed the creation of monastic military orders such as the Templars (1119), celibate knights under strict communal discipline and dedicated to keeping the Holy Land under Christian control. St. Bernard's treatise on the Templars positively exults in the order's martial purpose: "How glorious are the victors who return from battle! How blessed are the martyrs who die in battle! Rejoice, courageous athlete, if you live and conquer in the Lord, but exult and glory the more if you die and are joined to the Lord." Such sentiments have failed to impress a good many historians. Neill reflects a fairly standard view when he declares that "the Crusades involved a lowering of the whole moral temperature of Christendom."[8]

Eventually a Crusade would be launched against heretics in the south of France, with massacres (on both sides) rivaling those in the Middle East. Soon the Inquisition was up and running. The papacy's own pet wars, mainly to hold or reclaim vast Italian estates, would eventually consume nearly two-thirds of papal income in the High Middle Ages.

There is, however, another perspective on the Crusades that bears consideration, as Piers Paul Read explains:

> Because most histories of the crusades tend to start with the First Crusade, it is common to see it as the first of many waves of aggression of the Christian West against the Islamic East. However, it was Islam, not Christianity, that from its inception promoted conversion through conquest. . . . From the time of the Prophet Muhammad's first *razzia,* the Christians' perception was that wars against Islam were waged either in defence of Christendom or to liberate and reconquer lands that were rightfully theirs.[9]

Indeed, it was this conviction that infused the Crusades with their extraordinary popular appeal. "Unlike the Muslim jihad," Read points out, "the crusade was always voluntary. For a secular knight, a period of adventure and subsequent chivalrous renown may have been an inducement to take the Cross: but for the knight who joined a military order, the austere rule of the barracks-*cum*-cloister was quite likely to lead either to a long period in captivity or to an early death."[10]

The Crusades certainly did not give moral pause to many in the Christian West at the time. Indeed, the recapture of Jerusalem by Saladin in 1187 reinvigorated the crusading spirit among knights and royalty alike, and induced Pope Gregory VIII to plead for a truce among warring Christian kingdoms so they could focus their martial attention on Palestine. Europe's truly traumatizing experience of crusading warfare was yet to come, and it turned Western culture forever against another outbreak.

The Wars of Religion that followed the Reformation in the sixteenth century and lasted until the Treaty of Westphalia in 1648 cost hundreds of thousands of lives, and watered the landscape with the blood of martyrs who were exploited in propaganda battles between Protestants and Catholics for centuries to come. At times these wars were mainly national affairs, as the clashes between Huguenots and Catholics in France. At other times the struggles spread until they became a free-for-all convulsing practically the whole continent, specifically, the Thirty Years' War of the seventeenth century. During this period, even the most open carnage could find a distinguished apologist, while animosity was expressed in the most uncompromising terms. Martin Luther's fiery goodbye to his former church provided a preview of the era's mood: "Farewell, unhappy, hopeless, blasphemous Rome. The wrath of God come upon thee, as you deserve." And such sentiments were fully reciprocated. After the Saint Bartholomew's Day Massacre of French Huguenots by Catholic mobs in 1572, Pope Gregory XIII actually commissioned a commemorative medal for those involved.

Yet a marvelous thing happened as a result of these convulsions. Western society reconsidered holy war as a political option—and rejected it. "Increasingly it came to be felt that what was needed was . . . an atmosphere in which the notion of concord could flourish. Now that persecution on religious grounds had been extended from Jews and suspect converts from the Koran to the Bible, to men of sober and sincere Christian conscience and intellectuals themselves . . . the first need was religious toleration, an air that would be breathed unfurtively and with confidence," explains John Hale.[11] Full toleration within nations was a long time coming, but religious toleration between states took root with surprising speed. As James Turner Johnson observes, "The ongoing civil strife in Northern Ireland aside, the last time wars were fought for religion in the West was during the century after the Protestant Reformation, a period that included the religious wars in France, the Dutch Revolution, the Thirty Years War, and the Puritan Revolution in

England."[12] From that point forward, religion would remain what the British sociologist David Martin calls "one marker of national identity,"[13] more or less important depending on the enemy. But never again would wars be fought in the name of the Christian faith, let alone to impose a doctrine on unbelievers.

Indeed, Johnson is straining when he identifies Northern Ireland as a religious conflict. It is no more reasonable to blame religion for the contemporary strife in Northern Ireland or, for that matter, the former Yugoslavia, than it is to blame people for having different cultural traditions. As Martin wryly observes, "Nobody need suppose that the razing of Catholic churches in Krajina from 1991 to 1995 had anything whatsoever to do with a disagreement over the filioque clause in the Creed."[14]

Of course, if the last religious war in the West was fought more than 300 years ago, and if Christians were largely pacifist for more than 300 years of their early history, that still leaves 1000 years in which religious motives were sometimes at play in state-organized violence. Yet even during those remaining centuries, Christianity's record is far more ambiguous, and often more praiseworthy, than the critics suppose.

How Christianity Toned Down the Violence

It was churchmen who often restrained the worst instincts of the converted barbarian kings, counseling mercy where none had been known. It was church officials who mainly spurred the great medieval movements to suppress private violence and impose rules on the conduct of war: the Peace and Truce of God around 1000, and the Second Lateran Council in 1139. And it was church canon law, reinforced by the code of chivalry, that provided the basis for a right of immunity for noncombatants.

Even the original Christian ethic of total nonviolence survived and was carried forward through the centuries—here by Catholic monks, there by Anabaptists, Mennonites, Moravians, Quakers, Dukhobors, Brethren, and many others. It was religious agitation that convinced the British government to grant exemption from military service for reasons of conscience as early as 1802. And when secular governments embarked on imperial adventures that eventually circled the globe, it was men and women expressing their Christian conscience who decried the often naked exploitation accompanying these enterprises.

Even the Wars of Religion, upon closer review, turn out to be more complicated affairs than some assume. Secular motives were everywhere at play, and often held the upper hand. They involved political rivals contending for power, local leaders resisting central government or a foreign state, and one class or region pitting itself against another. The suppression of the Irish under Oliver Cromwell, for example, looks like a religious war from one perspective, yet from another, it resembles nothing so much as an old-fashioned imperial conquest in which the natives are dispossessed and massacred while the victors seize the spoils. Or consider the English Civil War. Generations of historians have argued over its causes, but no one doubts that the clashing forces of King versus Parliament reflected not only political and religious disagreements, but economic and regional differences, too.

According to Johnson, the common theme throughout Europe was "a link between the religious reformers and forces seeking more local autonomy. The result was what we would today recognize as an ideological use of religion to bolster claims essentially political and economic in nature."[15] Revolutionary warfare—which is what some "Wars of Religion" actually were—tends to be merciless with or without spiritual disputes. It is no wonder these conflicts left a deep wound on the Western mind. But their memory should not obscure the fact that although religious fervor sometimes has stoked conflict, it also has motivated attempts to bring violence under control. Indeed, whenever Western society failed to live up to humane and noble ideals—spectacularly so during the colonizing of the New World—it was the expression of Christian values that provided the primary, and sometimes the only, dissent.

How Christian Conscience Found Its Voice Defending Indians

Only a special brand of courage, or folly, prods a man to look his neighbor in the eye and declare that he is damned.

Antonio de Montesinos was such a man. "I am the voice of one crying in the wilderness," said the Dominican priest when he confronted startled settlers on the island of Hispaniola in 1511. "This voice says that you are in mortal sin and live and die in it because of the cruelty and tyranny that you use against these innocent peoples," he informed them. "Tell me, by what right or justice do you hold these Indians in such cruel and horrible slavery? By what authority do you wage such detestable wars on these peoples.... Are these Indians not men? Do they not have rational souls? Are you not obliged to love them as you love yourselves?"

Two thousand miles to the southeast, Antonio Vieira would eventually be asking the same questions of equally indignant colonists in Brazil. Horrified by the exploitation of Indians, this Jesuit missionary in 1653 laid out for the settlers of Maranhao exactly where they stood in the eyes of God: "At what a different price the devil buys souls today compared with what he used to offer for them," Vieira declared in mock awe. "There is no market in the world where the devil can get them more cheaply than right here in our own land.... All he has to do is offer a couple of Tapuia Indians and he is immediately adored on both knees. What a cheap market! An Indian for a soul! That Indian will be your slave for the few days that he lives; but your soul will be enslaved for eternity, as long as God is God."

The conscience of the English colonies did not wear a black robe, but its Christian foundations were no less striking. Consider the evidence of William Penn's letter of October 1681 to the chief of the Delaware Indians.

> There is one great God and power that has made the world and all things therein.... Now this great God has been pleased to make me concerned in your parts of the world, and the king of the country where I live has given unto me a great province therein, but I desire to enjoy it with your love and consent, that we may always live together as neighbors and friends, else what would the great God say to us....
>
> Now I would have you well observe, that I am very sensible of the unkindness and injustice that has been too much exercised towards you ... and caused great grudgings and animosities, sometimes to the shedding of blood, which has made the great God angry. But I am not such a man, as is well known in my country.

To be sure, Penn *was* a man who could rationalize African slavery—unlike some of his fellow Quakers. But right up until his final departure for Britain in 1701, Penn's particular concern for Indian welfare never wavered. His original negotiation with the Indians was, in Arthur Quinn's words, "colonization as it should have been; his principle of religious tolerance an ideal of the republic that would be.... [I]f history has any power, the name of Penn and what he tried to achieve on the Delaware will never be taken from human memory—if history has any power."

John Eliot is rarely remembered with as much favor as Penn, but the "Apostle to the Indians" of colonial Massachusetts should be. This Puritan missionary empathized with the tribes around Boston more than perhaps any of his seventeenth-century contemporaries. His mastery of an Indian language was rare enough. No doubt more important to the "praying Indians," as villages of converts were called, was his defense of their rights. Shortly after the outbreak of King Philip's War in 1675, for example, Eliot wrote to John Winthrop Jr., "I humbly request that one effect of this trouble may be to humble the English to do the Indians justice and no wrong about their lands."

Some historians censure Eliot for failing to treat Indian life with the deference and detachment of a modern anthropologist. They are correct that he did not. Yet he also did not attempt to engineer a wholesale uprooting of Indian culture. If he had, it is inconceivable that natives would have thanked him as some did in a letter written in 1684 for "about forty years" of effort on their behalf.

Farther north in Quebec—to cite one last example—the dogged Bishop François Laval waged a running war with secular authorities over the ruinous brandy trade with Indians. In Laval's view, the violent Indian binges were evil enough. Just as bad was the way some Indians would trade their entire supply of furs for drink, leaving them bereft of necessities as the winter descended. In 1678, this meddlesome French cleric took his case right to the door of the king—and extracted a compromise that banned the sale of brandy outside the settlements.

These men of conscience, and the literally thousands of men and women like them who squared off against the inhumanity they witnessed in Europe's colonies, failed to save the natives from social and physical collapse. For that matter, their cultural arrogance is sometimes shocking to the modern mind. Yet their motives were undeniably humane, and even a *little* respect for a strange and alien people went a long way five hundred years ago. As David Landes has noted, the power of sympathy "is a particular virtue of ethnological scholarship. But one must not expect to find it generally. In sixteenth century Europe, it was confined to a few clerics."[16]

At least it was in the settlements of Spain, Portugal and France. In this regard, the deeds of Father Vieira and his fellow Jesuits deserve a special word. Famous throughout Europe for his eloquent sermons, a personal friend to the Portuguese king, a literary stylist of still-enduring distinction, Vieira was just about the last person one might expect to forsake the comforts of Lisbon for the rigors of the New World. Yet forsake them he did, at age forty-five, to return to the land of his youth, where he would become history's most determined advocate on behalf of the Brazilian aborigines.

Vieira was not as faultless as we might wish our saints to be. He was as resolved as any missionary of the era to undermine and suppress Indian customs that he found obnoxious. He supported the fatal policy of encouraging natives of the Amazon basin to settle downriver in missions, where diseases cut them down. As a concession to the colonists, he and other Jesuits even accompanied slaving expeditions to ensure they fulfilled the letter of Portuguese law, thus giving the expeditions the cover of official approval.

But such blind inconsistencies were part and parcel of the New World missionary way. Even had missionaries wanted to, they could hardly have bypassed the political realities of the time. Let modern moralists dismiss Vieira as a hypocrite if they like. The fact remains that he and his fellow Jesuits harassed and berated the colonists literally to the point of eruption for their ill treatment of the Indians. In 1661, settlers invaded the Jesuit college in Belem, threw the priests including Vieira into jail, and shipped them back to Portugal.

It was ecclesiastical lobbying, after all, that prompted edicts by Spanish and Portuguese kings curtailing or banishing Indian slavery—mainly in theory, granted—while it was the outraged reaction of settlers that convinced those same kings to relent. And it was priests who tried to shield natives from the legendary *bandeirantes* of Sao Paulo who roamed hundreds of miles over brutal terrain in search of slaves. Even Spanish missions in what is now Paraguay and the far reaches of southern and western Brazil did not escape these stone-hard woodsmen. But Jesuits at least tried to soften the blows, in some cases by arming and training Indians for defense, so that more than one slaving expedition was routed by a disciplined force of armed natives.

Mostly, though, the victories went the other way, and a host of seventeenth-century missions were destroyed or abandoned.

Eventually, several of the Jesuits' remote Indian towns found themselves on the wrong side of an international border drawn in the Treaty of Madrid, and this became one of several excuses for that religious order's expulsion from the New World. When Indians in the "Seven People" missions refused to pack up and move, a joint Spanish-Portuguese army swept down upon them in 1756.

"The Jesuits were condemned, by both Spanish and Portuguese authorities, for having incited their Indians to resist," writes John Hemming in *Red Gold: The Conquest of the Brazilian Indians, 1500–1760.* "This may not have been a fair criticism: senior Jesuits certainly tried to make the Indians move, although there was a suspiciously large number of Jesuit Fathers in the missions when they were conquered."[17]

For two centuries, the Jesuits had been the Indians' principal defenders throughout vast regions of the Americas. Whatever their shortcomings, they at least sprang from lack of understanding, not lack of good will. "If the Indians were doomed to incorporation in colonial society," Hemming concludes, "they were vastly better off under missionary protection than adrift in settler society."[18] This was a principle that held true outside of Latin America as well. In the United States, according to Sydney Ahlstrom, Christian missions were "almost the only American institutions to deal constructively with the situation [of Indian treatment]" right up to the Civil War.[19]

How Dominicans Routed Defenders of Indian Enslavement
When Spaniard and Taino first stood blinking at each other across the sand of a tropical beach, no society on earth embraced a commitment to universal human rights as we understand that term today. Some tribes and nations were less violent and predatory than others, but slavery and torture were endemic around the globe—in some cases with a Christian seal of approval. Just a few decades before Columbus's first voyage, for example, a papal bull briskly authorized the King of Portugal "to subdue Saracens, pagans, and other unbelievers inimical to Christ, to reduce their persons to perpetual slavery and then to transfer for ever their territory to the Portuguese Crown." This was just the sort of invitation to get a ruler's juices flowing.

For thousands of years, empires had come and gone, with conquerors rarely betraying the slightest qualms about the suffering they caused, let alone instigating a high-level public debate over their campaigns. But something new was afoot in the sixteenth century. Thanks to the persistence of a number of Dominican friars, the Spanish crown launched an inquiry into the morality of its own empire, sparking an ethical revolution that reverberates to this day. As Samuel Johnson would quip some two hundred years later, "I love the University of Salamanca; for when the Spaniards were in doubt as to the lawfulness of their conquering America, the University of Salamanca gave it as their opinion that it was unlawful."

Dr. Johnson was exercising his famous wit, but he came closer to the truth than he knew. Within twenty years of European landfall in the West Indies, Dominicans like Montesinos and Pedro de Cordoba were already insisting that the natives were humans with inviolable rights. Montesinos took his case back to Spain and, before King Ferdinand himself, debated a noted university professor, Juan Palacios Rubios, on the merits of Indian slavery. The professor, having drunk too deeply of Aristotle, thought the Indians qualified as "slaves by nature." This argument became the weapon of choice for those inclined to defend the conquistadors. But opponents of Indian enslavement were developing more potent intellectual firepower, which eventually carried the day.

What one historian has described as "the first unequivocal defense of the Indians against their conquerors"[20] was unleashed in the 1530s by the Dominican theologian Francisco de Vitoria. In careful reasoning that apparently electrified educated opinion of the time, Vitoria concluded that "even if the Christian faith has been announced to the barbarians with complete and sufficient arguments, and they have still refused to receive it, this still does not supply a reason for making war on them and despoiling them of their goods." Such head-clearing tolerance was only the beginning, for as important as Vitoria's contribution was, it paled beside that of the single greatest conscience of the sixteenth century, Bartolomé de Las Casas.

Las Casas came to his cause from regrettable experience. As a priest in Cuba in the early sixteenth century, he operated a grant of land complete with Indian serfs. But his complacency took a jolt when a Dominican—from the order that Las Casas himself would eventually join—confronted him in the confessional over his treatment of the natives. One qualm led to another, until finally, with that special fervor peculiar to the repentant sinner, Las Casas turned on the colonial system with a fanatical passion.

The arguments of Las Casas were familiar to Pope Paul III, as is evident in *Sublimis Deus,* issued in 1537, declaring that "Indians and all other people who may later be discovered by the Christians are by no means to be deprived of their liberty or the possession of their property, even though they be outside the faith of Jesus Christ . . . nor should they be in any way enslaved." Indians should be converted by "preaching the word of God and by the example of good and holy living." It was papal pressure, along with the influence of a number of clerics, that prompted the royal proclamation of the "New Laws of the Indies" in 1542. Those laws, which met with such fierce opposition from colonists that they could never be enforced, forbade Indian enslavement and ill treatment, and even ordered a phase-out of all private *encomiendas,* or plantations.

Las Casas' most memorable moment, however, occurred in 1550 when he defended the Indians in a famous debate at Valladolid arranged by King Charles V. His learned opponent, Juan Gines de Sepulveda, justified Indian enslavement on the ground that so long as Indians had no knowledge of the Christian faith, they could not be living in a state of "political liberty and human dignity," and therefore they fit Aristotle's category of "slaves by nature."

These were fighting words to Las Casas, whose case on behalf of the Indians lasted literally days and included every possible proof that they were rational creatures who must be treated as all other men. "Las Casas's testimony bore fruit," concludes Robert Royal in *1492 and All That.* "His central views, shared by many Dominicans in the New World and Spain, slowly reshaped Spanish activity."[21]

Granted, it is easy to identify numerous religious figures who rubber-stamped colonial barbarism in the New World. But to the extent Indian rights and culture were defended, the work was done by men and women spurred by religious motives. They were a minority, even a small minority, but such work is always done by a small number. The Peruvian novelist Mario Vargas Llosa remarks that Las Casas and his allies "fought against their fellow men and against the policies of their own country in the name of the moral principle that to them was higher than any principle of nation or state. This self-determination could not have been possible among the Incas or any of the other pre-Hispanic cultures. In these cultures, as in the other great civilizations of history foreign to the West, the individual could not morally question the social organism of which he was a part."[22]

The New World's Capital of Cruelty

It is unfortunate that the Indians did not have their own Las Casas, Vieira, Eliot or Penn, for they clearly needed such enlightened figures as much as the Europeans did. Actually, they needed them more, unless we are prepared to accept human sacrifice, cannibalism and exquisitely refined torture as acceptable cultural options.

In his monumental account of the fall of Old Mexico to the Spanish conquistadors, *The Conquest,* Hugh Thomas warns that "to read into the past the morality of our time (or the lack of it) may not make the historian's task any easier."[23] Lord Thomas is no doubt correct, yet the morality of our time is read into the conquest with almost every telling. We are supposed to understand that the Europeans were cruel, and so they were, but compared with whom? Primarily compared with us, it turns out, and not the indigenous peoples with whom they collided.

Consider the Aztecs, who may have been not only the cruelest society in the New World, but perhaps also the cruelest high civilization in history. Certainly they hold the distinction of being the only large-scale civilization to indulge in wholesale human sacrifice and cannibalism. "Mercy was as foreign to the Mexica [Aztecs] as it had been to the ancient Greeks," Thomas concedes.[24] But his comparison is misleading; for unlike the Greeks, the Aztecs lorded over one of the most savage empires on earth, one that required annual warfare just to grab enough captives to sate the blood lust of Huitzilopochtli, god of the sun and of war, as well as a variety of other pitiless deities.

The temple offerings to Xiuhtecutli, god of fire, were typical of the grisly ceremonies. As related by Fray Bernardino de Sahagun, prisoners were thrown into the fire at the top of the temple. "The poor captives at once began to twist and turn in that fire and to suffer from nausea ... and big blisters would rise all over the body. While in this agony, the priests called Qualquacuiltin pulled him out with gambrels and placed, one after the other on the block they called techcatl, and at once cut the breast from nipple to nipple or a little below, and tore the heart out." The body was then dumped by a statue of Xiuhtecutli, god of the fire.

Spanish chroniclers claimed to have seen more than a hundred thousand skulls of victims in the Aztec capital of Tenochtitlan alone. Even if they exaggerated, as some historians now believe, a more conservative accounting of Aztec butchery is sobering enough. In *The Killing of History,* Keith Windschuttle concludes that the "most plausible estimates are that the numbers executed every year ran to several thousand." He describes the most common execution as "a messy affair, with priests, stone, platform and steps all drenched by the spurting blood. The head of the victim was usually severed and spitted on a skull rack while the lifeless body was pushed and rolled down the pyramid steps. At the base of the pyramid, the body was butchered and, after being distributed to relatives and friends of the warrior who had offered the sacrifice, the parts were cooked and eaten."[25]

The brute killing and eating of humans is the easiest part of Aztec ceremonies for the modern mind to grasp. Other practices, such as priests donning the flayed skins of their victims, quite simply defy our understanding.

Human sacrifice and other Aztec religious practices genuinely appalled the hardened Spaniards. They reeled at the extent to which the shocking rituals pervaded everyday existence among these otherwise sophisticated people. Here blood was sprinkled like holy water within temples and homes alike. The European invaders were hardly untutored in institutionalized cruelty, of course; they were living during the heyday of the most notorious instrument of religious oppression in all of Christian history: the Spanish Inquisition. Yet that Inquisition, which was founded in 1480 (and which later had functional counterparts in other European nations), was child's play compared with what the Spaniards discovered in Old Mexico. Indeed, their Inquisition probably put to death fewer people during its entire history than the Aztecs sacrificed in an average year.

Henry Kamen, who has spent a lifetime in the study of Golden Age Spain, summarized the body count in his 1997 book, *The Spanish Inquisition.* "In rounded terms," Kamen writes, "it is likely that over three-quarters of all those who perished under the Inquisition in the three centuries of its existence, did so in the first half-century.... Taking into account all the tribunals of Spain up to about 1530, it is unlikely that more than two thousand people were executed for heresy by the Inquisition."[26] Perhaps more surprising, given the legend of an Inquisition holocaust within the Spanish empire that stokes popular rhetoric to this day, "it would seem that during the sixteenth and seventeenth centuries fewer than three people a year were executed by the Inquisition in the whole of the Spanish monarchy from Sicily to Peru, certainly a lower rate than in any provincial court of justice in Spain or anywhere else in Europe."[27]

The Inquisition's use of torture was not unusual. In fact, torture seems to have been applied less frequently to prisoners of the Inquisition than to inmates of ordinary European criminal courts, where the practice was "universal." Even that most grotesque public spectacle of the Inquisition, the auto-de-fé or "act of faith" leading up to burning at the stake, was not usually all that it appeared to be. Those who "repented" before the flames were lit—apparently the vast majority—were quickly strangled to spare them the far worse ordeal of being roasted alive.

It is not even the case that the Catholic Church was robustly behind the Spanish Inquisition. It had been introduced by the Spanish crown, and Kamen believes "there is much to be said for the argument that ... Ferdinand ... wished to use it to consolidate his power."[28] Pope Sixtus IV quickly became alarmed at the events in Spain and issued a bull in which he charged that the "Inquisition has for some time been moved not by zeal for the faith and salvation of souls, but by lust for wealth, and that many true and faithful Christians, on the testimony of enemies, rivals, slaves and other lower and even less proper persons, have without any legitimate proof been thrust into secular prisons, tortured and condemned as relapsed heretics ... setting a pernicious example, and causing disgust to many." This warning provoked an indignant reaction from Ferdinand, and the pope backed down. He then made the fateful appointment of Tomas de Torquemada, a one-man scourge, as chief inquisitor. Even so, Kamen says, "The next half-century or so witnessed several attempts by Rome to interfere in questions of jurisdiction and to reform abuses that might give the Inquisition a bad name."[29]

The Spanish Inquisition did get a bad name, of course, and like the original medieval version, deserved it. The Inquisition blighted Spanish intellectual life, made special targets of converted Jews and Muslims, and was probably behind the expulsion of the Jews in 1492. But its horrors were almost penny ante compared with those endured by the residents of Mesoamerica. During most of its existence, the Inquisition was irrelevant to the vast majority of Spaniards, who rarely if ever saw an inquisitor, let alone were hauled before one. By contrast, the conquistadors discovered blood-spattered shrines even in minor Indian villages during their march to the Aztec capital in 1519.

It was not just the Aztecs in the New World who were partial to human sacrifice or cannibalism. Tribes in all directions from central Mexico—the Tlaxcalans to the east, for example, and Mayans to the south—ritually killed and ate humans. So did the Tupi tribes along the coast of Brazil, for whom incessant warfare was basically a hunt for captives to stock their ceremonial meals.

Archeologist Johan Reinhard believes some children in the Incan empire may actually have been raised for sacrifice. Whether or not the theory is true, Reinhard's discoveries have left little doubt that the ritual killing of children on mountain peaks was common among the Incas. (They held no monopoly on child sac-rifice: Both Mayans and Aztecs butchered children by the legion.)

North America, too, was not exempt from such terrifying cus-toms. Tribes as diverse as the Pawnee, Muskogean Natchez, Huron and Iroquois indulged in similar practices. Indeed, some of the ceremonies are better documented than we might like. Consider, for example, what French Jesuits witnessed after a Huron village had captured an enemy Iroquois warrior. "First each person burned the captive's body in a different place," recounts Arthur Quinn in *A New World.* "When little skin was left uncharred, red hot hatch-ets were applied to the bottoms of his feet, and hung from about his neck to sear through the flesh of his chest and back. Burning sticks were forced into his ears and rectum.... The torture had taken much of the night, and the finishing touches were made in honor of the dawning sun.... First his eyes were gouged, then a foot chopped off, then one hand, then the other. Throughout he was still conscious.... Finally there was nothing left to do but reluctantly end his misery by severing his head."[30]

And after that, nothing left to do but roast him for a meal.

So strong is the popular desire to see Native Americans as deeply spiritual, peaceful people that contrary evidence is often resisted even when it stares observers in the face. Some of the first to excavate Anasazi ruins in the Southwest, for example, suspected the Ancient Ones of ritual cannibalism; heaps of bone fragments with telltale markings pointed the way. Yet mainstream archeology rejected that view for virtually the entire twentieth century. Its blinkers were finally torn away in 1999, with the publication of *Man Corn: Cannibalism and Violence in the Prehistoric American Southwest,* by Christy G. Turner and Jacqueline Turner. The Turners identified dozens of sites in four states where cannibalism almost certainly was practiced. They concluded that it endured for nearly four centuries (900 to 1300, when Anasazi culture collapsed), and suggested it involved the killing of children, at least in Chaco Canyon.[31] One year after their book appeared, its argument was vindicated by irrefutable evidence published in the journal *Nature.*

"The land of the Anasazi was not a pleasant place to be, after all," Christy Turner says. "It was just as violent as any place else in the world."[32]

War and the State of Nature

The myth of the peaceful native has been around, in one form or another, for nearly five hundred years. Even the brute fact of cannibalism has rarely deterred those intent on romanticizing and sanitizing native culture, such as the sixteenth-century French essayist Michel de Montaigne. Without a trace of irony, Montaigne actually titled his paean to Indians, "On the Cannibals." Montaigne's modern successors merely carry on the tradition of locating paradise in the midst of shattered bones.

The anthropologist Lawrence H. Keeley has described how "prehistorians have increasingly pacified the human past. The most widely used archeological textbooks contain no references to warfare until the subject of urban civilization is taken up."[33] (A 1995 study of high school history textbooks found only one that mentioned human sacrifice in discussion of the Aztecs, too.) This resolve to see no evil, Keeley explains, is so pronounced that "a Belgian archeologist who has excavated many Iron Age burials was criticized by several colleagues ... for referring to burials from this period as 'warrior' graves, even though they contained spears, swords, shields, a male corpse clothed in armor, and in some instances the remains of a chariot."[34]

In his book *War before Civilization: The Myth of the Peaceful Savage,* Keeley marshals a wealth of research to demolish one cherished popular myth after another. Among his conclusions:

• There is no peaceful state of nature for humans. With few exceptions, virtually all societies have engaged in warfare.

• Bands, tribes and other non-state groups have been as likely to make war as civilized states, and probably more so. One study involving 25 tribes found that 20 of them, or 80 percent, fought all the time. They were engaged in warfare literally every year.

• The proportion of war casualties in primitive societies "almost always exceeds that suffered by even the most bellicose or war-torn modern states."

• Native Americans did not learn such barbarous tactics as scalping and wholesale massacre from Europeans. A site at Crow Creek in South Dakota, circa 1325, contains five hundred scalped and butchered bodies, and similar sites have turned up elsewhere. For that matter, only fairly advanced civilizations bother to adopt rules intended to temper war's brutality, such as recognizing noncombatants, accepting the surrender of an enemy force and taking prisoners. In most pre-state societies, captured males were almost always killed, either on the spot or after ritualized torment. Surrender under such a threat was unthinkable. War between nations, for all its horrors, is a form of organized killing hemmed in by definite rules.

Keeley's views should not be startling. Anthropologists at the Human Relations Area Files, a nonprofit research organization at Yale University, have found war "rare or absent" in only 9 percent of 186 societies they have studied. (The most common reason for conflict? Not religion, but fear of shortages or impending natural disaster.) Marvin Harris, one of America's best-known anthropologists, told the 1999 meeting of the American Anthropological Association that he doubted whether war could ever be abolished precisely because it has been so universally practiced.

It is simply absurd, in other words, to maintain that serious warfare was unknown to most Native American tribes until the incursions of the Christian West. And it is equally misleading to claim that those same Indians were the victims of an intentional genocide. No sober historian believes this. Native Americans fell by the millions, but mainly to diseases against which they had no resistance. Cortes and Pizarro were great and ruthless soldiers, with a marvelous instinct for the main chance. Yet they never could have triumphed without the unexpected help of the microscopic armies of infection that landed with them, smallpox most of all. "Had it not been for these diseases," Hugh Thomas concludes, "the history of Mexico might have been closer to that of British India than that of New Spain."[35]

Given the rudimentary state of medical knowledge, no one ever quite grasped why a disease would carry off so many of one people and not another. Christian missionaries would pray over an epidemic's victims, hauling them water and offering comfort, but still the piles of bodies grew. "Because of the microbes they carried, Europeans who arrived in and spread throughout North America were an invading force that took no prisoners," writes Shepard Krech III. "There is no need to accuse Europeans, as some have, of mass continental genocide—assuming that requires intent. These diseases did not need conspiracy to spread."[36]

Christianity and the Most Pitiless Century
Whatever Christianity's role in the conflicts of the past two millennia, its hands were clean during the bloodiest century on record—the one just past. The body count from the two great barbarisms of the twentieth century, communism and Nazism, is extraordinary enough on its own. Communism's toll ran to perhaps 100 million: 65 million in China, 20 million in the Soviet Union, 2 million in Cambodia, 2 million in North Korea, 1 million in Eastern Europe and 10 million in various other spots around the globe, according to Stephane Courtois' authoritative *Black Book of Communism*.[37] Adolf Hitler's death machine was equally efficient, but ran a much shorter course.

"For the historian of the year 3000, where will fanaticism lie? Where, the oppression of man by man? In the thirteenth century or the twentieth?" asks Regine Pernoud.[38]

Communism was and is proudly atheistic, while Nazism (as explained in the next chapter) embraced a form of neopaganism. Both were hostile to the organized religions in their midst, and neither genuflected before any power other than man himself. Yet these movements exterminated their victims with an efficiency that clearly exceeded the most grisly achievement of states prodded by Christian zealotry. In that sense, they were worthy heirs to the French Revolution, which erected altars to the Goddess of Reason before the backdrop of a guillotine.

Other state ideologies, including nationalism, seem equally ferocious with or without a religious component. Even the brutality of ethnic rivalry appears unaffected by religious differences. The worst explosion of violence in modern Africa, for example, in Rwanda, had nothing to do with religion. Meanwhile, where religious difference does seem to heighten conflict, for example in the long-running warfare in Sudan, it is impossible to say how much better the clashing ethnic groups might have gotten along if they had been of one faith. David Martin makes a similar point in another context: "Turks, Iraqis, and Iranians can slaughter Kurds, and vice versa, with an enthusiasm entirely unaltered by the presence or absence of religious difference. In Turkey Turks are largely Sunni, Kurds often Alawite. In Iraq Kurds are Sunni, like most Iraqis, and in Iran they are Sunni and the Iranians mostly Shia. But the degree of conflict remains fairly constant."[39]

It was understandable that Europeans three hundred years ago would feel a special revulsion for warfare fought over religion, given their recent experience. It is less understandable that even seemingly well-informed people today assert that religion is the primary cause of war. Anthropology does not support this view. The universal nature of warfare contradicts it. Even a casual review of conflicts around the globe debunks the idea that strife is any less energetic when combatants share the same religion than when they do not.

For that matter, wars proclaimed explicitly for religious reasons often have a secular purpose below the rhetoric. Classic Islamic tradition requires a jihad, or holy war, upon unbelievers once a year if possible, yet it is striking how consistently these holy calls to arms have dovetailed with temporal aims. One scholar, Rudolph Peters, categorically states that "Historical research . . . has proved that the wars of the Islamic states were fought for purely secular reasons."[40] Peters clearly exaggerates, unless faith and ideology (and the religious preaching of warfare) have no effect on behavior—a conclusion that would strike most people as inconceivable after the suicide hijackings of September 11, 2001. Yet his argument does suggest how difficult it can be to disentangle secular from religious motivations.

It may be that the only honest assessment of the overall influence of religion—or at least of Christianity—on violence and warfare is an admission that no one quite knows how to add up the lives saved versus the lives lost. Bainton believes:

> the Christian religion makes in some respects for the reduction and in other respects for the intensification of strife. Many of the cleavages which divide men are removed. There is no longer Jew nor Greek, circumcision nor uncircumcision, Hellene nor barbarian, bond nor free. A racial war, a cultural war, a national war, a servile war, are unthinkable if Christianity be taken seriously. But there are new divisions. The believer stands over against the unbeliever, and Paul's anathema upon any who should preach another gospel foreshadows, however dimly, the wars of orthodoxy.[41]

Yet surely Bainton has missed something equally important. If ideas matter, then a religion that intones "blessed are the peacemakers" has more likelihood of restraining human aggression than one that demands a parade of captives be dragged up the steps of a temple for sacrifice. And a religion whose central rite included prayers for peace even during the Crusades has a better chance of fostering subcultures of antiwar dissent than religions that lack such ambiguity. The New Testament Gospel is dead set against killing, and stubborn literalists in every era have taken its message to heart. Their failure to create peace on earth is not nearly so surprising as the fact that against such overpowering odds, they tried.

FIVE

CHRISTIANITY
AND. THE THIRD REICH

*The gravest charge against Christianity of the past three hundred years,
and certainly since the Wars of Religion, is that it failed to resist the Nazi
extermination of six million Jews. Not only did Christian leaders within
Germany quietly submit to Nazi aims—or even embrace them outright—
but Christian protest elsewhere was disgracefully weak and ineffective.
Most scandalously of all, Pope Pius XII refused to exert his moral authority on behalf of the Jews, either because of cowardice and indifference,
or because he favored a German victory over Soviet communism. In its
extreme version, this indictment not only links Nazi ideology to Christianity itself, but claims that the movement was the natural fulfillment
of centuries of anti-Semitism.*

At the National Prayer Breakfast in February 1999, President Bill
Clinton spoke solemnly about the religious roots of Nazi philosophy as he understood them. "Throughout history," the president
said, "people have prayed to God to aid them in war. I do believe
that even though Adolf Hitler preached a perverted form of Christianity, God did not want him to prevail."

The politicians, world leaders and other luminaries in attendance let the president's history lesson pass unchallenged. So did
the vast majority of media and even religious commentators after
it appeared in news accounts. If Americans were dismayed or bewil-
dered to hear that Hitler embraced a form of Christianity—perverted or not—few gave any hint that this was so. Yet perhaps
their placid response is not surprising, given what they see and

hear from other respected sources regarding the Christians' responsibility for Nazi crimes.

Not far from where the president spoke that day in Washington, D.C., stands the United States Memorial Holocaust Museum, whose powerful exhibits have been viewed by millions of visitors. Among the lessons many have learned is one consistent with Clinton's statement: The Holocaust was engineered by a Christian on behalf of Christian ideals.

This message has never been stated directly by the museum, but for years it was unmistakably promoted by a version of a film titled *Antisemitism,* available to visitors at the outset of the tour. Not only did the film present anti-Semitism as a uniquely Christian phenomenon, including references to the Crusades and Martin Luther, it implied that Hitler himself was a religious militant. "Enter Adolf Hitler," the film intoned, "Austrian born and baptized a Catholic." Hitler's mission? "In defending myself against the Jews," he was quoted as saying, "I am acting for the Lord. The only difference between the church and me is that I am finishing the job."

If film viewers didn't know better, they could easily have concluded that Hitler was a devout Catholic. After all, Hitler cast himself as a pious son of Christianity, at least at one point in his life, and no dissenting voice in the film contradicted him.

In the spring of 2000, the museum introduced a revised version of the film without the Hitler quotation. But the film's premises remain, in the words of the Hudson Institute's Michael Horowitz, that "Christian anti-Semitism is the principal if not singular source from which the Holocaust arose" and that Nazi anti-Semitism does not differ fundamentally from its Christian predecessor. When such a prestigious institution as the Holocaust Museum presents Nazism in this way, and when the president of the United States considers Hitler a perverted Christian evangelist, the idea of the "religious" Hitler is well on its way to becoming conventional wisdom. Or perhaps it already has achieved this status. How else to explain the ease with which popular commentators such as Maureen Dowd of the *New York Times* resort to the theme? Writing in June 1999, Dowd included the Führer in a list of examples of violent Christian zealotry. According to Dowd, "History teaches that when religion is injected into politics—the Crusades, Henry VIII, Salem, Father Coughlin, Hitler, Kosovo— disaster follows."

It is a wonder Dowd did not include Pope Pius XII in her roll call of calamity. For if there is one other popular theme involving Christian complicity in the Holocaust, it is the claim that Christians in general, and the Roman Catholic pope in particular, did little or nothing to aid the Jews, or, even worse, connived in their tragic fate; that Pius XII was either criminally indifferent to the Jews' plight or possessed by even darker motives.

That allegation burst into the public arena in the early 1960s by way of Rolf Hochhuth's play *The Deputy*. It has been updated numerous times since, most stridently by John Cornwell in his 1999 book, *Hitler's Pope: The Secret History of Pius XII*, whose lurid title accurately reflects its contents. Even Cornwell, whose thesis received an uncritical hearing on *60 Minutes*, draws short of calling Pius XII and the Catholic Church active Nazi collaborators. Others haven't hesitated, however. In a column in *The Guardian*, for example, Professor David Cesarani of England's Southampton University contends that "once Hitler invaded the Soviet Union in 1941, the church was effectively on his side." *Time* magazine concurs, announcing flatly in its January 26, 1998, edition that "in 1997 the Roman Catholic Church finally said it was sorry for collaborating with the Nazis in World War II."

Ironically, the Vatican's own assessment of the church's role in the Holocaust was not released until two months later, under the title *We Remember: A Reflection on the Shoah*. This fourteen-page statement acknowledges that Christian anti-Semitism was a historical fact and issues a "call to penitence" on behalf of those who were silent in the face of Nazi crimes. It also deplores "the sinful behavior" of some members of the church. Meanwhile, however, it credits many Catholics, including the much-vilified Pope Pius XII, with rescuing Jews during World War II—a qualification that makes the apology hard for many observers to swallow. The *New York Times*, for example, characterized the Vatican's statement as a virtual whitewash.

In the eyes of Pius XII's most vehement critics, he was a calculating cynic who preferred National Socialism to communism and was thus prepared to dawdle as the death toll climbed. Rabbi Marvin Hier of the Simon Wiesenthal Center in Los Angeles reflected this perspective when he declared that Pius XII "sat on the throne of St. Peter in stony silence, without ever lifting a finger, as each day thousands of Jews were sent to the gas chambers with his full knowledge."

— — —

Adolf Hitler might have been a baptized Catholic, but he didn't preach a "perverted" form of Christianity, or any form at all. He was a blood-and-soil primitive, a pagan determined to save and ennoble Germany by sweeping all trace of Judaism and Christianity from the national stage.

"My pedagogy is strict . . . ," Hitler once explained. "I want a powerful, masterly, cruel and fearless youth. . . . There must be nothing weak or tender about them. The freedom and dignity of the wild beast must shine from their eyes. . . . That is how I will root out a thousand years of human domestication."

What else could he have meant by "a thousand years of human domestication" save for the influence of Christianity on the German people?

There is no need to speculate about whether this was the case, since Hitler was frequently far more explicit in his contempt for Christianity. "It is through the peasantry that we shall really be able to destroy Christianity," he confided in 1933, "because there is in them a true religion rooted in nature and blood." His countrymen would have to choose: "One is either a Christian or a German. You can't be both."

Not that Hitler was especially worried about the eventual choice. "Do you really believe the masses will ever be Christian again?" he wondered in mock seriousness. "Nonsense. Never again. The tale is finished . . . but we can hasten matters. The parsons will be made to dig their own graves"—just as Polish priests would be forced to do.

When the Reich minister for church affairs, Hanns Kerrl, died in 1941, Hitler remarked that "Kerrl, with the noblest of intentions, wanted to attempt a synthesis between National Socialism and Christianity. I do not believe this is possible, and I see the obstacle in Christianity itself. . . . Pure Christianity—the Christianity of the catacombs—is concerned with translating the Christian doctrine into fact. It leads simply to the annihilation of mankind. It is merely wholehearted Bolshevism, under a tinsel of metaphysics."

Such jarring anti-Christian sentiments naturally were not regular fare in Hitler's public pronouncements, especially in the early years, when he adopted a pious front for political advantage. But they always represented his true feelings and the feelings of the Nazi leadership he assembled, which teemed with Christian-haters of stunning virulence. "The Nazi ideology was never fully articulated or made systematic," writes J. S. Conway in *The Nazi Persecution of the Churches*.

> The claim to be the representatives of a new paganism was, nevertheless, not just a personal idiosyncrasy of a few minor figures in the Nazi hierarchy. The conviction of being the vanguard of a new ideological force in European culture was an integral part of all Nazi thinking. Among the most prominent features of this new paganism can be discerned the exaltation of the personality of Hitler, the propagation of the "religion of the Blood" and the attempts to provide pagan equivalents for "outdated" Christian ceremonies.[1]

Both SS chief Heinrich Himmler and his thuggish confidant, Reinhard Heydrich, "the hangman of Europe," were fanatical racists and anti-Christians who repeatedly advocated a crackdown on the clergy. It is no wonder the SS practiced, according to Richard Grunberger, "neo-paganism in its purest form."[2] Special ceremonies not only replaced Christian sacraments and holidays, but tended to emphasize the precise opposite of Christian themes. An SS groom handed his bride a dagger as the final act of the marriage ceremony, while an infant ready for christening was carried to the gathering on a battle shield.

Himmler and Martin Bormann, Hitler's personal secretary, actually favored abandoning monogamy—a Christian tenet laid down in the New Testament—for the Nazi elite once Germany won the war. And they were as shrinking violets compared with Alfred Rosenberg. His half-baked treatise *The Myth of the Twentieth Century* pounded Christianity with such violence ("the Christian-Jewish plague must perish") that even Hitler felt obliged to distance himself from it before his seizure of power. Not that Rosenberg's career ever suffered. This crude propagandist, who never muffled his hatred for the churches, was rewarded time after time with high Nazi posts. "I imagine," he once speculated, "that in place of many of these tormented 'saints' we could erect statues of the German heroes." By the late 1930s Rosenberg was exulting that "the curriculum of all categories in our schools has already been so far reformed in an anti-Christian and anti-Jewish spirit that the generation which is growing up will be protected from the black swindle."

The problem with Christianity was that it was too soft. It preached patience, humility and understanding, whereas self-conscious Aryans who fancied themselves on a march of destiny could have no truck with such qualities. As one swaggering loud-mouth put it before a Munich rally in 1935, "Christianity has failed us in the social question, the racial question and in the educational question.... Can one imagine one of our Hitler Youth lads with a rosary? Or an SA or SS man taking part in a pilgrimage along with a lot of old women?... Our faith is in blood and earth, we want to be pure heathen, not contaminated with Christian ingrafts."

Little by little, such sentiments were used to squeeze the churches onto an ever-shrinking patch of ground. Although religious instruction was at first mandated even in schools that had lacked it, this ploy lasted only while the Nazis were consolidating power. By the mid-1930s, religious instruction was discouraged, school prayers had been made optional, and denominational schools were under attack. Such schools disappeared altogether by 1940.

The effort to drive Christianity from the public square took many forms. The Catholic German Center Party was extinguished; Christian trade unions were undermined; religious youth groups were bullied and vilified, and their sporting events, camps, parades and uniforms banned. Monks and nuns by the hundreds were brought up on bogus charges of currency violations and sexual perversion. Carols and nativity plays were barred from classrooms; crosses gradually stripped from hospitals and schools; the religious press censored and circumscribed; pilgrimages ridiculed and harassed; and theological faculties at the universities starved of replacements. "By 1939," Conway reports, "only 2 percent of the university student body was enrolled in theological studies, as compared with 6 percent in 1933."[3]

In the Soviet Union, a desperate Stalin, similarly antireligious, granted the Orthodox Church a bit of breathing room during World War II in order to stoke nationalist flames, but in Germany the vise on churches actually tightened. Wholesale confiscation of property—monasteries, convents, abbeys, hospitals, charitable institutions—began in 1939 and accelerated with the war. Moreover, as Grunberger notes in *The Twelve-Year Reich: A Social History of Nazi Germany, 1933–1945,* "the very expression 'Christmas' was officially proscribed during the war, to be replaced by the term 'Yuletide,' semantic manipulation being an essential feature of dechristianization."[4]

Admittedly, the Nazis never launched an all-out, open suppression of German Christianity. That would have been too difficult and risky. Yet their ultimate intentions are not difficult to describe, for they put them into practice in Poland. It was there—and especially in the region bordering Germany known as Warthegau—that the Nazis saw fit to deal with Christianity as the ideological enemy they believed it was.

Poland was the proving ground because Poles counted for nothing. In no other country, writes John Morley in *Vatican Diplomacy during the Holocaust,* "was the Christian population treated as it was in Poland. In Poland, both Jews and Christians were objects of Nazi oppression and manipulation."[5] The Christian clergy was a chief target from the outset, secondary only to the Jews. Conway provides some idea of the scope of this assault: "In West Prussia, out of 690 parish priests, at least two-thirds were arrested, and the remainder escaped only by fleeing from their parishes. After a month's imprisonment, no less than 214 of these priests were executed.... By the end of 1940 only twenty priests were left in their parishes—about three percent of the number of parish priests in the pre-war era."[6]

The toll of murdered Polish priests would rise into the thousands by war's end—an estimated one-fifth of the clergy—while thousands of religious brothers and nuns perished as well. And the far smaller Protestant churches in Poland fared no better. Many of their clergy were packed off to Buchenwald, Dachau and other concentration camps.

The Nazis were not content only to exterminate church leaders. In Warthegau, they also restructured what religious life they allowed to survive. Churches were forbidden to own property other than church buildings. (Monasteries, for example, were outlawed.) They were stripped of official status and designated as mere religious associations, with the Catholic Church being severed from Rome. They were also barred from engaging in any social or welfare work and from organizing any group not directly associated with church worship. Adults could join only by taking the potentially hazardous step of signing a declaration, and children were not allowed to join at all.

In short, the churches were marginalized and harassed when they weren't simply liquidated. Finally, the occupying Germans seized control of all church finances, including the collection plate. Protestant leaders who objected to the local Nazi warlord were told, "Here the National Socialist state is being constructed."

Martin Niemoller and the Confessing Church

It is easy for those who do not live under a totalitarian regime to expect heroism from those who do, but it is an expectation that will often be disappointed. Christians in Germany did not fall over one another defying the Nazi state. That is a fact, and a melancholy one for sure. A significant number welcomed the advent of Hitler. Yet it is equally true that the price of defiance could be very high, involving death or deportation. In such a context it should be less surprising that the mass of Christians were silent than that some believed strongly enough to pay for their faith with their lives.

Pastor Martin Niemoller, who voted for the National Socialists in 1933, attracted the menacing attention of the Gestapo before the year had passed. As a German nationalist and former U-boat captain, he was a principled Christian who opposed attempts by enthusiasts who called themselves "German Christians" to seize control of the Protestant churches and adulterate the Gospel with a crude infusion of German mythology and "heroic piety." Niemoller decided to check them.

On January 25, 1934, as a member of a Protestant delegation to see Hitler, Niemoller admonished the Führer personally. He did so even after a harrowing introduction by Hermann Göring, who revealed the contents of an incriminating phone conversation involving Niemoller that the secret police had tapped. This revelation was followed by an equally alarming rant by Hitler himself.

Yet the pastor would not be silenced. "A moment ago, Herr Reich Chancellor," Niemoller responded at last, "you told us that you would take care of the German people. But as Christians and men of the church, we too have a responsibility for the German people, laid upon us by God. Neither you nor anyone else can take that away from us."

By nightfall, the Gestapo were raiding Niemoller's home. Within days, he was arrested and ordered to report every twenty-four hours to the secret police. Within a week, a bomb exploded inside his house, igniting the roof. In the years that followed, Niemoller was arrested repeatedly, for the last time in 1937. He was tried in 1938 on charges so obviously trumped up that he was in most respects acquitted, but was held afterward as the Führer's personal prisoner and spent the next eight years in Sachsenhausen and Dachau concentration camps.

To be sure, not many clergymen had the courage or even the desire to go as far as Niemoller. Many were ardent patriots, and either indifferent or hostile to democracy. It was fine with them if an authoritarian regime promised a moral renewal of the German nation while battling Bolshevism and restoring national pride. A decade earlier, some had begun to search for a theological basis for German ambitions. By the 1930s, these extremists had gathered in several factions, all racing to embrace the Nazis.

It was not hard for such zealots—and a good many mainstream Christians, too—to dismiss the anti-Christian subtext of the Nazi movement. Even if they discerned it, they discounted the thought. Surely Hitler himself did not endorse such unpleasant notions, they told themselves. Had not the Nazi Party platform since the mid-1920s committed itself to respect the independence of religious denominations? Did not Hitler declare, shortly after assuming power, that "the National Government ... will seek firmly to protect Christianity as the basis of our whole morality, and the family as the nucleus of the life of our people and our community"? Had he not pledged one month later in the Reichstag that Protestants and Catholics both were "important factors in the preservation of our nationality"?

For that matter, wasn't Hitler himself the picture of piety, invoking providence and the moral foundations of German greatness at every turn? And speaking of greatness, hadn't Hitler's economic program begun to bear fruit?

By such self-delusions, devout Germans reconciled themselves to a criminal regime that was committed, in Hitler's own words, to "stamping out Christianity in Germany, root and branch." It helped, of course, that many Christians shared, to one degree or another, the anti-Semitism that infused Nazism with a distinctive fervor. The responsibility of Christian anti-Semitism for the

Holocaust is a question that will never be settled, even among careful historians without an ax to grind. No doubt the history of anti-Semitism—the oldest, ugliest stain on the church—helped to provide a climate in which the Nazis could thrive. Not only were Jews still blamed for the death of Jesus and for attempting to thwart the progress of Christianity during its years in the wilderness before it wound up ascendant in Rome, but many Christians also condemned Jews for spreading unwanted modern influences, including "cosmopolitanism" and Bolshevism. Niemoller later admitted that he too had harbored such thoughts.

No such admission was necessary from some of Niemoller's anti-Nazi colleagues. Their words are on the record, crude and jarring. For example, Otto Dibelius, the brave pastor who succeeded to Niemoller's pulpit and was arrested by the Gestapo two weeks later, once declared, "It cannot be denied that in all manifestations of disintegration in modern civilization, Jewry has always played a leading role." (Hitler's animus toward Jews was political in its origins, too: he blamed them for the Marxist revolt in Germany near the end of World War I, which he characterized as a stab in the back of the German army.)

Yet however much anti-Semitic Christian folklore and sentiment were exploited by the Nazis, the fact remains that their neo-pagan hatred of Jews (and of the handicapped and the Gypsies, the other special victims of their genocide) broke with Christian tradition. As scholars like Marc Saperstein, professor of Jewish history at George Washington University, have pointed out, Christians historically had identified Jews in religious, not racial, terms. Baptized Jews were considered true Christians (however much the Spanish Inquisition briefly disagreed) and neither Christian states nor Christian teachings had advocated or condoned the slaughter of Jews.

Indeed, pogroms and violent outbursts were typically the product of mobs, their powder fired by hotheads and zealots. If the state intervened, it was usually on the side of the victims. That is not to say that some clergy didn't sympathize with the mobs, but theirs was hardly the only attitude. Through the worst excesses of the Middle Ages, church leaders insisted that Jews must not be harmed. "No medieval pope or council authorized or incited the murder of Jews," observes medievalist Thomas F. X. Noble, while "many clerics and councils thundered against the preposterous blood libels."[7]

"The Jews survived 1,600 years of Christianity," notes Cornell professor Steven T. Katz. "They almost didn't survive four years of World War II. Something different must have happened."[8]

The difference was that the murderous, race-based anti-Semitism of the Nazis represented a break from Christian anti-Semitism, and many Germans realized it. That is why when pro-Nazi "German Christians" proposed adoption of the "Aryan paragraph" in the Protestant churches in April 1933, it set off tumultuous debate. The paragraph was pure Nazi racism: "Anyone who is not of Aryan descent or who is married to a person of non-Aryan descent may not be appointed as a pastor or official. Pastors or officials of Aryan descent who marry non-Aryans are to be dismissed. The only exceptions are those laid down in the state law." At stake were the livelihoods of twenty-three Jewish-Christian pastors, as well as a number of other pastors in "non-Aryan" marriages. Also at stake, of course, was the fundamental Christian principle that every man, woman and child of any background may be "saved" through embrace of the faith. With the Aryan paragraph, race would trump baptism. Moral equality would be uprooted and lost.

Niemoller bolted into action, inviting fellow pastors throughout Germany to join a Pastors' Emergency League to resist the Aryan paragraph and all other attacks on church doctrine. Within a few months, more than two thousand pastors had signed the pledge—and that was still before one of the most revealing spectacles of the first year of Nazi rule.

On November 13, more than twenty thousand "German Christians" thronged the Berlin Sports Palace to demonstrate for religious renewal. This evening of high excitement climaxed with a speech by Dr. Reinhold Krause, a high party official and leading German Christian of Berlin. To ecstatic applause, Krause called for creation of a "German people's Church" that would expunge Christianity of "the Old Testament with its Jewish morality of rewards, and its stories of cattle-dealers and concubines." The New Testament would need some judicious pruning, too, Krause maintained, especially the theology of "Rabbi Paul."

Krause's speech was a wake-up call for many Protestant clergy not in attendance. By mid-January, more than seven thousand— or nearly 40 percent of all German Protestant pastors—had signed on to Niemoller's Emergency League. The Aryan paragraph was scuttled. Hitler himself soon had second thoughts regarding the usefulness of the "German Christians"; he would never again provide them with the full support they would need to carry the day in their theological adventures.

Karl Barth, the Swiss Protestant theologian who was expelled from Germany in 1935 for refusing to take an oath of allegiance to Hitler as a condition for employment at the University of Bonn, later recalled a critical legacy of that early battle: "In the struggle against the Christianity à la mode of 1933, under Martin Niemoller's direction first the so-called Pastors' Emergency League came into being and then, on a broader basis, the Confessing Church." Barth was being uncharacteristically modest. In fact, he helped push the budding German Confessing Church into open challenge of German Christians through his role, in May 1934, in drafting what became known as the Barmen Declaration. It quickly became the rock of principle upon which the new Confessing Church stood. No one who accepted the Barmen Declaration could doubt the scriptural—thus the non-German—basis of the Word of God.

Confessing Church leaders presented their new church structure not merely as an alternative to the Protestant church structure now controlled by pro-government German Christians, but as the only legitimate church. And while the Confessing Church never pulled a majority of German Protestants into its orbit, it was far from marginal, and even achieved majorities in such regions as Hanover and Hamburg. As James Bentley has observed, "The Confessing church membership in Rhineland-Westphalia alone soon amounted to 800 thousand. Niemoller sometimes despaired, temporarily, over its vacillations, but the Confessing church undoubtedly presented the sole coherent opposition to Hitler's religious (and therefore racial) policies within Germany."[9]

No doubt one reason the Confessing Church vacillated and failed to grow after its impressive early surge in membership was that it was stifled and harassed. When the Prussian Confessing Synod warned against the neo-pagan idols of race, blood and nation in a March 1935 manifesto, for example, seven hundred Prussian pastors were jailed or confined to their homes, and the rest warned to keep silent.

Had Protestant leaders been the wholly compliant sheep they are sometimes portrayed as, such numbers would never have dared speak out at all. Admittedly, without heroes like Neimoller, it is possible that German Protestants might have marched en masse away from the roots of their faith, replacing the Jewish foundation with a tribal Teutonic substitute. Some clearly yearned to do so. When all pastors of the Evangelical Church were ordered in 1938 to swear a loyalty oath to the Führer or be dismissed from their posts, the bishop of Thuringia could not contain his enthusiasm. "In a great historic hour," he declared, "all the pastors of the Thuringian Evangelical Church, obeying an inner command, have with joyful hearts taken an oath of loyalty to Führer and Reich." Yet despite such squalid displays, a wholesale embrace of darkness never occurred. Hitler had been right: One thousand years of Christian "domestication" would have to be rooted out.

The Confessing Church never fancied itself a political force in opposition to the government. Its concerns were political threats to church prerogatives, doctrine and the foundations of Christianity. And while its leaders' expressions of solidarity with the Jews were timid and rare given the severity of the crisis, the sincerity and courage of those who did speak out is not in doubt. In 1936, for example, Confessing Church leaders protested the treatment of the Jews in a memorandum sent directly to Hitler, part of which warned that "if Christians are pressed to adopt an anti-Semitic attitude as part of the National Socialist ideology, which will incite them to hate the Jews, then this is against the Christian commandment to love one's neighbor." And in 1943, the Confessing Church's synod in eastern Prussia issued a declaration that "the extermination of human beings merely because they ... belong to another race is not a [proper] exercise of the power that has been given to the authorities by God."

To the theologian Dietrich Bonhoeffer, who was hanged for his role in the plot to overthrow Hitler, the plight of the Jews was in fact the main catalyst to action. "Beyond question the deprivation of rights and the persecution of the Jews which followed soon after the Nazi seizure of power were the decisive stimulus to his repudiation of the regime from the beginning and his fight against it," writes Renate Wind.[10] (Lieutenant Colonel Klaus von Stauffenberg, who carried the explosives into the room with Hitler, was a devout Catholic who actually confided in Berlin's Cardinal Konrad von Preysing before the attempt.) Bonhoeffer had no patience with those in the church who wished to avert their eyes from the moral challenge before them, declaring, "Only those who cry out for the Jews may sing Gregorian chant."

The Wary Catholic Church

In 1937, the papal encyclical *Mit Brennender Sorge* ("With Burning Anxiety") was smuggled into Germany and read from Roman Catholic pulpits on Palm Sunday. This unique document was the most forceful repudiation of Nazi paganism and racism issued up to that time. It denounced the "superficial minds" that "could stumble into concepts of a national God, of a national religion; or attempt to lock within the frontiers of a single people ... the Creator of the universe." It ridiculed those who wished "to see banished from church and school the Biblical history and the wise doctrines of the Old Testament." It warned that the church "needs lessons from no one in heroism of feeling and action," while declaring that "Whoever exalts race, or the people, or the State ... above their standard value and divinizes them to an idolatrous level, distorts and perverts an order of the world planned and created by God." The church, it said, is a "home for all peoples and all nations."

Infuriated, the Führer responded with various hammer blows, including a show trial of Franciscans on charges of immorality.

This was merely the latest episode in the sour relationship between the Roman Catholic Church and the Nazis. As Conway recounts, almost from the beginning "a number of clearsighted theologians saw the incompatibility between Christian doctrine and the Nazi notion of so-called 'positive Christianity.' In several parts of Germany Catholics were explicitly forbidden to become members of the Nazi Party, and Nazi members were forbidden to take part in such Church ceremonies as funerals." Right up to January 1933, the church's attitude "was one of reserve. With a few minor exceptions, the Catholic clergy and laity had given no open support to the Nazi movement, and the Catholic doctrinal position remained unaltered."[11] Catholic publications were particularly fierce in denouncing Nazi doctrine as "deceptions" and "lies."

All this began to change in the spring of 1933, when German bishops, in response to overtures from Hitler, declared their hope that their "previous warnings and prohibitions" against National Socialism "need no longer be considered necessary." Still more dramatic was the concordat signed by the Vatican and Berlin a few months later, which granted the church unprecedented rights—on paper, at least—in return for a pledge to steer clear of politics.

Why did Pope Pius XI, who would authorize the blazing sentiments of *Mit Brennender Sorge* four years later, try to do business with Hitler? Although Catholic-bashers think they know the answer (sympathy for the devil), the truth is more prosaic. The Vatican had been seeking a concordat with the German state for years, even before Hitler swaggered onto the political stage. It had signed no fewer than nine such agreements with other states, ranging from Poland to Romania, between 1922 and the summer of 1933, in order to ensure control over education, appointment of bishops and other fragile church rights. Nazi hostility only reinforced the Vatican's desire to cut a deal and solidify church prerogatives.

The church simply didn't have the stomach to wage all-out cultural warfare with yet another German ruler; the first so-called *Kulturkampf,* fought with Bismarck half a century before, had been ugly enough. And who knew whether the bulk of the Catholic laity would even follow the clergy this time, especially given Hitler's clarion promise to respect the church's traditional rights and autonomy? Defiance risked exposing a shrunken church to full-scale persecution and an unscheduled return to the catacombs. Besides, some in the clergy rather liked the idea of a strong national leader sweeping away the socialist Left and its anticlerical obsessions. These priests and bishops would defend the church if it came to a showdown, but they were not convinced that such a crisis was at hand.

And so the church allowed the Center Party—the Catholics' historic vehicle for self-preservation—to be maneuvered into extinction, along with trade unions and a host of Catholic civic groups. Meanwhile, the clergy hunkered down for a treacherous ride.

Even so, when Hitler appointed Alfred Rosenberg to a critical post in 1933, the church retaliated by placing the rabid bigot's *Myth of the Twentieth Century* on the Index of Prohibited Books and cranking up its denunciations of the "New Heathenism." And while the Catholic hierarchy generally confined themselves to a defense of their coreligionists and the church's institutional rights, there were exceptions. Perhaps the most inspiring moment of outright defiance occurred in July 1941, when Cardinal Clemens August von Galen of Münster challenged the Nazi euthanasia program—the mass murder of the handicapped, mentally ill, retarded and terminally sick—through an impassioned public appeal from the pulpit of St. Lambert's Church. His indictment was precise and unrelenting, revealing details the state had never acknowledged and which it could not possibly admit in its rebuttal.

"Woe unto the German people," von Galen declared in a direct attack on the regime, "when not only can innocents be killed, but their slayers remain unpunished."

His words provoked a sensation. They were copied and distributed to a nationwide audience, including front-line troops uneasy about their fate in the event of grievous injury. Martin Bormann, Hitler's private secretary, favored von Galen's execution (and three priests who distributed his sermon were promptly liquidated), but Hitler wisely refused to create a prominent martyr. Instead, he accepted Joseph Goebbels' counsel to settle accounts after the war. "I am quite sure," Hitler said later, "that a man like Bishop von Galen knows full well that I shall extract retribution to the last farthing. . . . No 't' will remain uncrossed, no 'i' undotted." For all his menace, however, Hitler left von Galen alone.

The Nazis apparently did pull back somewhat from euthanasia in late 1941, while attempting to conceal the program more carefully from the public. Yet the killings nonetheless continued— an awkward fact for those inclined to believe that moral protest could have decisively influenced Nazi policy in other areas. Moreover, von Galen had spoken truth to an audience primed to hear it. Average Germans could empathize with the victims of euthanasia, who might be their own families, neighbors and friends. But most did not empathize in the same way with Jews.

Yet that is not to say no Christians objected to the Nazi genocide. Archbishop Joseph Frings of Cologne, for example, issued a pastoral letter in December 1942 declaring that the "right to life, to inviolability, to freedom, to property" extended to someone "who is not of our blood or does not speak our language." The dean of St. Hedwig's Cathedral in Berlin, Msgr. Bernhard Lichtenberg, protested so forcefully on the Jews' behalf that he was arrested in October 1942, and died on his way to Dachau. Nor was Lichtenberg's experience unique. Indeed, Dachau eventually became the site "of the largest religious community in the world," writes William J. O'Malley in *America* magazine, interning upwards of 2,750 clergymen. The vast majority were "Catholic priests, lay brothers and seminarians" who hailed from nearly every nation under Hitler's thumb. And they included—contrary to the image of a doormat German Catholic church—447 from Germany and Austria. Among other things, "they had run underground presses and underground railways to rescue retarded children from the euthanasia laws and Jews from deportation," O'Malley writes. "German priests and pastors were exiled to Dachau for preaching love of neighbor, for insisting that Jesus was a Jew, for warning S.S. men that they could not abjure their faith to achieve promotion, for offering requiem Masses even for relatives of Communists."[12]

In *The Catholic Martyrs of the Twentieth Century,* Robert Royal recounts that "In 1932, just prior to the Nazi rise to power, there were about twenty-one thousand Catholic priests in Germany. Of these, more than a third (over eight thousand) clashed with the Reich, and several hundred have been documented as having perished at Nazi hands."[13]

Such resistance must not be washed from memory just because it represented a minority of those who *could* have protested, or because German Christian leaders spoke out so rarely in organized force on behalf of the Jews. In the name of the German Catholic bishops, Cardinal Adolf Bertram did write a letter to the government in November 1942 insisting that people of all races should be treated humanely—the year before the Confessing Church of Prussia issued its public protest of the treatment of Jews. But it was too little, too late. Insofar as the German Jews were concerned, this admirable expression of conscience might as well have been a funeral dirge.

The Case of Pius XII
The gravamen of the charge that Christians appeased Hitler finally falls on Pope Pius XII. Even for his day, this wellborn Roman's style was archaic, his language guarded, his instincts monarchical in the extreme. His papal world of self-abasing courtiers has vanished, probably never to return. Yet among the many things Eugenio Pacelli was sure of were the divine wisdom of the church, the historic rights of the Holy See, and the urgent need for papal guidance in a world broken by decadence and despair. And it was precisely this self-confidence and sense of destiny that made the pope the inevitable antagonist of anyone bent on total domination of a Christian society—particularly anyone so violently primitive as Adolf Hitler.

The pope's contempt for Nazism is an incontestable fact. Before a gathering at Lourdes in 1935, the future pope (then Vatican secretary of state Cardinal Pacelli) indicted National Socialists as "miserable plagiarists who dress up old errors with new tinsel. It does not make any difference whether they flock to the banners of the social revolution, whether they are guided by a false conception of the world and of life, or whether they are possessed by the superstition of a race and blood cult." Pacelli's attitude was reflected in *Mit Brennender Sorge,* to which he contributed and to which he referred with approval upon becoming pope.

Pius XII's inaugural encyclical of October 1939 renewed the Vatican's assault on racism and materialism. He spoke of the "law of human solidarity and charity that is dictated and imposed ... by our common origin and by the equality of rational nature in all men, regardless of the people to which they belong." It is true that the pope did not mention National Socialism by name, but there is no doubt what he meant. Nor was there doubt at the time. The *New York Times* headline declared: "Pope Condemns Dictators, Treaty Violators, Racism; Urges Restoration of Poland."

This would be the style of the Vatican throughout the war: to deplore racism, oppression and injustice in a manner unmistakably aimed at Nazi persecutions, but without mentioning the Third Reich by name. The pope did this, for instance, in an address in June 1943 intended for distribution to the Poles, and in his wartime encyclical *Mystici Corporis Christi.* The best-known example of this theme was his Christmas message of 1942, in which he sympathized with those "persons who, through no fault of their own and by the single fact of their nationality or race, have been condemned to death or for progressive extinction." The reaction has been described by Ronald Rychlak:

> Mussolini ... was greatly angered by the speech. The German ambassador to the Vatican complained that Pius had abandoned any pretense at neutrality and was "clearly speaking on behalf of the Jews." An official Nazi report stated: "In a manner never known before the Pope has repudiated the National Socialists' New European Order. . . . His speech is one long attack on everything we stand for. . . . God, he says, regards all people and races as worthy of the same consideration. Here he is clearly speaking on behalf of the Jews. . . . He is virtually accusing the German people of injustice towards the Jews, and makes himself the mouthpiece of the Jewish war criminals."[14]

Officially, the Vatican was neutral during the war. Desperately wanting to protect the Catholic Church in every national home, the pope put his trust in diplomacy rather than public gestures. It was the same policy as that pursued by Pope Benedict XV during World War I, but it became increasingly difficult to sustain as the later conflict wore on. After all, the historian Eamon Duffy observes, it was "a different war, and a different world. To many of those around him, the moral circumstances seemed qualitatively different, and Pacelli himself sometimes felt it."[15]

Yet if Pius XII was officially neutral, he nonetheless had chosen sides. His closest confidant within Germany was the anti-Nazi Cardinal Konrad von Preysing of Berlin, who favored a far more combative attitude toward the Nazi regime than several other top-ranking church officials the pope could have heeded. In the very first year of his papacy, the pope even connived at Hitler's downfall. The otherwise venomously anti–Pius XII author John Cornwell acknowledges:

> In November 1939, in deepest secrecy, Pacelli became intimately and dangerously involved in what was probably the most viable plot to depose Hitler during the war. The plot centered on a group of anti-Nazi generals committed to returning Germany to democracy. The coup might spark a civil war, and they wanted assurances that the West would not take advantage of the ensuing chaos. Pius XII agreed to act as go-between for the plotters and the Allies.[16]

This was but the beginning of extensive efforts by Pius XII to thwart Nazi designs. Even stern critics sometimes acknowledge as much. Robert S. Wistrich, who faults the pope for a "paucity of moral courage" and failure to act decisively during the Holocaust, admits that "in those Catholic countries where Pius XII had some leverage, he tried to intervene at times to halt the deportation and mass killing of Jews by Nazi puppet governments.

> In Slovakia, he ordered bishops to intercede with President Jozef Tiso and other high officials. In fascist Croatia, the papal representative, along with the Croatian Archbishop Stepinac, worked behind the scenes to deter the savage Ustashe regime of Ante Pavelic from committing further murders. To Admiral Nicholas Horthy, the regent of Hungary, Pius XII sent an open letter asking that he do everything in his power to "save as many unfortunate people as possible from further pain and sorrow." In addition, when the Nazis

occupied Rome in October 1943 and began deporting the city's Jews to Auschwitz, the Pope quietly opened buildings within Vatican City to offer refuge to those who managed to escape the manhunt.[17]

To say the pope "opened buildings" in Vatican City doesn't nearly convey what actually occurred. The Vatican waived ancient rules barring laypeople from entering monasteries and convents, and shielded some five thousand Jews within their walls and within a host of other buildings owned by the church—including Castel Gandolfo, the pope's summer home. That number was more than half of all the Jews who remained in Rome at the time the Germans marched in. Other Italians wanted by the Nazis were also protected. At one point, Rychlak reports, "almost the entire National Committee of Liberation was hidden in the Roman Seminary at St. John Lateran."[18] Meanwhile, the pope personally offered the Roman Jewish community fifteen kilos of gold as part of a ransom demanded by a German official in return for their safety, and protested through his representatives when the Nazis began a general roundup of Jews in Rome in late 1943. The roundup was halted.

Such efforts extended well beyond Rome, for example to Romania. According to John Morley, another often-quoted critic of Vatican efforts, "the nuncio in Bucharest was possibly the most active of the Vatican diplomats in matters concerning the Jews. . . . He did not hesitate to protest openly, in August and September 1942, the impending deportation of the Jews from Romania proper."[19] In addition, the pope's refugee program, headed by the tireless Father Anton Weber, assisted thousands of Jews in escaping from Europe. As Robert A. Graham, one of four Jesuit historians given unhampered access to Vatican archives beginning in the mid-1960s, briskly remarks, "Such assistance was not sporadic or incidental or perfunctory but consistent—and persistent. It was not the accidental product of some curious circumstance, but the result of policy and principle."[20]

If Pius XII had been indifferent to the fate of Jews, he hardly would have sent money to the cardinal archbishop of Genoa for support of a Jewish rescue organization known as DELASEM. And he never would have embraced the scheme of Father Pierre-Marie Benoit, whose feats read like a work of adventure fiction, to transfer tens of thousands of French Jews to North Africa in 1943. Philip Friedman notes that even when the plan collapsed, "Father Benoit, aided by the Vatican, prevailed upon the Spanish government to authorize its consuls in France to issue entry permits to all Jews who could prove Spanish nationality."[21] An "impartial arbiter" would have final say on an applicant's nationality. Wonder of wonders, the arbiter turned out to be the wily Father Benoit.

The pope privately signaled his support for those inside Germany who aided Jews, too. This was acknowledged, for example, by the three Catholic and three Jewish scholars on the International Catholic-Jewish Historical Commission, appointed by the Vatican and the world Jewish community, in a document made public in October 2000. Here they noted:

> On 30 April 1943, the Pope indicated to [Cardinal] von Preysing that local bishops had the discretion to determine when to be silent and when to speak out in the face of the danger of reprisals and pressures. Although he felt that he had to exercise great prudence in his actions as Pope, he made it clear that he felt comforted that Catholics, particularly in Berlin, had helped the "so-called non-Aryans" (*sogenannten Nichtarier*). He particularly singled out for "fatherly recognition" Father Lichtenberg, who had been imprisoned by the Nazis and who would die shortly afterwards.[22]

The Vatican and the church in general are frequently belittled for focusing attention almost exclusively on the jeopardy faced by Jews who had been baptized as Christians. Even if the charge were true—and it is not—such a policy would still have represented a thrust at the heart of racial ideology. In Croatia, for example, Archbishop Aloysius Stepinac protested fiercely when the Nazis ordered several priests and nuns of Jewish descent to wear the Star of David. His protest continued even after the Nazis backed down, at which point he cantankerously declared, "I have ordered the priests and nuns to continue wearing this sign belonging to the people from whom the Savior came." Stepinac had transformed the yellow star, that sign of Jewishness, into a badge of honor. He would go on to set up an organization to aid imperiled Jews.

Naturally the pope, as head of the Catholic Church, had a special interest in baptized Jews, but there was legal logic to this interest, too. In countries such as Hungary, Pierre Blet points out, the concordat between that government and the Vatican "offered [the papal nuncio] a more solid basis for becoming involved."[23] At the very least, as Joseph L. Lichten observed some years ago, there is "an element of naiveté on the part of those who alleged that papal nuncios engaged in preferential treatment of baptized Jews, because a countless number of baptismal certificates were not genuine."[24] Church authorities usually knew this, yet nevertheless attempted to protect the bearers of the certificates as if they were genuine converts. A single church in Budapest, for example, "averaged about four or five conversions a year before the occupation," Rychlak recounts, yet "three thousand Jews became Catholics at this one small church in 1944."[25]

In Romania, ethnic Germans actually complained to the nuncio there that the Vatican's Information Service was assisting too many Jews. When told of this, the pope's secretary of state, Cardinal Luigi Maglione, replied that the service would continue to process inquiries without regard to race or religion. This indeed it did, both during and after the war, handling literally millions of missing-person requests.

It is equally difficult to make the case that the pope soft-pedaled the Nazi threat because of his special loathing of communism, which was certainly real enough. According to Blet, another of the four Jesuit scholars who spent more than fifteen years sifting through Vatican archives to compile twelve volumes of documents related to the Holy See's activities during the Second World War, "Pius XII did not change his position when Germany began its war with Russia, and he never spoke, even by means of allusion, about a 'crusade' against Bolshevism or of a 'holy war.'"[26] Hitler and Mussolini tried to cast the invasion as such a crusade, but the Vatican would not be seduced. When the Italian ambassador asked the Vatican for a word of encouragement to those fighting Soviet communism, the secretary of the Congregation of Extraordinary Ecclesiastical Affairs dismissed the idea out of hand, noting that "the swastika is not the cross of a crusade." By contrast, when Myron Taylor, the U.S. representative to the Holy See, asked the pope to confirm to wary American bishops that Vatican condemnation of communism did not rule out aid to the Soviet state, Pius XII willingly complied.

Critics of Pius XII are correct that the Vatican's statements during the war were often so cautious that they seem to many today to lack a definite sense of moral purpose. Not only did the pope refuse to single out the Nazi oppressor by name, he never publicly attempted to rally Catholics under occupation to oppose Nazism, let alone excommunicate Catholics who did Hitler's bidding. Fairminded people may disagree regarding the wisdom of these decisions. What should not be in dispute, however, are the pope's motives. He feared the loss of what little leverage he had, and he also worried that a full-throated protest would provoke devastating retaliation against Catholics under occupation and others the church sought to protect and rescue.

The pope's behind-the-scenes approach was not particularly controversial at the time. While the Allies naturally would have preferred a more robust denunciation of Germany from the pope, they appreciated why it wasn't forthcoming, as did most contemporary commentators including prominent Jewish observers. "At Pius' death," writes William D. Rubinstein, "there was a serious move in Israel to dedicate a forest in his honor, while Golda Meir, Israel's Foreign Minister, eulogized that 'when fearful martyrdom came to our people in the decade of Nazi terror, the voice of the Pope was raised for the victims.'"[27]

Criticism of Pius would have more weight if there were reason to believe that he could have been another Pope Leo the Great and, by sheer force of moral authority, checked the barbarians at the gates. Yet this is fantasy. Hitler's hatred of the Jews was all-consuming—indeed, as Rubinstein explains, he was "plainly deranged on the subject of the Jews. . . . From early 1942 until literally the day of his suicide, Hitler repeatedly described the war as a life-or-death struggle between the Jewish and Aryan races."[28] Which is why, Rubinstein adds,

> In all likelihood—a likelihood probably amounting to a near certainty—Hitler would have paid no heed whatever to any pronouncement on the Jews made by the Vatican. . . . Theoretically, and in hindsight, the Pope might have excommunicated all Catholic members of the SS (or the Nazi Party) although the only likely effect of such a pronouncement would have been that the Nazis denounced the Pope as an agent of "Judeo-Bolshevism" and an impostor. The Vatican had more influence on Catholic satellite states such as Hungary, which it used to good effect whenever it could.[29]

Pius XII had no leverage whatsoever with a Nazi government that cordially despised him, and to which he had been sending notes of protest, in one capacity or another, since 1933. Not only had Berlin denounced Pacelli's elevation to the office, it stonewalled every one of the many diplomatic inquiries that the Vatican made on behalf of individual Jews.

In any event, wonders Michael Novak, "what exactly was unclear about what the pope did say? More than once, he drew the portrait of the brutal jackboot of racism, unjustified violence, and the gross slaughter of human beings. He did not, of course, point out which powers the portrait described. To figure that out did not take rocket science; the propagandists at BBC knew instantly how to put those papal condemnations at Hitler's feet, and did so within hours."[30]

If Pius XII is to be judged as indifferent to the fate of the Jews, how then are we to rate Franklin Roosevelt and Winston Churchill, the State Department and British Foreign Office, the Red Cross, the bulk of the American press and the vast majority of American intellectuals? In other words, how are we to rate those very individuals, institutions and groups rendering unto Caesar that might have been expected to protest loud, hard and without rest against such a catastrophe as the Holocaust? In many cases, they were no more vocal than the pope, and their active efforts often so much inferior to the Vatican's that they hardly bear serious comparison.

Anthony Eden, the British foreign secretary, seemed genuinely horrified at the prospect of hordes of homeless Jews escaping from Axis territories. What would be done with them, after all? "The British learned of the Holocaust almost at its inception when they intercepted German military cables," Deborah E. Lipstadt observes.

> They did not or would not warn Jews who might have escaped because to do so would have revealed that they had cracked the enemy code. While this decision could be justified on strategic grounds, harder to explain is the satisfaction some British diplomats expressed when Jews were thwarted in their escape attempts. In 1943, a British diplomat expressed relief that a boatload of Jews escaping the Final Solution had sunk because this would prevent other Jews from trying to do the same thing.[31]

The State Department was only slightly more energetic, or so David S. Wyman argues in his influential book, *The Abandonment of the Jews: America and the Holocaust, 1941–1945*. "By far the most important cause for State Department inaction," he writes, "was fear that sizable numbers of Jews might actually get out of Axis territory. (Sizable numbers meant more than a very few thousand.)"[32] Roosevelt himself "did nothing" about the Holocaust for fourteen months after it had been verified by United States officials, and finally responded only because of political pressure. The War Refugee Board was not established until January 1944, yet even then had to be funded mainly through private Jewish donations. Pius XII is repeatedly bludgeoned for failing to speak out publicly against the extermination of the Jews, but FDR also "had little to say about the problem," Wyman writes, and he "gave no priority at all to rescue."[33]

The United States failed to bomb the Auschwitz gas chambers when it became possible in 1944, although scholars disagree on the wisdom of such a strike and whether it could have been launched in time to save lives. For that matter, scholars at the Simon Wiesenthal Center in Los Angeles uncovered a cable in 1999 suggesting American officials knew about the Nazi euthanasia program by late 1940, but neglected to sound an alarm. Another pertinent disclosure by the center: The Protestant bishop of Württemberg, Theophil Wurm, had protested euthanasia in a letter to the Reich Interior Ministry dated July 10, 1940, about a year before Bishop von Galen's electrifying intervention.

It would be unseemly to push these comparisons too far, lest they imply moral culpability for the Holocaust where none exists. The essential point is that despite the literary assault on Pius XII, the Christian conscience at the Vatican did not slumber silently through the long night of Nazi barbarism, any more than the Christian conscience slept in many other locales. Sometimes the Good Samaritans operated in dreadful isolation; sometimes they rode forth to find others, equally oblivious to danger, on their left and on their right. But wherever one looks—both where resistance to Nazi racial policies was shamefully limited and where it evoked broad support—Christians acting out of religious duty were in the forefront.

In France, for example, Catholic and Protestant clergy "played a role second to none in their opposition to the anti-Jewish decrees and in their rescue activities on behalf of the persecuted," Philip Friedman concludes.[34] It was there, Wyman adds, that "nearly 8,000 Jewish orphans" were hidden "in Christian homes, schools, and convents."[35] In his book *Lest Innocent Blood Be Shed,* Philip P. Hallie describes how the southern French village of Le Chambon became "the safest place for Jews in Europe." Why was this? "When you try to understand the peculiar spirit of Le Chambon, you find that all roads lead to Andre Trocme, just as all roads led to him when Vichy was trying to punish and wipe out the Resistance in Le Chambon in February 1943."[36] Trocme was a Protestant pastor, a man who located his uncompromising belief in nonviolence in the Bible and who boldly told the first official threatening to hunt down Jews in Le Chambon, "We do not know what a Jew is." Trocme estimated that 2,500 Jews sought refuge in the village and its environs at one time or another. His congregation's allies in stealth were the Darbyites, a militant Christian sect with a fierce contempt for unbridled state power that numbered perhaps one-third of the region's Protestants.

And if Le Chambon was notable for its activities, it was not alone. In the region of Lyons, Father Chaillet founded Christian Witness, a network of Catholics dedicated to helping Jewish refugees, while publishing an important underground journal. And in Toulouse (to mention only one more French example) Archbishop Jules-Gérard Saliège penned a pastoral letter for reading in diocesan churches on Sunday, August 30, 1942, saying in part: "Jews are men and women. Foreigners are men and women. It is just as criminal to use violence against these men and women, these fathers and mothers with families, as it is against anyone else."

Religious motives were equally prominent in the opposition to Nazi racial policies in Belgium and the Netherlands. In Holland, both Protestant and Catholic churches protested the deportation of Jews. The resistance of Corrie ten Boom may be best known: a middle-aged, single, seemingly unremarkable woman who found herself, step by step, drawn into terrible risks in order to satisfy the demands of her Christian ethics. First she sheltered Jews in the home where her equally devout sister and aged father also resided. Then she began to secure refuge for Jews in homes and farms in and around Haarlem. Her father, who considered Jews "God's people," died a few days after the three of them were seized by the Gestapo. Corrie survived Ravensbruck concentration camp, but not before she had watched her sister Betsie worked and starved to death.

A similar pattern of Christian resistance characterized Denmark. "As soon as the sobering news of the impending action against the Jews got around," Friedman recounts, "a secret meeting of the Protestant higher clergy was convened in the home of

the Bishop of Copenhagen, Fogelsang-Dagmar. With swift una-
nimity, the clergymen present resolved to form an organization
whose avowed purpose it was 1) to rescue Jews and 2) to rescue
Jewish devotional objects."[37] Polish Catholic anti-Semitism could
be profound, and historians have recently discovered that four
massacres of Jews in towns in western Poland were carried out by
Poles themselves (at German instigation). Yet Polish Catholics also
sheltered some hundred thousand Jews at one time or another
during the war. In Britain, it was the archbishop of Canterbury
who raised the alarm about possible genocide against the Jews. He
and the entire Anglican high clergy broke with the British government over the question of refugees, urging the politicians in
January 1943 to accept as many Jews as needed asylum.

Like others who answered the roll call of Christian conscience,
they might just as easily have lowered their eyes. Pastor Dietrich
Bonhoeffer could have stayed in the security of New York rather
than return to Germany in 1939; the Jesuit Rupert Mayer, who
ended up in Sachsenhausen concentration camp for his outspo-
ken rejection of Nazi beliefs, might have gone quietly about his
business in Bavaria without attracting notice; the young Hungar-
ian priests and nuns who distributed reams of safe-conduct papers
on behalf of the papal nuncio could have cowered in their homes
and convents; Corrie ten Boom's elderly father, Caspar, might have
renounced his Christian duty to shelter Jews when given the chance
by his German interrogator; Sisters Maria Ewa Noiszewska and
Maria Marta Wolowska could have turned away the Polish Jews
who sought sanctuary with them in Slonim, knowing that an
expression of mercy could lead—as it did—to their execution;
Father Krupovitchius, deported from Lithuania to a forced-labor
camp for protesting the murder of Jews, might have kept quiet,
realizing as he certainly did the futility of his defiance.

The wonder is not that many Christians failed to bear witness
to the imperatives of their faith—to do good is noble, but also
hard—but that those who did do good were plentiful enough to
give us hope, and resolute enough to have earned a more hallowed
place in memory than they have been granted by those eager to
saddle Christianity with the evil of Nazism.

SIX

CHRISTIANITY
AND CHARITY

Christianity, it is often said, is a refuge for smug hypocrites who preach love of neighbor but practice adoration of self, who revile riches in public while plundering their neighbors the rest of the week, and who extol charity, sexual restraint and self-sacrifice, but are loath to practice these virtues themselves. These Christians pay lip service to the Gospel but never embrace its fundamental message, let alone the radical demands that Jesus placed upon his followers—that they abandon their possessions and even their loved ones to come, follow him.

Charges of religious hypocrisy and phoniness go back to the Pharisees, and before. Then it often took a brave man—like Jesus—to make these charges. Today it is relatively easy.

"In the bullshit department, a businessman can't hold a candle to a clergyman," George Carlin told an HBO audience in a live performance in 1999. " 'Cause I gotta tell you the truth, folks. When it comes to bullshit, big-time, major league bullshit, you have to stand in awe of the all-time champion of false promises and exaggerated claims, religion. No contest. No contest. Religion."

The assault on religious hypocrisy usually homes in on lust or greed. A gag-packed episode of *Ally McBeal* highlighted a nun dismissed from her order for having a lover; at one point she quipped, "A priest has sex with a boy, he gets transferred. . . . At least my lover was of legal age." In the same show, McBeal joked that "nuns are not supposed to have sex except with other nuns," while a priest videotaped confessions about sex for a film titled *World's Naughtiest*

Confessions. Woody Allen exploited an even more raucous theme in his Cinemax TV movie *Picking up the Pieces.* It featured a priest who was having sex with a prostitute and who bilked the faithful by advertising the alleged cure-all properties of a severed hand—and those are just a couple of the film's highlights. Comedic assaults on religious hypocrisy are so pervasive, in fact, and frequently so over the top in tone, that they sometimes have more in common with gags from *National Lampoon* than serious satire.

Naturally, some of this humor has been at the expense of genuine religious hypocrites—outright mountebanks like Jim and Tammy Faye Bakker, for example, whose PTL ministry collapsed in the rubble of a 1980s sex and financial scandal; garish sinners like Jimmy Swaggert; or brazen swindlers like the Reverend Henry Lyons. But even well-aimed gibes tend to reinforce the notion that the deviant is the norm, and that the entire Christian enterprise is a refuge for the insincere and grasping. This is the cultural premise, for example, that allowed travel writer Jason Goodwin to explain to readers of the *New York Times* that in southern France, "Even the enemies of the Cathars [a movement of medieval heretics] agreed that they behaved like good Christians, which is no doubt why the church resorted to such dramatic measures to exterminate them."

A "money-grubbing preacher," a "buck-grubbing hypocrite," a TV evangelist who froths "over sin, hellfire and donations," a philandering priest whose eyes glint at the collection plate, a "mean-spirited" leader of the Christian Right—all are stock images of Christianity in contemporary entertainment and culture. Those who exploit them with enough skill, such as authors Dario Fo and José Saramago, may even find themselves awarded a Nobel Prize.

■ ■ ■

The question of wealth has been an awkward one for Christians from the beginning. Jesus' injunctions to his followers to turn their backs on worldly goods were among his most provocative statements, both at the time and ever after. They seemed to have been tailored for the truly saintly, yet they have functioned as a moral yardstick for believers since the advent of the church.

The Emperor Julian (331–63) ordered his pagan priests to match Christian generosity because he instinctively knew what contemporary social scientists have since quantified: People are initially drawn to new religions not so much by doctrines as by the qualities they see in others already within the fold. Christian generosity played a crucial role not only in the survival and growth of the early church, which eventually won the demographic contest against Julian's pagan masses, but in the later survival and stability of Western civilization, too.

Even in the modern era, as the historian Arnaud Marts notes, "The church is the chief agency which systematically tries to teach people to give, starting this unique process even with its youngest children."[1] In this context, child is truly father to the man, and children who learn to contribute to the common good often carry that practice into adulthood.

The story of Christianity's attempt to deal with wealth begins with the words of Jesus, whose teachings in this area are mutually reinforcing: First, he demands that his followers devote themselves to the care of the poor and desperate; and second, he promises that those who ignore his demand should expect punishment in the world to come. Charity is a non-negotiable requirement for entrance into his eternal kingdom. "If you love those who love you, what is that to you?" Jesus asked.

> Even sinners love those who love them. And if you do good to those who are good to you, what credit is that to you? Even sinners do that. And if you lend to those from whom you expect repayment, what credit is that to you? Even sinners lend to sinners, expecting to be paid back in full. But love your enemies, do good to them, and lend to them without expecting to get anything back. Then your reward will be great, and you will be sons of the Most High, because he is kind to the ungrateful and wicked. Be merciful, just as your Father is merciful. (Luke 6:32–36)

The fate of those who follow his teachings on charity and those who do not is most starkly foretold in the parable of the sheep and the goats:

> Then shall the King say unto them on his right hand, Come, blessed of my Father, inherit the kingdom prepared for you from the foundation of the world: for I was hungry and you gave me meat: I was thirsty and you gave me drink: I was a stranger and you took me in: naked and you clothed me: I was sick, and you visited me: I was in prison and you came unto me. Then shall the righteous answer him, saying Lord, when saw we thee hungry and fed thee? or thirsty,

and gave thee drink? When saw we thee a stranger and took thee in? or naked and clothed thee? or when saw we thee sick, or in prison, and came unto thee? And the King shall answer and say unto them, Verily I say unto you, Inasmuch as you have done it unto one of the least of these my brethren, you have done it unto me. Then shall he say unto them on the left hand, Depart from me, ye cursed, into everlasting fire, prepared for the devil and his angels: For I was hungry and ye gave me no meat: I was thirsty and ye gave me no drink: I was a stranger, and ye took me not in: naked and ye clothed me not: sick and in prison and ye visited me not. (Matt. 25:34–43)

These words were taken quite literally by early Christians, who expected the sheep to be separated from the goats within their lifetimes.

This is not to suggest that Christianity introduced the concept of good works to the world, or that the Christian religion has been alone in its concern for the poor. The ancient Hammurabic code, for instance, instructed that "justice be done to widows, orphans, and the poor," and similar concern was also shown by the Buddha and Islam's Prophet, among other religious leaders. And the Old Testament certainly taught a high regard for love with charity. Yet Christians placed the poor at the center of their theology, which often put them at odds with the world into which their religion was born.

"The Roman empire was no welfare state," writes John McManners, "and before Christian times in the West (unlike the East) care for the poor was rare."[2] Classical philosophy, adds Rodney Stark, "regarded mercy and pity as pathological emotions—defects of character to be avoided by all rational men. Since mercy involves providing unearned help or relief, it was contrary to justice."[3]

Christianity turned this classical notion on its head. Whereas the poor were formerly thought of, for the most part, as victims of a cruel destiny, a Christian was told that to look closely at a poor woman, for instance, was to see the face of God. "Pagans had never seen any spiritual merit in the status of the poor," Robin Lane Fox explains, "whereas Christianity idealized poverty."[4] More to the point, perhaps, one's eternal destiny suddenly depended on one's relationship to that crippled child in the gutter. That was a profound shift in perspective.

"There was nothing new in the idea that the supernatural makes behavioral demands upon humans," says Stark, for the prevailing gods had always required sacrifices and devotion. Nor was there anything new in the belief that the gods would sometimes pat a supplicant on the head in return for devotion, whether by curing a disease, dropping rain on a parched field, or routing an antagonist. "What was new was the notion that more than self-interested exchange relations were possible between humans and the supernatural. The Christian teaching that God loves those who love him was alien to pagan belief.... Christians cannot please God unless they love one another. Indeed, as God demonstrates his love through sacrifice, humans must demonstrate their love through sacrifice on behalf of one another.... These were revolutionary ideas."[5]

These were ideas that soon attracted attention. The Christian writer Tertullian (c. 200), noting that "we Christians have everything in common except our wives," also observed, "It is our care of the helpless, our practice of loving kindness that brands us in the eyes of many of our opponents. 'Only look,' they say, 'look how they love one another.'" Others viewed such practices with mockery. The pagan writer Lucian (130–200), very much a man of his world, was slack-jawed over the beliefs of those Christian misfits, easily seduced by con artists. "The earnestness with which the people of this religion help one another in their needs is incredible. They spare themselves nothing for this end. Their first lawgiver put it into their heads that they were all brethren!"

Such a critique was reasonable from the pagan perspective. Christians had convinced themselves not only that their Master had risen from the dead, but that the way to true wealth was to give away worldly possessions. What could be odder? There was also the fact that many Christians practiced their creed with what could only be called a devout fanaticism. Christian generosity went far beyond giving a beggar a few coins or a spare crust of bread. Many actually forfeited their own bread to provide food to the hungry.

"If the brethren have among them a man in need," wrote Aristides of Athens, "and they have not abundant resources, they fast for a day or two, so as to provide the needy man with the necessary food." Another contemporary, Hermas, explained that "On the day when you fast, take only bread and wine. Calculate the amount of feed you would have taken on other days; put aside the money you would have spent on it and give to the widow, the orphan or the poor." Said Origen of Alexandria: "Let the poor man be provided with food from the self-denial of him who fasts." Large numbers of Christians fasted on behalf of the hungry, writes historian Michel Riquet. "It has been calculated that at Rome in 250, under Pope Cornelius, ten thousand Christians obliged to fast could provide, from a hundred days' fasting, a million rations a year. These more or less regular offerings were supplemented by gifts made to the Church by rich converts."[6]

Charity was not an option. Riquet notes a third-century message to leaders of the church in Syria, who were instructed that "As then you have undertaken the burden of all, so also ought you to receive from all your people the ministration of food and clothing and of other things needful.... For it behoove thee, O bishop, as a faithful steward, to care for all." St. Justin spoke to the crucial role Christians played in this pre-welfare era: "What is collected is deposited with the president, and he takes care of orphans and widows, and those who are in want on account of sickness or any other cause, and those who are in bonds, and the strangers who are sojourners among us, and, briefly, he is the protector of all those in need." Similar instructions permeate early church documents.

These sacrifices did nothing to dissuade pagans from concluding that the Christians had handed themselves over to irrational beliefs. That they were sometimes prepared to die in order to do their God's will added to this perception of madness. One of the early church's most popular saints was Lawrence, a deacon arrested by Roman authorities during the same persecution in 258 that resulted in the martyrdom of Pope Sixtus II. According to oral tradition later recounted by St. Ambrose, the deacon was instructed to hand over the Christians' poor fund, which he agreed to do, at least if the authorities would provide him three days to accomplish the task. Once freed, Lawrence distributed this much-desired fund among Rome's poor and cripples, many of whom he gathered before authorities at the close of his grace period, proclaiming that "This is the church's treasure, these poor who are rich in their faith."

This was not the sort of currency the authorities were hoping for, and so Lawrence was soon to perish, according to legend, upon a white-hot gridiron.

Fate—or, Providence—appears to have determined that a more general sort of death and suffering would play a major role in bringing Christianity to full flower. In fact, two epidemics helped Christianity expand its reach. The first took place in the second century and was known as the Plague of Galen. It claimed the lives of perhaps a quarter to a third of the Roman Empire's citizens. A century later another terrible epidemic killed as many as five thousand people a day in Rome alone. Some accounts say that as much as two-thirds of Alexandria's population perished. Had it not been for these two withering epidemics, argues Stark in *The Rise of Christianity* (from which much of the following information is taken), the Jesus movement might have died early on. Instead, against a backdrop of immense suffering the supposed illogic of the Christian creed—that one must give of oneself in order to become rich—would suddenly reveal itself as the cornerstone of life itself. By practicing the virtues that promised them a heavenly reward, Christians reaped worldly benefits of the most dramatic nature.

Not unreasonably, any pagan who could leave town when major epidemics struck quickly did so. This was, after all, an age that had little understanding of the origins of diseases, but understood very well the wisdom of putting as much distance as possible between oneself and a stricken neighbor. The terror that epidemics unleashed was all but indescribable. Dionysius, bishop of Alexandria, paints a heart-rending picture of the resulting stampede: The pagans "pushed the sufferers away and fled from their dearest, throwing them into the roads before they were dead and treating unburied corpses as dirt, hoping thereby to avert the spread and contagion of the fatal disease; but do what they might, they found it difficult to escape."

The Christians' response was different from their neighbors'. They tended to stand fast in the cities and nurse the stricken. Providing food, water, and basic sanitation was not enough to save all of the diseased, by any means, and cost many Christians their lives. Stark notes that Dionysius, who called the second plague a period of "schooling and testing," spoke of these sacrifices in an Easter letter:

> Most of our brother Christians showed unbounded love and loyalty, never sparing themselves and thinking only of one another. Heedless of danger, they took charge of the sick, attending to their every need and ministering to them in Christ, and with them departed his life serenely happy; for they were infected by others

145

with the disease, drawing on themselves the sickness of their neighbors and cheerfully accepting their pains.

Stark believes this rudimentary care may have cut the mortality rate by two-thirds or more. This left a number of surviving pagans in an interesting situation. Many who had been succored knew they owed their lives to their Christian nurses, but they also had a deeper matter to consider: How was it that these Christians were able to survive in greater numbers than anyone else? Did Christianity enjoy an endorsement from on high?

The mere fact that pagan survivors found themselves living among a higher concentration of Christians resulted in increasing numbers of them converting to a religion that seemed to confer survival benefits on its adherents, thus initiating a process that fed on itself. As Stark explains, a significant percentage of conversions to any fledgling religion results not from attraction to its creed, but from knowing people who have already joined. Put another way, people do not come to a creed so much as to a community. "As mortality mounted during each of these epidemics," says Stark, "large numbers of people, especially pagans, would have lost the bonds that once might have restrained them from becoming Christians."[7] Each time a plague subsided, Christians were a larger proportion of the general population, and continued to grow at a rapid pace.

The plagues clearly revealed what C. S. Lewis calls the "shrewdness" of Christian doctrine, which allowed the religion to prosper in the face of calamity. Eventually, pagan authorities attempted to respond in kind. The Emperor Julian ordered that "every city establish numerous hospices, so that strangers may be able to praise us for our humanity, and not only those of our own religion, but all others too, if they have need. . . . It would be shameful, when the Jews have no beggars, when the impious Galileans feed our people along with their own, that ours should be seen to lack the help we owe them."

Yet there was a key element missing in Julian's call to arms. He could not offer a reason for sacrifice as compelling as could Christians; for while the hope for some form of existence after death was common among pagans, and philosophers had developed various concepts of the soul, pagan gods did not offer eternal life or any promise of salvation. So while pagan philosophers could encourage charity as an ethical ideal and justify it on practical grounds, they could hardly claim that the gods demanded generosity. One can imagine a typical pagan, in the quiet of his rooms, rhetorically responding to St. Justin's admonitions: "Tell me again why I should risk my life for a stranger?" As a moral force, classical paganism could not keep up with the competition.

Residents of the Roman Empire also noted differences in how the competing creeds disbursed their funds. Unlike pagan offerings, Tertullian observed, Christian funds were not "spent on feasts, and drinking bouts, and eating houses, but to support and bury poor people, to supply the wants of boys and girls destitute of means and parents, and of old persons confined to the house; such too as have suffered shipwreck; and if there happen to be any in the mines, or banished to the islands, or shut up in the prisons for nothing but their fidelity to the cause of God's Church, they become nurslings of their confession." There is much evidence that Christians were indeed spending their money this way. John McManners estimates that by the mid-third century, the Roman church alone was feeding more than 1,500 widows and distressed persons. Twice that number were fed in Antioch by the late fourth century, and the numbers in some locales seemed to increase as dramatically as the Gospel's loaves and fishes.

The "testing" periods, as Bishop Dionysius called the epidemics, left in their wake a human prototype, the Christian charity worker, and also directly linked Christianity, which professes itself eternal, with a constant of human existence: suffering. At first glance, this would appear to be a deadly relationship for any religion, but it has proved otherwise, in part because Christianity promises to rob the grave of its victory. For that matter, a nun tending to lepers, or a Presbyterian deacon ladling soup, has turned out to be a religious symbol with immense recruitment power.

How Christianity Helped Create the Idea of the Hospital

Historians can't seem to agree on when genuine hospitals first appeared, but it seems the early ones were little more than ambulatory clinics—for soldiers and other valuable citizens, for example—before Christians arrived on the scene. Apparently Christian hospitals were unique in their mission of caring for the sick without regard to status, as rudimentary as that care might have been. Documents believed to come from the first Council of Nicaea (325) ordered that "hospitals should be erected in every city of the Empire." In the late fourth century, Basil the Great, bishop of Caesarea, founded general philanthropic institutions called the Basileias, which are believed to represent the first charities of their type in the Christian Greek East. In a letter, Basil explained his dedication to this pursuit:

> Whom have we injured in any way by building these places of refuge to shelter strangers who come to this country, or those who need some special treatment because of their health? It is for them that we have arranged in our house the means to provide them with the necessary aid, with nurses, doctors, porters, guides. It has been indispensable to add to it the industries necessary for life, and the arts designed to adorn it. For this reason it has been necessary to construct buildings where these various kinds of work could be carried out.

Another prelate dedicated to establishing hospitals (whose original mission was simply to provide hospitality to travelers) was John Chrysostom, bishop of Constantinople (398–402), a city with a destitute population of fifty thousand. Although no modern judgment of Chrysostom can ignore his vicious anti-Semitism, the fact remains that his dedication to the poor reaped lasting benefits. The early hospital, notes G. C. Pournaropoulos, made significant contributions to our understanding of surgery, orthopedics, obstetrics/gynecology, epidemiology, pharmacology, toxicology, and a number of other disciplines.[8]

The foundation of the famous Hotel-Dieu, the Hostel of God, was laid about 651 in Paris, and it gradually took shape as a hospital recognizable to a modern eye. By the later Middle Ages, hospitals "were grand affairs which were specifically built to be hospitals," and usually under control of the church, writes Dr. E. J. Mayeaux Jr. "The Hotel-Dieu in Paris had regular nurses (nuns), only two people per bed, good ventilation (for the time) and good waste disposal."[9]

Hospitals were not the only centers of mercy operated by this expanding faith. In a truly heroic development, Christians also established leper houses, or lazar-houses, beginning in the fourth century. Working with lepers was not a job for the half-convinced; besides fear of contracting the disease, the smell of the festering sores was overpowering, the sight of the putrefying flesh was horrifying and there were no miracle cures to offer. The caregivers had a double purpose: To make these outcasts as comfortable as possible and, more importantly, to attend to their spiritual needs. Documents from the period, writes Riquet, "show that the life of the lazar-house was organized like that of a religious house, but also that a substantial diet was provided for the lepers."[10] One estimate puts three thousand lazar-houses in Europe and Asia.

The multiplication of monasteries (in sixth-century Gaul there were more than six hundred) also provided an enormous resource for the poor, offering everything from aid and comfort during famine to schooling for children. "Let special care be taken in reception of the poor and strangers, because in them Christ is more truly welcome," exhorted an early Benedictine document. Riquet notes that "In a single year at Cluny 17,000 poor persons were provided for. Certain poor persons had their names on a register and lived all the year round on the alms of the monastery."[11]

The explosive growth in religious establishments was in part a result of the faith-spurred philanthropy of a rough-and-tumble aristocracy. As Richard Fletcher observes, "The directing elites in the barbarian kingdoms were prepared to divert colossal, staggering resources into the service of new spiritual ideals. These adjectives are not used loosely. The number of monasteries founded, and the extent of their aggregate endowments, in seventh-century Francia and elsewhere, strain credulity. But the facts are well attested."[12]

The charitable ethic, concludes Christopher Dawson, was almost entirely church-based:

> All the social services which we regard as natural function of the state, such as education and the poor relief ... were fulfilled, in so far as they were fulfilled at all, by the action of the Church. ... There were in fact two societies and two cultures in early medieval Europe. On the one hand, there was the peace society of the Church, which was centred in the monasteries and episcopal cities and inherited the tradition of later Roman culture. And, on the other hand, there was the war-society of the feudal nobility and their following, whose life was spent in incessant wars and private feuds. Although the latter might be affected personally by the influence of the religious society, whose leaders were often their own kinsmen, they belonged socially to a more primitive order.[13]

Although widespread disease sometimes created almost chaotic conditions, caregivers countered by establishing order through a combination of piety and battlefield discipline. Indeed, orders of knighthood were established specifically to tend to the stricken. Raymond Le Puy, who is thought to have founded the Great Orders of Hospitallers in 1182, declared in its founding statutes that "Wherever there are hospitals of the sick, the commanders of the houses must serve the sick with good courage and provide them with all they need, and do them service without murmuring or complaint, so that by this ministry they may have part in the glory of heaven. And if any of the brothers frets at keeping the commands of the Master in these matters, the Master must be told of it, and punish him according to the discipline ordered by the house."

Similarly, Article Four of the statutes for the Order of St. John of Jerusalem (also 1182) established a strict regimen of care: "Every patient must have a cloak to wear, and boots, for going to and from the privy, and a woolen cap." Also required were "little cradles for the children of women pilgrims, born in the hospital, so that they may rest separately, by themselves, so that the children at the breast may not be troubled by the illness of their mothers." Three days each week, the sick were to be given "fresh pork or mutton, and chicken for those who cannot eat this." Riquet also reports a policy of providing two bowls for impoverished newly-wed couples and a small purse to discharged prisoners.

Eventually, the principle of strictly organized and disciplined charity would find its greatest practitioner in the person of Vincent de Paul (1580?–1660), whose spirit remains strong among Catholic relief workers of our era. Devoted to detail, Vincent appears to have considered no task too trivial for his attentions. "Each sick person," he wrote to one of his groups of volunteers,

> should have as much bread as he needs, with a quarter pound of boiled mutton or beef for dinner, and the same amount of roast for supper; except on Sundays when they may be given some boiled chicken for their dinner, and two or three times a week their meat may be chopped. Those who have no fever should have a pint of wine each day, half in the morning and half in the evening.... If fish can be found at an honest price, this shall be given them only at dinner. Permission to eat meat in Lent and on other forbidden days should be obtained for those who are very ill; and if they are

> unable to eat solid meat, they should be given bouillon, bread-soup or toasted bread, barley gruel and fresh eggs, twice or thrice a day.

Each orderly was instructed to treat invalids "all with love, as if it were her son she were treating, or rather God, who counts as done to himself the good she does to the poor."

Perhaps Vincent's greatest contribution was the founding of the Daughters of Charity in 1633, an extraordinary development for the time. As Henri Daniel-Rops notes in *Monsieur Vincent,* "In his day no one conceived of a feminine vocation outside the cloister: Claretians, Carmelites, Dominicans were nuns living out of the world, enclosed in their convents.... When Monsieur Vincent disclosed his plan both the religious and lay authorities were uneasy; it took all his influence and astuteness to carry the matter to its conclusion."[14] Thus was born the legendary Gray Sisters, who would labor in hospitals, hospices, foundling homes, armies (as the first female nurses) and even among the debased and brutalized royal galley slaves.

"The poor are our masters," instructed Vincent, who had himself been a slave for a brief spell after his capture by Barbary pirates in 1605. "They are our kings; we must obey them; and it is no exaggeration to call them this, since Our Lord is in the poor."

The plagues and famines associated with the Thirty Years' War were the occasion to which Vincent rose. "He lodged and sheltered thousands of refugees," writes Riquet, "and some eight hundred orphans 'who were put to a trade or in service.'"[15] During the 1650s his various enterprises fed as many as fifteen thousand people. (Many times that number are fed by the St. Vincent de Paul Society today. Founded in 1833 by eight students at the Sorbonne along with Professor Frederick Ozanam, the society has grown to 875,000 members in 132 countries, according to its officials.)

These were brutal times, admittedly, and mercy could be fleeting, especially when Catholics and Protestants took their differences to the battlefield. Christians nonetheless maintained their impressive pattern of charitable giving, if often in a strategic or partisan manner. So despite massive upheavals of war, famine and plague, Europe continued building charitable networks of notable proportions. "From huge institutions like the Albergo dei Poveri at Genoa and the Hotel-Dieu at Paris down to tiny three-bed hospitals in villages, from orders expert in surgery to others specializing in ransoming slaves from the Barbary corsairs, Catholic Europe was covered with a network of organizations to help the poor and sick, with parish priests and committees of devout ladies organizing outdoor relief," writes McManners.[16] And in time, Protestants would establish their own networks in the areas where they held sway. "In Protestant Europe, voluntary societies arose to fill the gap left by the abolition of the religious orders.... The list of societies—something like a hundred—to which [William] Wilberforce subscribed indicates the scope of the movement."[17]

One area of special importance to Protestant charity was the establishment of schools, providing an education that coupled evangelical religion with humanist learning. This motivation would lead to the founding of many of Europe's colleges and universities, and many of America's, too. The Protestant interest in humanistic studies was very much present in the grand Protestant himself. Martin Luther wrote that "If I had children [he eventually would have six] and could manage it, I would have them study not only languages and history, but also singing and music together with the whole of mathematics.... The ancient Greeks trained their children in those disciplines:... they grew up to be people of wondrous ability, subsequently fit for everything." Meanwhile, he provided a boon to growing literacy by translating the Bible into German. John Calvin, agreeing with Luther's view, founded the school that would become the University of Geneva for the purpose of teaching the Way, Truth and Life alongside a humanist curriculum. In this spirit, Calvinists also founded universities in Montauban, Nimes, Saumur, Sedan, Edinburgh, Leiden, Amsterdam, Gronigen, Utrecht and Franeker—to mention but a sample of the institutions established by Protestant educators.[18]

How the Charitable Spirit Enriched America

In 1636, Connecticut passed a law that "no young man that is neither married nor hath any servant ... shall keep house by himself, without consent of the town where he lives." Plymouth had a similar law, and all told, reports Leland Ryken, "Massachusetts took action against sixty people for living alone."[19]

Critics of the Puritans point to a zeal for social control in that enforced togetherness, but it had a larger purpose as well. Early colonists wanted to be part of a community of saints, not a loose grouping of rugged individualists. This desire for community grew out of the desire to please their God, who had promised to bless those who live not for themselves, but for others. John Winthrop said in his famous "Model of Christian Charity":

> We must be knit together in the work as one man, we must enter-
> tain each other in brotherly affection . . . , we must uphold a famil-
> iar commerce together in all meekness, gentleness, patience and
> liberality, we must delight in each other, make others' conditions
> our own, rejoice together, mourn together, labor and suffer together,
> always having before our eyes commission and community in our
> work, our community as members of the same body, so shall we
> keep the unity of the spirit in the bond of peace, the Lord will be
> our God and delight to dwell among us.

Looking out for Number One was not the Puritan way, as William Perkins stressed: "He abuseth his calling, whosoever he be that . . . employs it for himself, seeking wholly his own, and not the common good. And that common saying, Every man from himself and God for us all, is wicked." Besides elevating the individual to dangerous heights of arrogance, focusing on the one obscured the needs of the many less fortunate. This could lead, among other things, to profiteering. Increase Mather complained that "A poor man cometh amongst you and he must have a commodity whatever it cost him, and you will make him give whatever you please, and put what price you please upon what he hath to give . . . without respecting the value of the thing."

In fact, authorities did more than merely cast disapproving glances. In one famous case, a merchant named Robert Keayne was prosecuted and fined 200 pounds for charging excessive prices.

If Puritan divines were quick to denounce an unseemly lusting after profits, they were equally forceful in their enjoinders to care for the poor. An anonymous tract called "St. Paul the Tent-Maker," for example, insisted that "the more diligently we pursue our several callings, the more we are capacitated to extend our charity to such as are in poverty and distress." Contemporary Christians who squirm in their pews during a yearly "stewardship sermon" should find some relief in considering the level of exhortation they would have faced in earlier times. John Ashley, for example, delivered this ringing call to charitable arms in "The Great Duty of Charity, Considered and Applied," preached in

Boston on November 28, 1742: "Whatever attainments we may arrive so in religion, if we are void of charity, we are no real Christians, nor will they profit us any thing. This charity or divine Love, the Apostle tells us, is the Fruit of the Spirit.... To love all Men, even our enemies as ourselves, is above the utmost reach of human nature, and only the spirit of Christ can enable us to do so."

This same charitable spirit informed sermons and actions elsewhere around the Colonies. In Charleston, South Carolina, the city's Fellowship Society (established April 4, 1762) based its good works on the belief that among "the many duties which man from his creation was by his very nature enjoined to observe, the most essential one next to what he owes the Supreme Being, is that whereby he is bound to contribute to the relief of all those miseries, afflictions and infirmities, which from the time of Adam have been entailed on mankind."

With a dedication to order that would have met with the approval of Vincent de Paul, the Fellowship Society carried out its duties according to well-established rules. Dues and fines included a ten-shilling levy for anyone who attended meetings "disguised in liquor." The chief organizing principle was "the poor come first." After that, some provision could be made for those of healthier means. If "there shall be room in the Hospital to spare, after as many poor patients are accommodated, as the interest of the general fund can support, the society shall take in other patients at such reasonable rates as they can agree for." Proceeds would be used to care for the poor. Additionally, a minister would be hired from the Church of England, and at each gate were tin collection boxes stamped in gold letters with the words CHARITY FOR THE HOSPITAL.

Christians in Charleston also organized on behalf of orphans. On October 18, 1797, Rev. William Hollinshead marked the fifth anniversary of the city's Orphan House with a rousing (and lengthy) address including an explicit reminder that good works in this world might pay off handsomely in the next: "There, those small expressions of generous tenderness to the widow and the orphan, which a good man performs with exquisite pleasure, shall be acknowledged, as done to Christ himself."

It is no coincidence that the only two American-born Catholic saints, Elizabeth Ann Seton and Katharine Drexel, each made her name succoring the needy and neglected—most notably through the establishment of schools. Mother Seton not only founded the Sisters of Charity, whose work in schools, hospitals and orphanages would become legendary, but in 1810 she started the free school that was the seed of the American parochial school system. Drexel likewise founded a religious order, the Sisters of the Blessed Sacrament, while devoting a huge inheritance to sustain more than a hundred schools serving Indians and rural and inner-city blacks—including Xavier, the only Catholic university established for African-Americans. So prodigious was Drexel's charity that the income tax code was actually changed to accommodate it. As Mary J. Oates explains in *The Catholic Philanthropic Tradition in America,* "With the introduction of the federal income tax in 1913, Katharine Drexel's large annual income from her father's trust fund was taxed, even though she was using almost all of it for philanthropic purposes. In 1924, in recognition of this unusual circumstance, Congress passed the Income Tax Reduction Bill, soon known as the Philadelphia Nun Amendment, exempting from payment of federal income taxes persons who for each of the immediately preceding ten years had given 90 percent of their incomes to philanthropy."[20]

Christians of course had been founding colleges in North America since the seventeenth century. A document dating from 1643, entitled "New England's First Fruits," discusses the motivation behind the founding of Harvard University: "After God had carried us safe to New England, and we had builded our houses, provided necessities for our livelihood, reared convenient places for God's worship, and settled the civil government, one of the next things we longed for and looked after was to advance learning and perpetuate its posterity."

The goal of a Harvard education was indisputably Christian: "Let every student be plainly instructed and earnestly pressed to consider well the main end of his life and studies is to know God and Jesus Christ which is eternal life, John 17:3, and therefore to lay Christ in the bottom, as the only foundation of all sound knowledge and learning." This goal was to be achieved by a great deal of Bible reading: Every student "shall so exercise himself in reading the Scriptures twice a day that he shall be ready to give such an account of his proficiency therein . . . as his tutor shall require, . . . seeing the entrance of the word giveth light, it giveth understanding to the simple, Psalm 119:130."

Meanwhile, public-spirited Christians were establishing colleges throughout America, though these denominational links are little mentioned today (and in some cases have been completely severed). The religious devotion of the founders is indisputable. James Duke, whose family founded Duke University, was a deeply committed Methodist. "My old Daddy," he recalled in later years, "always said that if he amounted to anything in life, it was due to the Methodist circuit riders who so often visited his home, and whose preaching and counsel brought out the best that was in him. If I amount to anything in this world I will owe it to my Daddy and to the Methodist Church." Duke would no doubt be disturbed by recent protests that ended the practice of giving Duke University graduates a Bible along with their diplomas—a change defended (to the surprise of no one familiar with the ethos of the contemporary university) on grounds of religious tolerance.

William and Mary College, whose most illustrious student was Thomas Jefferson, was founded by Episcopalians so that "the Church of Virginia may be furnished with a seminary of ministers of the Gospel, and that the youth may be piously educated in good letters and manners and that the Christian faith may be propagated amongst the western Indians, to the glory of Almighty God; to make a place of universal study, or perpetual college of divinity, philosophy, languages and other good arts and sciences."

Elihu Yale volunteered financial aid to found Yale University after receiving a solicitation in 1718 from none other than Cotton Mather, who understood that charity is not confined to physical want. Yale was to be a school "wherein Youth may be instructed in the Arts and Sciences, who through the blessings of Almighty God may be fitted for public employment both in Church and Civil State." Similarly, Columbia University was founded "For Instruction and Education of Youth in the Learned Languages and in the Liberal Arts and Sciences ... to lead them from the Study of Nature to the Knowledge of Themselves, and of the God of Nature, and their Duty to Him."

Arnaud Marts comments, "There are those who tend to minimize the religious motive back of the founding of our early colleges; but had there been no such motive it seems only fair to conclude that few, if any, would have been established in those rugged days, in the face of such difficulties." With rare exceptions, he adds, "practically all the colleges founded between the Revolution and the Civil War were organized, supported, and, in most cases, controlled by religious interests."[21] By his count, before the Civil War various religious denominations established 150 of the 180 permanent colleges and universities.

• Presbyterians founded, among others, Princeton, Hampden-Sydney, Lafayette, Union, Hamilton, Washington and Jefferson of Pittsburgh, New York University, Wabash, Davidson, the University of Buffalo, and the College of Wooster.

• Baptists founded Brown, Colby, Colgate, Bucknell, Wake Forest, Baylor, Hillsdale, Rochester, Vassar, and Chicago.

• The Methodists started Randolph-Macon, Wesleyan, Emory, DePauw, Northwestern, Boston, Duke, and South Union.

• Catholics established an immense educational system at all levels, at one time maintaining 233 colleges, including Holy Cross, Fordham, Villanova, Georgetown, Notre Dame, Loyola, and St. Louis.

• Besides William and Mary, the Episcopalians founded Columbia, Trinity, Hobart, and Sewanee.

• The Quakers are most noted for Swarthmore, Haverford, Earlham, Guilford, and Wilmington.

The slow but significant crusade for higher education for black Americans also has Christian roots. General Samuel Armstrong, the son of a Congregationalist minister, founded Hampton Institute in 1868 with help from the American Missionary Society. George Peabody provided $3 million that year for funding education for blacks and whites, and the announcement of this effort was made in Washington at an event attended by Ulysses S. Grant and various other worthies, including vanquished Confederates. According to a contemporary account, "After reading his deed of gift to them for the children of the South, there is a solemn hush, and then it is proposed that the blessing of Almighty God be called upon his solemn act. They kneel there in a circle of prayer—the Puritan of New England, the pioneer of the West, the financier of the metropolis, and the defeated veterans of the Confederacy. With bended knee and touching elbow, they dedicate this great gift."

As their counterparts did in Europe, American Christians established hospitals, too; the oldest may be Philadelphia's Old Blockley, founded in 1731 as a sick ward for the Alms House. Catholics alone had established more than five hundred hospitals by the 1920s.

Christians also came to the aid of those with specific chronic ailments. In 1817, Rev. T. H. Gallaudet founded the Connecticut Asylum for the Education of Deaf and Dumb Persons; by 1880 the movement included sixty-one asylums with eight thousand members. Similarly, in 1832, Dr. S. G. Howe founded the Perkins Institute for the Blind, and also pioneered education for the "feeble-minded." Howe hailed from a family of deep religious faith. (His wife, Julia Ward Howe, wrote the "Battle Hymn of the Republic.") Dorothea Dix's Christian compassion and unflagging energy transformed the treatment of the mentally ill, convincing many states of the need to upgrade their hospitals for the insane or to create them in the first place. And it was the likes of Rev. Louis Dwight of Boston who not only agitated against brutal prison conditions but managed, through the promotion of such modern notions as cell blocks, to make the United States an international leader in civilized incarceration.

Meanwhile, droves of Christian activists ministered to the growing concentrations of urban poor, a few making themselves well-known figures in the process. Jane Addams, the pacifist founder of Chicago's Hull House (1889), may be the best known, for her career culminated in a Nobel Peace Prize.

Charity has taken other directions in our age, with government and the great foundations assuming much of the burden of social welfare. That said, Christians continue their good works to an impressive degree. In 1999, the Salvation Army led all charities in the country in fundraising for the eighth straight year, collecting $1.4 billion in cash and donated goods, according to the *Chronicle of Philanthropy*.[22] The YMCA of the USA was second, Lutheran Services in America sixth, and Habitat for Humanity International ninth—to cite the Christian-oriented groups in the top ten. Many other groups, from the International Union of Gospel Missions to Catholic Charities USA, raised hundreds of millions of dollars as well.

Direct financial contributions are not the only manifestations of the giving spirit. The *Independent Sector* reports that an estimated 109 million Americans participated in volunteering in 1998, which "represented the equivalent of over 9 million full-time employees at a value of $225 billion," and that a "strong relationship exists between religious involvement and the total level of giving and volunteering."[23] *The Chronicle of Philanthropy* confirms this relationship between religious belief and the charitable impulse, noting that "a region's economy and its religious and community traditions are often indicators of how much money residents give away."[24]

Indeed, according to Laurence R. Iannaccone, writing in the *Journal of Economic Literature,* total church contributions alone "appear to have remained around 1 percent of GNP since at least 1955. Religious giving consistently accounts for about half of all charitable giving in the United States (approximately 64 billion dollars in 1995); religious volunteer work is more common than any other form of volunteer work ... and the majority of non-profit institutions are or were religiously based."[25]

Nonetheless, it would be misleading to suggest that Christian philanthropy has not been transformed in some ways by the rise of gigantic secular counterparts. The twentieth century saw many church charities turn over their fundraising to professional, centralized bureaucracies increasingly distant from the rank-and-file laity, with predictably mixed results. Reliance on government funds grew, too, along with government influence. Oates points out that by the 1960s, Dorothy Day warned that "uncritical acceptance of government policies and goals by diocesan charities was weakening the foundations of Catholic philanthropy," and she "urged that parishioners return to a standard of 'true efficiency' that measured charity not by budget or agency size, but rather by the extent of personal exchange between local parishioners and the poor."[26]

Yet despite the worrisome trends, a still significant number of Christian charities managed to hold true to their spiritual and historical traditions. Certainly the best known of these, and also the largest, was founded by a remarkable man named William Booth.

A Methodist street preacher and former pawnshop employee, Booth established his Christian Mission in 1865 to serve the destitute in London's East End. Robust in his beliefs, which included a strong disdain for alcohol, he reputedly attracted the attention of his future wife, Catherine, by a dramatic recitation of "The Grog-Seller's Dream," a temperance mainstay. In 1878, the mission recast itself along military lines, with Booth as its first general. As commanders of the Salvation Army, William and Catherine took up not only the cause of the poor, but that of women's and children's rights as well. Indeed, "as the first Christian group in modern times to treat women as men's equals, the Army offered a compelling, if sometimes contradictory, vision of gender," according to Diane Winston in *Red-Hot and Righteous: The Urban Religion of the Salvation Army*.[27]

This multiplicity of interests did not endear the upstart organization to the reigning powers. Initially, the Church of England was hostile, as was the evangelist and political figure Lord Shaftesbury, who referred to Rev. Booth as the "Anti-Christ." The Salvation Army's gaudy style and apparent success no doubt inspired some degree of this hostility. According to the Army's historian, Edward H. McKinley, an 1882 London survey found that on one weekend night there were nearly 17,000 people at an Army worship service, compared with 11,000 in established churches.

The Salvation Army's first American meeting took place in Philadelphia on October 5, 1879. Promotional posters announced "Two Hallelujah Females" who would "speak and sing in behalf of God and Precious Souls." The posters also asked that "Rich and Poor, Come in Crowds." A total of twelve people showed up, most of them friends of the evangelists. The next meeting began with hymn singing and ended in a riot after patrons of local saloons investigated the source of the unexpected commotion. "When they tried to deliver a message to the gathered crowd," writes Edward McKinley, "it dispersed in a cloud of oaths and gibes." Returning later that evening, the missionaries "were greeted by many of the same crowd with a shower of insults, mud, and garbage."[28]

Yet as required by their faith, the missionaries persisted and soon found their first convert in a drunk named Reddie. From this wretched fellow soon grew a formidable organization, active in evangelizing the poor and determined to serve their physical wants as well. In 1891, Salvationists established their first American men's shelter. By the turn of the century they operated more than sixty shelters in the United States, including several for women. They also ran numerous workshops, rescue homes and other philanthropic enterprises, including farm colonies. By the height of the Great Depression, the Army had grown to the point where it could provide "100,000 meals and 25,000 lodgings free of charge for needy New Yorkers each week."[29]

Today the Salvation Army operates in 80 countries, maintaining 16,000 evangelical centers and more than 3,000 social welfare institutions, hospitals, schools and agencies. Public confidence in its activities is reflected in the fact that the Army attracts more contributions than any other single charity, including such broad-based organizations as the American Cancer Society and the American Red Cross.

"I am not a Salvationist and I began with no brief for or against the movement," Diane Winston acknowledges in the introduction to her book on the Salvation Army. "However, my research has given me a deep appreciation for the selfless work Salvationists have done and continue to do. Their compassion and dedication are truly compelling."[30] And what is the "big idea" that has consistently inspired them? It is, Winston relates, "evangelical Christianity."

There is no denying that Christian charity has enriched the world to a remarkable and singular degree. H. G. Wells, famously non-Christian, paid eloquent tribute to this contribution more than three-quarters of a century ago:

> It is only within the last three or at most four thousand years that we have any clear evidence that voluntary self-abandonment to some greater end, without fee or reward, was an acceptable idea to men, or that anyone propounded it.... We have seen the idea become vivid as a beacon, vivid as sunshine caught and reflected dazzlingly by some window in the landscape, in the teaching of Buddha, Lao Tse, and, most clearly of all, Jesus of Nazareth. Through all its variations and corruptions Christianity has never completely lost the suggestion of a devotion to God's commonweal that makes the personal pomp of monarchs and rulers seem like the insolence of an over-dressed servant and the splendors and gratifications of wealth like the waste of robbers.

SEVEN

CHRISTIANITY
AND THE ENVIRONMENT

Among all the world's religions, it is alleged, Christianity has proved uniquely dangerous to the environment. This it has accomplished in part by insisting that the Creator is separate from the creation, and therefore streams could be dammed and forests razed without fear of angering the spirits that other people believed dwelled within them. Further, Christianity teaches that there is a hierarchy among living things, with humans on top, supreme in worth. Finally, Christians have been instructed to be fruitful and multiply, and to dominate all other creatures of the Earth— suggestions they have taken seriously to the detriment of the natural world. More than any other people, Christians, because of their insular and egocentric vision of the world, have manipulated the environment for their own selfish purposes. It is a habit that continues to this day.

When St. Boniface chopped down a pagan sacred oak in his eighth-century mission to the Germans, little did he know that he would someday become the poster boy of supposed Christian hostility to the environment. "To a Christian," charged historian of science Lynn White in a famous 1967 article in *Science* magazine, "a tree can be no more than a physical fact. The whole concept of the sacred grove is alien to Christianity.... For nearly 2 millennia Christian missionaries have been chopping down sacred groves, which are idolatrous because they assume spirit in nature." White asserted that "by destroying pagan animism, Christianity made it possible to exploit nature in a mood of indifference to the feelings of natural objects." As the "most anthropocentric religion the

162

world has ever seen," he added, Christianity "bears a huge burden of guilt" for the ecological ills of the modern world.

These remarks caused a sensation when they were published, and have continued to resonate in the ecology movement ever since. Although leading conservationists going back to Ralph Waldo Emerson, Henry David Thoreau and John Muir had sometimes embraced a form of animism in their writings on nature, White brought a straightforward anti-Christian thesis out of the closet. His *Science* article was greeted with hearty approval, and has been widely quoted ever since. Its critique has worked its way into the canon of environmentalism.

In *A Green History of the World,* Clive Ponting asserts that "The early and medieval Christian thinkers accepted, almost without demur, the view inherited from Jewish writing that God had given humans the right to exploit plants, animals and the whole world for their benefit. Nature is not seen as sacred and therefore it is open to exploitation by humans without any moral qualms." Jeremy Rifkin echoes this theme in *Biosphere Politics,* arguing that "By stripping people of their close bonds with nature, the Church left Western man and woman without any secure grounding in the physical world." Kirkpatrick Sale, an exponent of "deep ecology," concedes that a desire to master nature was "not exclusive to early modern Europe.... But it had seldom developed to this degree.... The roots of this attitude are essentially biblical, found in the creation myth which is central to any society."

Sale means, of course, the story of Genesis, where God instructs humans to "be fruitful and multiply, and fill the earth and subdue it; and have dominion over the fish of the sea and over the birds of the air and over every living thing that moves upon the earth." This "Dominion Covenant" comes under fire from those who want to "resacralize" nature because it sets humans apart from other creatures and thus, they say, erodes our respect for them. "Man's greedy impulse to exploit nature used to be held in check by his pious worship of nature," wrote Arnold Toynbee in the twilight of his career. But Genesis, according to some environmental activists like Tom Hayden, provided "a license to plunder the natural world."

Some target their censure especially at the Protestant Reformation, which suppressed the veneration of saints and angels and other rituals with links to a pagan past. Protestants "wanted to purify religion, and this purification involved the disenchantment of the world," writes Rupert Sheldrake. "All traces of magic, holiness, and spiritual power were to be removed from the realm of nature; the spiritual realm would be confined to human beings." The ultimate result, according to this argument, is a man-centered cosmology that creates, as a byproduct, an appetite for ecological destruction.

This critique has been influential not just in environmental circles, but even within the Christian establishment. In recent years, virtually every denomination has taken pains to teach stewardship of nature as opposed to dominion over it. Taking note of this trend, the executive director of the Sierra Club actually apologized to Christians attending a symposium in 1997 for the abuse they'd taken from the environmental movement. But such expressions of regret are rare, partly because the movement as a whole has embraced the belief that some form of animism or pantheism is most compatible with respect for nature.

Consider the reverential treatment that the literature of the environmental movement gives to the "environmental Indian," the native uniquely in tune with the natural world and loath to inflict the slightest scar on it. The *Gaia Atlas of First Peoples* is typical when it reports that indigenous people "consider the Earth like a parent and revere it accordingly." This image has become a staple in the wider culture, too. Its ideology appears in movies from *Dancing with Wolves* to *Pocahontas,* and in school textbooks. According to one high school history text, Indians "worshipped the gods who had created the world, and they viewed the land as a sacred trust that they were privileged to use but were obligated to pass on unspoiled to future generations." Advertisers use the imagery of the environmental Indian whenever possible; Keep America Beautiful's "Crying Indian" was a memorable early example of this. Even leading cultural and historical institutions have followed suit; a Smithsonian Institution exhibit in the early 1990s described pre-Columbian America as a place where "native people were transparent in the landscape, living as natural elements of the ecosphere."

It would seem that saving the world from ourselves requires thinking like Indians, or at least not like Christians. "I believe the earth has suffered from the perception that the sacred is no longer resident in its depths," declares Tom Hayden in *The Lost Gospel of the Earth.* "Only when we believe the sacred is present in the living earth will we revere our world again."

— — —

The indictment of Christians as earth's despoilers does rest on a kernel of fact, for Christianity supplied a philosophical framework that enabled people more readily to investigate, understand and manipulate the physical world, leading to the founding of modern science. Environmental understanding is a gift of that scientific quest, and so too is the luxury to be able to seek such knowledge on a comprehensive scale. As Stanley L. Jaki remarks, man before the Industrial Revolution "had been very much on the defensive vis à vis nature."[1] Technological progress changed that; and the romanticized disdain for technology and its fruits is, intentionally or not, an expression of indifference toward human welfare.

Residents of today's advanced societies have lost touch with the typical living conditions of the past. They no longer fear the famine that stalked every part of the world well into the eighteenth century, when the Industrial Revolution gathered force. They have forgotten that as late as 1730, three-quarters of all children born in London failed to reach their fifth birthday, while adults could be struck down in their prime by cholera, smallpox, tuberculosis and a host of other infectious diseases that no one fully understood, and which contemporary treatment often made worse. They fail to appreciate that as late as 1800, life expectancy in both England and Japan was about thirty-five years, although conditions were more tolerable than they had been for most of recorded history.

It is true that some ancient hunter-gatherer societies may have enjoyed healthier lives than many humans after the agricultural revolution. But even people in those ancient tribes did not achieve the health or longevity of those who live in the industrialized world today. And although a few premodern societies managed to create and spread modest wealth beyond a small elite, it wasn't until the past few hundred years, and beginning in the still largely Christian West, that humans discovered how to generate more-or-less steady economic growth that could withstand even the shock of major hostilities. Formerly, prosperity had usually been snuffed out by "corruption, wars, and inept government," in the words of economists Joyce Burnette and Joel Mokyr, or by a bureaucracy (as in China) that simply distrusted commerce.[2]

We described several of the catalysts for this economic transformation in previous chapters: the establishment of the rule of law, the extension of property rights, the flowering of an inventive and entrepreneurial spirit, an embrace of manual labor. Two more are central: a commitment to literacy and a recommitment to the sacred nature of all forms of work that took hold in the wake of the Reformation.

Literacy rates among both sexes rose dramatically where Bible reading became a general Christian duty, as it did in Protestant homes. And general literacy was one of those telltale indicators of Europe's emerging market economy. David S. Landes was so struck by such indicators that in *The Wealth and Poverty of Nations* (1998) he resuscitated and updated Max Weber's famous (but battered) thesis about the influence of the Protestant ethic on the rise of capitalism.[3]

Weber's original thesis had some flaws, as his many critics in the past eighty years have explained at great length. He failed to account for why groups of Calvinists and even entire nations like Scotland—Calvinist to the core—failed to get a jump on the industrial age. He slighted what arguably are the key ingredients for economic dynamism: an inventive spirit and entrepreneurial instincts. And he failed to give sufficient credit to the Middle Ages as the incubator for capitalism's takeoff and for the institutions that made it possible. Yet as Landes suggests, it is impossible to dismiss altogether the historical influence of religion—call it a Protestant ethic if you will—unless we are prepared to argue that cultural values and codes of conduct have nothing to do with success in a market economy.

If culture doesn't matter, then a great many Puritans (to cite one Calvinist group) wasted tremendous amounts of ink and energy exhorting their coreligionists to diligence, moderation, thrift and contentment in work—to the service and glory of God, they insisted, not to accumulate wealth. It is impossible to review this body of writing without concluding that such powerful beliefs must have influenced behavior, helping English and American Puritans alike to gain traction in a capitalistic world.

Many modern images of the Puritans are so much myth: their alleged narrow-mindedness, misogyny and self-flagellation, for example. In fact, Puritans were among the most educated people of their era, who elevated women's status and promoted the ideals of companionable marriage and romantic love. Yet their fabled disdain for idleness is no misconception. The comments of one John Robinson are fairly typical: "It is a blessing upon every one that feareth the Lord, and walks in His ways, that he shall eat the labor of his hands. And he that without his own labor either of body or mind eats the labor of other men's hands only, and lives by their sweat, is but like unto lice, and such other vermin." Elizabeth Joceline put the matter more briskly: "Be ashamed of idleness as thou art a man, but tremble at it as thou art a Christian." As Leland Ryken sensibly concludes, "It is obvious from such statements that the Puritan work ethic made work an individual responsibility as well as a social obligation."[4]

Modern social science research confirms, in the words of Laurence R. Iannaccone, "the links between religiosity and a wide range of economically important social behavior, such as criminal activity, drug and alcohol consumption, physical and mental health, and marriage, fertility, and divorce."[5] Why should religion's influence have been any less decisive in the past?

Luther, Calvin and their followers rejuvenated the Christian concept of the dignity and sanctity of every kind of work, no matter how humble—a notion which had eroded over time. Paul had twice counseled Christians to do everything to the glory of God, and the monks who brought so much of Europe into cultivation took him at his word. Although focused preeminently on spiritual work, they also embraced backbreaking labor as an integral part of a holy life. Similar attitudes, updated and even radicalized, would be crucial to the emerging economic order of capitalism. "There is no difference betwixt washing of dishes and preaching of the word of God; but as touching to please God, none at all," declared the Protestant martyr William Tyndale. Those who worked with their hands were entitled to hold their heads high, however they might be scorned by idlers with inherited status or even a clergy too often convinced of its own preeminence. Like the monks who plunged into the dark forests a thousand years before, these Christians of the Reformation helped to remake a civilization in the service of their faith—and to our ultimate benefit.

It is true that nature did not go unscathed in this unfolding drama of growing wealth, new technology and opportunity for body and spirit. But it is equally true that nature has not escaped unscarred from the activities of non-Western cultures, either, including those whose tools were fashioned of nothing more than stone.

How Non-Christians Regarded the Natural World

If aboriginal people were natural conservationists, this attribute is not evident in many of their works. On Easter Island, for example, the same natives who quarried the legendary stone statues that mark the landscape also stripped the island of trees, to the point that by 1500 their society was careening toward collapse. In the Hawaiian Islands, half of the endemic species of birds vanished after the Polynesians arrived. In New Zealand, the Maoris' ancestors drove more than a dozen types of flightless birds to extinction—the same fate that awaited a variety of species in Australia once the aborigines arrived.

The wages of ignorance and miscalculation fell upon people from the higher civilizations as well. The ancient Greeks razed the forests of Attica; the Phoenicians clearcut the coast of Dalmatia; the civilizations of Mesopotamia turned more than one agricultural breadbasket into half-sterile desert. Indeed, "Some of the worst ecological disasters of human origin occurred in the earliest civilizations," notes the scientist and philosopher Rene Dubos. By the fourth century B.C., China was so thoroughly deforested that "the Taoist Chuang Tsu looked back nostalgically to the golden age of the past."[6]

The historical record of early New World peoples is no less sobering. When game was abundant, explains anthropologist Shepard Krech III, Indians could be as indifferent to waste as any European faced with similar bounty. For hundreds of years, a favored technique of the Plains Indians for killing buffalo was to drive as many as possible off a cliff, leaving a huge number to rot untouched. Often the Indians—anticipating the rapacious white hunters who followed—took nothing more from slaughtered buffalo than such delicacies as the tongue.

Ironically, a conservation ethic was often incompatible with Indian religion. "Understanding that buffaloes were animated other-than-human persons helps make sense of two beliefs with implications for conservation and ecology," Krech writes in *The Ecological Indian: Myth and History.* "The first is that buffaloes that

escaped from an enclosure or jump would warn others away. . . .
A second Plains Indian belief . . . is that when buffaloes disappeared
for the season, they went to lake-bottom grasslands, and that when
they reappeared they came from those habitats. . . . If buffaloes
returned each year from the earth because they were of the earth,
how could they possibly go extinct? How could one kill too many
if one held to this belief?"[7] For the Plains Indians and for many
other New World natives, "waste and overkill (as understood by
today's conservationists) were apparently largely foreign concepts
based in Western science and practice."[8] Charles E. Kay makes a
related point in "Aboriginal Overkill: The Role of Native Americans in Structuring Western Ecosystems," explaining that

> a scarcity of animals or hunting failures were not viewed as bio-
> logical or ecological phenomena, but rather as a spiritual conse-
> quence of social events or circumstances. If a Native American could
> not find any game, it was not because he had overharvested the
> resource, but because he had done something to displease the gods.
> Since Native Americans saw no connection between their hunting
> and game numbers, their system of religious beliefs actually fos-
> tered the overexploitation of ungulate populations. Religious respect
> for animals does not equal conservation.[9]

After a devastating overtrapping of beavers in the seventeenth
and eighteenth centuries, it was European traders of the Hudson
Bay Company who encouraged Indians to adopt game manage-
ment techniques that would help restore depleted populations.
(Interestingly enough, one of the first recorded recommendations
for preserving beaver numbers by taking only large males had been
made two centuries earlier by a Jesuit priest, Paul Le Jeune.)

Recent scholarship is rapidly battering down the widespread
belief that Indians had little role in depleting the immense herds
of buffalo—perhaps thirty million creatures—that existed into
the mid-eighteenth century. Andrew C. Isenberg, author of *The
Destruction of the Bison*, estimates that by the start of the devastating Great White Hunt in 1870, the buffalo population had
already been decimated by the nomadic Indian hunters who had
taken to the Plains to exploit new trade opportunities with whites.[10]
The Indians also slaughtered buffalo because their own growing
numbers demanded it. "By 1850, you had more Indians on the
Plains than had been there in several hundred years," notes Elliott

West. The Indians moving onto the Plains in the first half of the century "quickly began creating their own problems by overestimating what the Plains' resources could support.... In a couple of generations, Indians faced a resource crisis of their own."[11]

Indian appreciation of nature was real enough, yet when land was abundant, it was often treated with indifference. The archeological record is replete with examples of tribes who sapped the fertility of good cropland by overfarming year after year. Then they either packed up their villages and moved on, or altered their diets to survive.

If Indian spiritual values had promoted environmental consciousness, the Anasazi and other tribes would not have hacked their way through the local wood supply with such abandon in pre-Columbian times. "The forests of the Americas, from Canada to Argentina, were so highly disturbed or modified by Amerindian use by 1492 that it is surprising that even the popular literature has missed this point," write B. L. Turner and K. W. Butzer in the journal *Environment*.[12]

Far from respecting a forest's or grassland's "natural" state, Indians everywhere manipulated nature to their advantage. Often they would do this with fire. They set fires to create habitat for favored game animals; fires to force animals into traps or onto land where they could be hunted with less trouble; fires to frighten or disperse their enemies; fires to signal their whereabouts. And if a fire raced out of control? Well, so be it. "The evidence that Indians lit fires that then were allowed to burn destructively and without regard to ecological consequences is abundant," Krech concludes.[13]

"To claim that Indians lived without affecting nature is akin to saying that they lived without touching anything, that they were a people without history," remarks Louis S. Warren. In fact, he adds, "the idea of 'preserving' land in some kind of wilderness state would have struck them as impractical and absurd. More often than not, Indians profoundly shaped the ecosystems around them."[14] This is not to say that native peoples were wanton abusers of the environment, but rather that they were merely human.

How Christians Regarded the Natural World

When the Roman Emperor Julian attempted to revive paganism in the mid-fourth century, he traveled about sacrificing animals with such zest that he sometimes distorted the local price of meat.

Say what you will about the Christian relationship with nature, it has never required the wholesale execution of living creatures in sacred ceremonies. The New Testament is fairly explicit in rejecting animal sacrifice: it is "impossible that the blood of bulls and goats should take away sin" (Hebrews 10:4). Christians believed that animal sacrifices have no purpose, given the incomparable sacrifice of Christ himself on behalf of human redemption.

To be sure, some ancient pagans could more than match any Christian in a respectful regard for nature. The Pythagoreans considered it a crime to kill animals because of the transmigration of human souls. Other pagan writers ascribed extravagant powers of reasoning and logic to animals, claiming they equaled the capacity of humans. Yet it was pagans who sustained the wretched slaughter of the amphitheater, in which vast numbers of wild animals clawed and tore one another—and humans—apart; and it was Christians who outlawed this spectacle as the degrading barbarism that it was. Christian societies would eventually indulge blood sports of their own, such as cockfighting and bearbaiting, but these never approached the grotesque, formal magnitude of the gladiatorial games.

Christian attitudes toward nature begin with Genesis, where God looked upon creation and "saw that it was good"—a sentiment that would be echoed over and over in later books (for example, Psalm 104:14–23). The Old Testament, as Rabbi Dr. J. David Bleich notes, "abounds in passages that reflect concern for animal welfare. Concern for the welfare of animals is clearly regarded as the trait of a righteous person."[15] Old Testament guidelines for the treatment of animals are remarkably detailed and humane. The books of Exodus and Deuteronomy caution against overworking animals, yoking two unlike animals together, and otherwise treating domesticated creatures with wanton brutality. And one cannot be more direct than this warning from Proverbs 12:10, "A righteous man has regard for the life of his beast, but the mercy of the wicked is cruel."

In *Replenish the Earth,* Lewis G. Regenstein observes that Mosaic law contains "one of the first and strongest nature protection regulations" outlawing the destruction of fruit trees even to aid a military campaign.[16] Meanwhile, several biblical passages foretell a future of universal harmony among God's creatures, such as the well-known promise from Isaiah that the "wolf shall dwell with the lamb, and the leopard shall lie down with the kid, and the calf and the lion and the fatling together . . . and the lion shall eat straw like the ox. . . . They shall not hurt or destroy in all my holy mountains: for the Earth shall be full of the knowledge of the Lord." Such passages are impossible to reconcile with the idea that nature exists for no purpose other than ruthless exploitation by humans.

The New Testament provides no specific guidelines for the treatment of animals or nature beyond what is laid down in the Old Testament. Paul does refer to the Mosaic law against muzzling an ox when it is treading out grain, but applies it as an allegory for the just treatment of humans. It is nevertheless striking how many New Testament references evoke sympathy for animals and speak of God's care for them. Christians are told that not a single sparrow falls to the ground without God's knowledge; that the Holy Spirit appears as a dove; that Jesus was born in a manger, no doubt among the sort of creatures that populate modern nativity scenes; that Jesus is "the good shepherd," and that a good shepherd "lays down his life for his sheep"; that the lamb is a symbol of suffering innocence. In the lyrical Sermon on the Mount (Matthew 5), Jesus repeats his assurance of divine concern for the humblest of earthly creatures: "Look at the birds of the air; they neither sow nor reap nor gather into barns, and yet your heavenly Father feeds them." Such elegant references to nature have rarely been rivaled: "Consider the lilies of the field, how they grow; they neither toil nor spin; yet I tell you, even Solomon in all his glory was not arrayed like one of these."

It is true that some, like Regenstein, get carried away when they attempt to reinterpret the Bible as something akin to an unappreciated tract for the environmental and animal rights movements. They even speculate hopefully on whether Jesus might have been a vegetarian. But their larger point is well taken: Those intent on presenting the Bible as a polemic against nature, based on scattered passages like the Dominion Covenant, are engaged in a highly dubious exercise. It is just as easy—indeed, a great deal easier and more accurate—to portray the Bible and the Judeo-Christian ethic as encouraging humane treatment of animals and respect for the natural world. As Jaki remarks, "according to Christian faith the primary purpose of nature is to reveal the glory of God. For this reason alone man, Christian man in particular, could not feel entitled to take willful advantages of nature. Could a Christian man not feel compunction of heart for turning forests into wastelands while repeating the Psalms about trees shouting to God for joy?"[17]

If early Christian evangelists chopped down sacred groves, it was hardly out of hostility toward trees. The church of the first millennium, when the tree chopping mainly occurred, regularly bestowed sainthood on men and women who showed profound affection for nature and its creatures—not specifically for that reason, granted, but for the goodness that was powerful enough, according to the hagiographers, to attract even wild animals.

Long before Francis of Assisi extracted a promise from the wolf of Gubbio that he would kill no more sheep, St. Colman's faithful companions had been a cock, a mouse, and a fly. "The cock announced the hour of devotion," explains William E. H. Lecky, "the mouse bit the ear of the drowsy saint till he got up, and if in the course of his studies he was afflicted by any wandering thoughts, or called away by other business, the fly alighted on the line where he had left off, and kept the place."[18] A holy man or woman befriending animals, and vice versa, is one of the most common themes of the lives of the saints, involving hundreds of stories down through the Middle Ages. St. Macarius of Alexandria (4th century) supposedly cured a young hyena of blindness. St. Cuthbert (7th century) revived a dead bird through his prayers. Lecky suggests these legends represent "the first, and at the same time one of the most striking efforts ever made in Christendom to inculcate a feeling of kindness and pity towards the brute creation."[19]

Nor has Christian concern for animal welfare been confined to individual holy people. The Catholic church has frowned on bullfights for centuries, from Pius V's condemnation of them in 1567 as "contrary to Christian duty and charity" to Pius XII's refusal in 1956 to accept gifts offered by the Spanish bullfighting industry. Meanwhile, several Protestant traditions have opposed cruelty to animals in a more pronounced and arguably more productive way.

Puritan hostility to bearbaiting is notorious, thanks to Thomas Macaulay's unfair claim that Puritans hated the spectacle "not because it gave pain to the bear, but because it gave pleasure to the spectators." In fact, at Puritan instigation, an explicit ban on cruelty to animals was written into the colonial Massachusetts legal code as early as 1641. To wit: "No man shall exercise any Tir-ranny or Crueltie towards any bruite Creature which are usuallie kept for man's use." According to Regenstein, "Massachusetts was thus the first Western governmental body to incorporate mercy for animals into law."

When the mother country finally considered following suit, religious conscience again led the way. Paul Johnson reports that "Between 1800 and 1835, Parliament debated no less than 11 bills seeking to make the deliberate ill-treatment of animals unlawful. All failed, mostly by narrow margins. Bear-baiting and bull run-ning were the prime targets of the lobby.... The reform move-ment was dominated by religious groups, overwhelmingly non-Conformist and Evangelical."[20] The great evangelical figure in the antislavery movement, William Wilberforce, was also active in meetings of the Royal Society for the Prevention of Cruelty to Animals, which itself had been founded by an Anglican priest. Clergymen and Christian activists continued to be heavily repre-sented in the humane movement in Britain and the United States right through the nineteenth century.

By contemporary standards, of course, a good deal of histori-cal Christian rhetoric about nature is fairly jarring. We no longer talk, as Puritan preacher Cotton Mather did, of a duty to subdue and transform the "howling wilderness," although our restraint has everything to do with the fact that wilderness for most of us is both remote and defanged. Rene Dubos explains,

> Ecologists define as wilderness any environment that has not been disturbed by human activities, but in the popular mind, the word still has a deep resonance with a feeling of alienation and insecu-rity.... In the past, nature in the wild has been usually regarded as alien and cruel.... Fear of the wilderness probably began to decrease as soon as dependable roads gave confidence that safe and com-fortable quarters could be reached in case of necessity. There were numerous good roads in western Europe by the time Jean Jacques Rousseau roamed through the Alps and Wordsworth through the Lake District.[21]

Aldous Huxley's assessment was similar, if more biting: "To us who live beneath a temperate sky and in the age of Henry Ford, the worship of Nature comes almost naturally. It is easy to love a fee-ble and already conquered enemy."[22]

It is easy, too, in an era of abundance and comfort, to accord animals ever greater sympathy and thus to disdain the attitudes of an earlier, needier age. We recoil, for example, at a nineteenth-century Catholic Dictionary's insistence that animals "are made for man, who has the same right over them which he has over plants or stones. . . . It must also be lawful to put them to death or to inflict pain on them, for any good or reasonable end, such as the promotion of man's knowledge, health, or even for the purposes of recreation." Yet the same dictionary added a limitation, one that has characterized Christian thought almost from the outset: "It is never lawful for a man to take pleasure directly in the pain given to brutes, because in doing so, man degrades and brutalizes his own nature." In other words, cruelty toward any living creature demoralizes and coarsens those who inflict it. That is the baseline position of any Christian ethics, as is the notion that creation itself has intrinsic value in the eyes of God.

Modern Christian attitudes toward the environment are almost as diverse as those of the public at large. Some Protestant congregations embrace language not very different from that of "deep ecologists" who wish to resacralize nature. Some Christians maintain that animals share a form of eternal life. Others hew to a more traditional view, noting that even Jesus' tribute to the birds of the air was followed by a lesson in nature's moral hierarchy: "Are you not of more value than they?" The official Catholic view remains that animals have no inherent rights, although the church's modern catechism instructs that "Animals are God's creatures. He surrounds them with his providential care. By their mere existence they bless him and give him glory. Thus men owe them kindness." For that matter, "man's dominion over inanimate and other living beings . . . requires a religious respect for the integrity of creation."[23]

Even the most traditional teaching does not prescribe what our actual treatment of nature and animals should be. But as the Anglican priest Andrew Linzey points out, "a hierarchy of valuable beings in God's sight" hardly means that "we must ascribe absolute value to humans or absolutely none to animals. . . . Human beings cannot affirm their own value within the created order without at the same time affirming the value of all created beings."[24] Contrary to Lynn White and his supporting chorus, there is not now, nor has there ever been, any fundamental reason why Christians should fail to esteem the natural world.

EIGHT

CHRISTIANITY
AND AMERICAN DEMOCRACY

Christian influence on the history of the United States, we are told, began with intolerant and narrow-minded Puritans, and has tended to reinforce authoritarian attitudes and political reaction ever since. Fortunately, the Founders were led by Deists and skeptics who knew the importance of keeping religion in its place—walled off from public life, where it would not contaminate politics with its absolutist beliefs. The wisdom of the Founders' judgment would be vindicated in the decades that followed. They witnessed frequent attempts by religious enthusiasts—often incited by unlettered revivalists—to resist intellectual and scientific advances and to impede social progress. To this day, the biggest threat to democratic maturity and the acceptance of competing views is Christian zealotry, most particularly on the political Right.

Slightly more than a decade ago, Paul Gagnon discovered that the most popular high school history textbooks invariably portrayed Puritan settlers as hypocrites who persecuted dissidents and possessed few redeeming qualities. In one book, for example, "the Puritans' religious notions [were] expressed mainly in a description of their hounding of Roger Williams and Anne Hutchinson and in a boxed account of the Salem witch trials that compares the trials to McCarthyism." Not much has changed since Gagnon wrote his critique. *America's Story,* Harcourt Brace & Co.'s 1997 elementary school textbook, is fairly typical of recent offerings. It devotes virtually all of its brief section on the Puritans to a discussion of those expelled from the Massachusetts Bay Colony for voicing dissent; the focus is on the Puritans' flaws, not their achievements.

Such treatment is not only a recent phenomenon. Indeed, textbooks from the 1950s through the 1980s contained even less information on religion than they do today, according to Gilbert T. Sewall of the American Textbook Council. In a report on ten civics and U.S. history texts published in the 1990s, Sewall concludes that religious coverage has actually expanded and been improved, partly in response to prior complaints. Still, their remaining defects in this area are notable: "Texts rarely comprehend religion as a motivating force in a 'rational' and 'scientific' world"; "textbook coverage of contemporary religion in the United States is uniformly scant, usually unsympathetic, and sometimes inaccurate"; and finally, "in some cases, especially at the elementary level, nonhistorical social studies actually displace history in the curriculum," and those courses "champion 'insurgent' values" that are sometimes "adversarial toward older moral systems."

While children in school are learning (indirectly, at least) that religion is somehow incompatible with modern life, elsewhere adults are often told so directly. This indictment is directed primarily at Catholicism and evangelical Christianity. The entertainment and arts world is particularly keen on painting Catholicism as antiquated and repressive. Movies such as *Dogma,* which ridicules the articles of Catholic belief, and *The Virgin Suicides,* which portrays a Catholic upbringing as dangerously stifling, are more blunt than most, but their themes are not unusual. More often, notes critic James Bowman, the expressions of "contempt for belief and believers are made along the way, in the course of doing other things."

Meanwhile, evangelicals more often take their lumps in the news media and academic circles. George R. Kaplan typified the tone a few years ago in a special report in the *Phi Delta Kappan,* a well-known journal for educators. "True believers usually materialize as a strident voice in favor of a turn-back-the-clock orthodoxy as our only hope against the sinister forces of modernism and progressivism in education," Kaplan intoned. "If you aren't with them, you might as well be the Antichrist." Kaplan's alarmist tone—he derided Christian conservatives as "paleolithic spear throwers"—has become standard among education professionals on the lookout for religious extremists.

177

These extremists, we are to understand, even threaten social peace. That was the premise of *Today* host Katie Couric's line of questioning in an interview with former Texas governor Ann Richards in April 2000. "Let's talk a little bit more about ... a climate that some say has been established by religious zealots or Christian conservatives," Couric said. "There have been two recent incidents in the news I think that upset most people in this country, that is the dragging death of James Byrd Junior and the beating death of Matthew Shepard. I just would like you to reflect on whether you feel people in this country are increasingly intolerant, mean-spirited, etcetera, and what, if anything, can be done about that."

Other prominent journalists voiced similar worries about intolerance among evangelicals after Senator Joseph Lieberman's selection as the first Jew on a presidential ticket. NBC's Forrest Sawyer, for example, wondered on air whether George W. Bush's campaign would "slap down" any outbursts of anti-Semitism from the "Christian Right." (The first significant eruption of anti-Semitism in campaign 2000, in fact, came from an NAACP official in Dallas, who was forced to resign.)

Indeed, some national journalists are so leery of evangelicals that the hiring of one as an ABC correspondent produced a mild sensation among her colleagues a few years ago. The Associated Press quoted correspondent Peggy Wehmeyer's boss, producer Sally Holm, as saying that other journalists at the network had trouble adjusting to the idea of working alongside a "Southerner, a born-again Christian." Network journalists are not alone in this unease. *Newsweek*'s assistant managing editor, Evan Thomas, has compared the Christian Coalition to the Spanish Inquisition. A Denver newspaper columnist—to cite a truly egregious outburst in the mainstream press—actually professed sympathy for "the frustration and general fatigue that compelled the Romans to throw select Christians to the lions. It's not just that the lions were hungry; it was that the Romans were tired of listening to the self-righteous babbling of the Christians who claimed to be experts on everything, and had egos the size of ... well ... God."

The implication is that American democracy, with its spirit of inquiry and tolerance, its liberties and rights, flourishes only to the extent that Christian meddling and influence are successfully put to flight. In the typically blunt words of Ted Turner: Christianity is "for losers."

■ ■ ■

Most of the English-speaking people who first settled North America were not merely religious; they were fiercely so, even by the reckoning of that time. As Calvinists and Puritans, they were also among the most stubbornly independent Christians alive. Aware of this background, Edmund Burke warned his colleagues in the British Parliament as they muddled toward war in 1775 that religion in "our Northern Colonies is a refinement on the principle of resistance." It was resistance to persecution, and despair over the course of church reform in England, that drove tens of thousands of Puritans—twenty thousand between 1629 and 1640 alone—to plunge into the wilderness of a new world.

This much of their history is more or less familiar. Today it is not the courage of these settlers that is unrecognized, but their relevance to the nation's fundamental principles. The headline version of colonial history recalled by most Americans—if indeed they were ever taught more—consists of two episodes: the founding of the Colonies in the early 1600s and the Revolution of 1776. Missing is the texture of the intervening century and a half. It is as if our historical memories skipped, say, from the outlawing of the importation of slaves in 1807, to Martin Luther King Jr.'s appearance at the March on Washington in 1963—and we were then asked to explain the origins of the modern civil rights movement. As far as we could tell, the concept of a colorblind society might have sprung from King like a divine gift, fully formed and without historical influence.

Given that kind of lacuna in the teaching of our nation's early history, it is no wonder that Americans usually consider Puritans good for little more than ritual acknowledgment at Thanksgiving, and for a quaint, yet deplorable, example of intolerance and cramped belief on the remaining days of the year. They seem so remote, so disconnected from the habits of mind that spawned the American rebellion and the liberties it enshrined.

In fact, the seeds of those liberties were planted by these religious dissenters themselves, at the moment of their arrival, in the Mayflower Compact of 1620:

> In the name of God, Amen. We whose names are underwritten ...
> having undertaken, for the glory of God, and advancement of the
> Christian faith, and honour of our king and country, a voyage to
> plant the first colony in the northern parts of Virginia, do by these
> presents solemnly and mutually in the presence of God, and of one
> another, covenant and combine ourself together in a civil body
> politic, for our better ordering and preservation, and furtherance
> of the ends aforesaid.

We have lost our sense of wonder at these words. Yet as Page Smith
reminds us, the Mayflower Compact, at the time, amounted to
"an extraordinary assertion of power by simple people who had
always experienced power as something 'outside'—the power of
the Church of England and its priests and bishops, power in the
form of edicts of the Crown and its officials, or in the statutes of
Parliament. So that to even imagine that they could state out of
their own free will ... the terms of their governance was astonishing and instructive."[1]

Smith's reference to "simple people" should not obscure the
fact that the first waves of settlers in New England were often
unusually well educated. E. Digby Baltzell says the Massachusetts
Bay Colony, with "at least 130 alumni of Oxford and Cambridge,"
boasted the "highest proportion of educated men the world had
ever seen."[2] And Kevin Phillips notes that "of England's nine 'pub-
lick libraries' outside London before 1640," six were in heavily
Puritan districts.[3] These Puritans were both educated and civically
involved. Smith points out that "for almost a hundred and fifty
years, covenanted communities dominated colonial life," not only
in New England but, with variations, in a number of Middle
Colonies as well, and these communities represented a summit of
participatory democracy.[4]

Not for everyone within them, surely. Not for the religious
mavericks Roger Williams and Anne Hutchinson, who were
expelled from the Puritans' midst; nor for the Quakers, who were
whipped, had their ears cropped and even, on four occasions, were
executed by Puritans; nor, of course, for the victims of the Salem
witchcraft trials. Puritans obviously did not advocate tolerance as
we understand it, but then almost no one else in the seventeenth
century did either, no matter what part of the globe they called
home. What the Puritans attempted to create, and for a time did
create, was a commonwealth of willing believers, a voluntary

association of both church and state that was, in fact, at least as democratic as any society of that era.

Far from being theocratic despots, the clergy were not exempt from this democratic discipline. Indeed, the Puritans "gave the clergy themselves less actual authority than any other government in the western world at the time," according to Paul Johnson. "The churches were, right from the start, managed by laymen. The religious establishment was popular, not hieratic."[5]

No wonder the town meeting, that quintessential local expression of American democracy, hails primarily from New England. In historian Stephen Foster's description, "few societies in Western culture have ever depended more thoroughly or more self-consciously on the consent of their members than the allegedly repressive 'theocracies' of early New England.... Every aspect of public life in New England demanded the formal assent of the public. Church members elected their ministers, town meetings their selectmen, freemen their deputies and magistrates, and militiamen their officers."[6] These democratic customs, Foster explains, sprang in part from the Puritans' unromantic view of human nature and its tendency toward corruption. "Because even magistrates, the most saintly of the saints, had a sizable residue of natural lust left in them, their power had to be limited by a codified body of laws [and] frequent elections," he writes.[7]

For all their largely mythical sternness, Puritans simply did not have the stomach for repression on a grand scale. It was never their goal to impose beliefs on others; instead, they ejected dissenters from their communities. (Foster quips that minorities were consigned "to Rhode Island in this world and the devil in the next.")[8] Even this policy began to break down when a few truly stiff-necked Quakers, who wouldn't depart and actually invaded Congregational churches in a bid for martyrdom, forced a showdown in the 1650s and 1660s. Puritan public opinion recoiled from the brutal punishments inflicted on Quakers, generating what Patricia Bonomi calls "a turning point in New England's attitude toward religious toleration."[9] It was the first evidence that religious competition in the United States wouldn't result primarily in strife, as it too often had in the Old World.

The Salem witch trials—turned into a metaphor by anti-Christians—were in fact uncharacteristic of Puritan behavior, as well as an enduring embarrassment to the Puritan leadership.

Those leaders believed in witches, admittedly, along with nearly everyone else of that era. But the Salem court ignored Cotton Mather's advice that "spectral evidence" (the devil taking on the form of people) not be used as the basis for convictions. In *The Story of the Salem Witch Trials,* Bryan LeBeau relates that "some of the most effective opposition" to the trials came from the ministers of Massachusetts. Indeed, when the Massachusetts General Court, deeply concerned by the Salem proceedings, called for a fast and a "convocation of ministers" to advise on "the right way as to the witchcraft," fourteen prominent Puritan divines again condemned the use of spectral evidence. In a classically liberal statement, Cotton Mather went so far as to declare that "it were better that ten suspected witches should escape, than that one innocent person should be condemned."[10]

As fascinating as an event like the witchcraft trials may be, such repressions were historical sideshows. The main event was the steady evolution of an American civic culture that would one day hold certain truths to be so self-evident as to be worth fighting a revolutionary war to protect. That development began with the Mayflower Compact, sometimes portrayed as the lucky handiwork of desperate emigrants who hit upon this social contract as a practical means of self-preservation. That is not what it was at all. Rather, it was a natural expression of covenant theology, and only the first of many in North America.

When R. H. Tawney declared that "the growth, triumph and transformation of the Puritan spirit" was the "most fundamental movement of the seventeenth century,"[11] he wasn't exaggerating. The Puritan emphasis on the "priesthood of every believer" sapped respect for empty titles, inherited privilege and unearned authority; it elevated the principle of merit; it functioned as a challenge to despotism and indeed to all arbitrary forms of governance. Consider how Robert Browne, an influential Congregational pastor of the time, defined a church: "a number of Christians or believers which by a willing covenant made with their God are under the government of God and Christ." There is no mention of a monarchy, or of the social hierarchy associated with it. Indeed, the Calvinist doctrine of "justification by faith" was a most powerful call to personal conscience. Individuals were directly responsible to God; they could form their own church, select their pastor, read the Bible without the mediating assistance of clerical superiors. Here indeed was the prototype of the modern self-directed citizen. When men and women are competent to make such decisions regarding their faith, sooner or later it will occur to them that they might be competent to act in a variety of other areas controlled by traditional elites. When that realization dawns, the result is a new kind of citizen: a man or woman with a democratic mindset.

These tendencies were concentrated in Puritanism, which Tawney called "the true English Reformation," adding, "it is from its struggle against the old order that the England which is unmistakably modern emerges."[12] If Puritan influence was so consequential in England, where Puritans in the early seventeenth century numbered no more than 20 percent of the population, it was even more decisive in early America. "Puritans provided the moral and religious background of fully 75 percent of the people who declared their independence in 1776," writes Sydney Ahlstrom.[13] For that generation, the language of social compact and a stubborn insistence on the consent of the governed was ingrained tradition—Christian tradition—with more than a century of practice behind it. The same Connecticut colony whose Fundamental Orders became, in 1639, the first written constitution in North America also announced, in that document, that the settlers' purpose was to "pursue the liberty and purity of the gospel of our Lord Jesus."

How Christianity Contributed to the Spirit of 1776

The rebels of 1776 were deeply indebted to their Puritan ancestors, although this is often overlooked in an attempt to portray the Founders as radicals breaking cleanly with the past. Puritan codes of law had, in fact, contained rudimentary bills of rights by the mid-seventeenth century, and such documents were not exclusively confined to New England, either. The General Assembly of New York enacted a bill of rights at least twice in the seventeenth century, to the enormous irritation of Mother England. "In an amazingly brief interval," writes M. Stanton Evans, "the founders of New England had created most of the features of representative, balanced government." They included "a theory of constitutionalism, power wielded by consent, annual elections with an expansive franchise, a bicameral legislature, local autonomies, and a Bill of Rights."[14]

Meanwhile, Roger Williams' iconoclastic strain of Puritanism inspired the founding of Rhode Island, the first modern commonwealth to enshrine religious liberty as a basic principle and to separate church and state in order to achieve that goal. "All men may walk as their consciences persuade them, every one in the name of his God," Williams wrote, and he evidently meant it. His royal charter confirmed this basic tenet: "No person within the said colony, at any time hereafter, shall be in any wise molested, punished, disquieted or called in question, for any differences in opinion in matters of religion."

Williams' theory of religious toleration had little to do with Enlightenment libertarianism, so he is never credited as a father of the First Amendment. Yet the fact remains that this devout religious dissident arrived at the same place—and did so first. (Not far behind was the equally devout William Penn, who made religious freedom the law of Quaker Pennsylvania in 1682 with the pledge that all citizens "shall in no way be molested or prejudiced for their religious persuasion or practice . . . nor shall they be compelled at any time to frequent or maintain any religious worship, place or ministry whatever.")

Steeped in covenant theology at its birth—"no commonweal can be founded but by free consent," declared John Winthrop, who himself founded the settlement that became Boston—America remained immersed in its influence through the Revolution. Bernard Bailyn confirmed this in the 1960s when he undertook a systematic review of revolutionary era pamphlets in *The Ideological Origins of the American Revolution* and found that the political and social ideas of New England Puritanism had a major impact on the men who made the Revolution. Bailyn concluded that covenant theology in particular "carried on into the eighteenth century and into the minds of the Revolutionaries the idea, originally worked out in the sermons and tracts of the settlement period, that the colonization of British America had been an event designed by the hand of God to satisfy his ultimate aims."[15]

Few Americans today would describe their nation's founding in such terms. But many of those who settled America conceived of their new country in precisely that way. So did many who would follow them, including a large number of those who one day would fight for independence.

Some scholars think Bailyn actually gives too little credit to religious influence. As Ellis Sandoz has written, "The meaning of equality and happiness as held by such 'aristoi' as Jefferson and Adams, and the esteem in which the people are held in the repeated references to them in the Constitutional Convention are quite mystifying unless the classical and Christian notions of a common human nature present to all men *qua* men and the dignity of man as created in the divine image and loved of God are borne in mind."[16]

The Founders' belief in a fundamental moral law, or natural law, bears a large debt to Christian tradition, too. Natural rights were God-given, not bestowed by philosophers or kings. The colonists' favorite common-law theorist, Sir Edward Coke, had been most specific about this. "The law of nature," Coke wrote, "is that which God at the time of creation of the nature of man infused into his heart, for his preservation and direction."

For America's Founders, such Christian attitudes were no mere backdrop for a largely secular worldview. The vast majority were Christians themselves, and many—such as John Jay and John Witherspoon—seriously so. Several decades ago, W. W. Sweet compiled a roll call of church affiliation among the framers of the Constitution. His breakdown was: nineteen Episcopalians, eight Congregationalists, seven Presbyterians, two Roman Catholics, two Quakers, one Methodist, one Dutch Reformed, and one deist—a term describing someone who rejected formal religion and the notion of divine revelation. Even the lone deist that Sweet identifies, Edmund Randolph, later became a Christian convert.[17]

Sweet's list is helpful, but somewhat misleading, too. We know Randolph was a deist because he said so. What of those Founders who preferred a more conventional public pose? Those most frequently described today as deists include Benjamin Franklin, Thomas Jefferson (who didn't attend the Constitutional Convention), George Washington, John Adams and George Mason. The description is plausible enough as applied to Franklin, Jefferson and Mason, but a serious misreading of the views of Washington and Adams.

Washington's religious moorings—raised Anglican, migrating to the Episcopal Church after the Revolution—are actually hard to ignore, although some historians have managed. Samuel Eliot

Morison once declared he could find "no trace of Biblical phraseology" in Washington's correspondence. Direct biblical quotations apparently didn't qualify. In fact, such references are numerous enough to provide a clear idea of what the first president believed.

"Washington's God was no watchmaker, who wound the world up and retired, but an active agent and force," concludes Richard Brookhiser.[18] No deist would author a message to the thirteen governors in which he suggested Americans "do Justice . . . love mercy and . . . demean ourselves with that Charity, humility and pacific temper of mind, which were the Characteristicks of the Divine Author of our blessed Religion, and without an humble imitation of whose example in these things, we can never hope to be a happy Nation." Yet that is what Washington wrote in 1783, while still commander in chief. Nor were such words unusual for him. John G. West observes that "The doctrine of God's providence, in particular, suffuses almost everything he wrote, from public addresses to private correspondence."[19]

Washington linked civic virtue directly to religion, stating that "reason and experience both forbid us to expect that National morality can prevail in exclusion of religious principle." Most of the other Founders concurred, including Adams. Indeed, despite personal religious views that took some liberties with orthodox Christian belief, Adams defended a public role for religion more emphatically than almost any other Founder. "Our Constitution was written for a moral and religious people," the stalwart Yankee said, "and it is wholly inadequate to the government of any other." For that matter, Adams had no doubt that the United States had been founded "on the general principles of Christianity."

How Religious Convictions Strengthened Revolutionary Sentiment

The original colonists had no real sense of a common American identity. They developed it only over time, with religion and clergy playing prominent roles. The first true celebrity of the colonial era, for example, was George Whitefield, a revivalist who stoked the Great Awakening of the late 1730s and 1740s. His appeal drew the largest crowds of any religious or secular figure in the pre-Revolutionary years. Whitefield was renowned "from New Hampshire to Georgia," Paul Johnson writes, "and his death in 1770 evoked comment from the entire colonial press."[20]

Johnson maintains that "religious evangelism was the first continental force, an all-American phenomenon which transcended colonial differences, introduced national figures and made state boundaries seem unimportant."[21] Alan Heimert makes much the same point in *Religion and the American Mind:* "The evangelical impulse ... was the avatar and instrument of a fervent American nationalism.... Whatever its manner of working, Calvinist doctrine succeeded in breaking down the local and particular allegiances of Americans."[22] Jonathan Edwards' celebrated defense of the Great Awakening, which appeared in 1742 as "Some Thoughts Concerning the Present Revival of Religion," was in one sense, Heimert believes, "the first national party platform in American history."[23]

Like revivalist movements to this day, the Great Awakening possessed an anti-establishment bite. The movement began, trivially enough, as a struggle between clerical factions in various denominations. But it evolved very quickly into something more significant. Insurgent ministers—on average far younger than their antagonists, and more likely to have been born or raised in the New World—soon developed an effective arsenal of invective that portrayed church authority as illegitimate, the established ministry as corrupt, and themselves as the purified voice of the common people. In effect, the Great Awakening became a dress rehearsal for the political revolution to come. It rekindled, reinforced and even enlarged the Protestant sense of individual responsibility in matters of conscience, and provided example after example of principled rebellion against established powers. The watchword of the day was defiance, not deference.

Years after he retired, John Adams would write that "the Revolution was effected before the war commenced. The Revolution was in the minds and hearts of the people; and change in their religious sentiments of their duties and obligations." Modern historians tend to agree. "In exhorting their followers to make personal decisions for God, and then to act on those decisions regardless of their effect on the larger society, the revivalists gave sanction to a new dynamic in human relationships," says Patricia Bonomi. "Defiant individualism ... was one of the most radical manifestations of the Awakening."[24]

This was not radical individualism in the modern sense—that corruption of self-reliance that acknowledges no rights or interests but its own, and no obligations but those of others. Eighteenth-century Americans still prized social cohesion and distrusted factions, but not quite so much after the Great Awakening as before.

Perhaps the most surprising byproduct of the Great Awakening—surprising at least to those tempted to equate Christian enthusiasm with intolerance—is its contribution to religious freedom itself. Separatists were forced to explain their divisiveness, and they swiftly developed arguments justifying the right of minorities to disobey church leaders whose rules, they believed, ran counter to God's law. Private conscience must not be trampled, some concluded, even when the minority was a party of one.

The Great Awakening propelled more people into the upstart Baptists than any other denomination, and they in turn took up the drumbeat for equal standing with the dominant churches. Isaac Backus and his New England Baptist colleagues who descended on the First Continental Congress in Philadelphia in 1774 to plead for unimpeded religious liberty are merely the best known of the agitators. (They were profoundly resented by both Samuel and John Adams, by the way, both of whom dismissed out of hand the notion that there could be religious intolerance in Massachusetts.) Baptists elsewhere intoned the same principle of minority rights, especially in Virginia and North Carolina. "With the war's end," Sweet reports, "Virginia was ready to pass Jefferson's Ordinance of Religious Freedom. In the final achievement of that goal the Baptists played the most consistent and persistent role."[25]

Thanks in part to the Great Awakening, the Christian church was still the dominant institution in America at the close of the colonial era—and dominant not merely in the antiseptic modern sense of being an irresistible lobby. Quite simply, it was the institution often closest to the people. That is not to say Americans were notable churchgoers. Historians have long known that formal church membership in the late eighteenth century was fairly anemic. Roger Finke and Rodney Stark's groundbreaking study *The Churching of America, 1776–1990* calculates that only 17 percent of the population at the time of the Revolution belonged to a church, although the authors hasten to add that this hardly means the rest were irreligious. America was, after all, a frontier society with the usual frontier problems: "transience, disorder, too many men, too many scoundrels, and too few effective and committed clergy."[26]

Yet even in such an environment, churches played an unsurpassed role "in the molding of colonial culture," according to Ahlstrom.[27] And their role would be equally vital in the political rebellion to come. It is worth quoting Bonomi at length on this point, since it is so important and yet so often ignored:

> Denominational politics forms the bridge between the Great Awakening and the American Revolution. From 1740 to 1776, thousands of provincials from every rank and section ... became embroiled in political activity as a consequence of their religious loyalties. Denominations organized committees of correspondence, wrote circular letters, adjusted election tickets for religious balance, voted en bloc, and signed political petitions "as a Sabbath Day's Exercise." ... Indeed, all that has been said and written about the New England town as the "school of democracy" can be applied with equal or greater force to the church congregation.[28]

Those who today so passionately denounce the intermingling of politics and religion, and who deplore the preachers and priests who stick their noses into secular affairs, would be scandalized by the rhetoric that cascaded from pulpits in the 1770s. Some preachers did avoid political questions altogether; others, in the manner of Enlightenment *philosophes,* popularized an abstract theory of the rights of man; and many others, especially those who hailed from the revivalist wing, might as well have been handing out weapons at the church door. Convinced that liberty was a divine gift, they exhorted their congregations to oppose British aggression as an expression of faith. They buoyed their listeners with reassurance that defense against advancing tyranny was righteous and just. One alarmed correspondent warned the Earl of Dartmouth after the war broke out, "Your Lordship can scarcely conceive what Fury the Discourses of some mad Preachers have created in this Country."

Again, Bonomi takes the full measure of the churches' impact:

> In an age of political moderation, when many colonials hesitated at the brink of civil war, patriotic clergymen told their congregations that failure to oppose British tyranny would be an offense in the sight of Heaven. ... By turning colonial resistance into a righteous cause, and by crying the message to all ranks in all parts of the colonies, ministers did the work of secular radicalism and did it better; they resolved doubts, overcame inertia, fired the heart, and exalted the soul.[29]

Many of these preachers, says Perry Miller, fused resistance with repentance: "What aroused a Christian patriotism that needed staying power was a realization of the vengeance God denounced against the wicked.... [W]hat kept them going was an assurance that by exerting themselves they were fighting for a victory thus providentially predestined."[30]

According to Kevin Phillips, the rebellion had three white-hot cores: the Congregationalists of New England, the "Greater Virginia tobacco lords" and the "Presbyterian Scotch-Irish of Pennsylvania, America's transplanted Ulster, who were also spreading south down the great valley into Maryland, Virginia, and the Carolinas." Although not as numerous, "descendants of emigrant Scottish Presbyterian Covenanters," notably in New Jersey, were equally ardent in their zeal for independence.[31]

The prominence of Congregationalists and Presbyterians is no accident: each group was steeped in a dissenting tradition that bridled at any arbitrary exercise of far-off power. Ulster Presbyterians, although arriving in the Colonies much later than the Puritans, were fired by a similar sense of persecution and hardy independence of spirit. The more devout they were, the more vehement their support of the Revolution.

This is not to say that the American Revolution was a religious war. But it can fairly be described as a war that would not have been fought, let alone won, without the energy and conviction of religiously based and religiously driven ideas. Christians, of course, filled the ranks of both sides in the struggle, as they would in any war between people largely of European stock. But religious dynamism in the Colonies aligned itself more often than not with independence, self-government and liberty, as indeed had been the case for more than a century and a half. As Miller sums up the matter, "A pure rationalism ... might have declared the independence of these folk, but it could never have inspired them to fight for it."[32]

There was, to be sure, an unpleasant dimension in the colonists' religious ethos that must be acknowledged: namely, a seething anti-Catholicism. The Reformation and its long, brutal aftermath had hardened Protestant views of Roman Catholics. This prejudice often took on an even stronger hue among dissenting Protestants of the sort so heavily represented among early American settlers. They denied Catholics the right to vote or hold office, and their descendants maintained this policy in most of the Colonies up to and through the Revolution—at least in formal statute. Thus, when the British Parliament established the Catholic Church in Quebec in 1774 by passing the Quebec Act, there was a convulsion of antipapist rhetoric, the point of which sounds preposterous to the modern ear. If Britain could establish Catholicism in Quebec, would its colonies to the south be next? The fear was groundless, but it was real.

The wonder is that any Catholic supported the revolutionary cause. Yet a number of them, perceiving where their broader interest lay, did just that. Charles Carroll of Carrollton, who famously wrote his town after his signature on the Declaration of Independence in order to remove any doubt regarding his identity, led the patriot movement in Maryland. His cousins John Carroll, who would become the new nation's first Catholic bishop, and Daniel Carroll, a delegate to the Constitutional Convention, were fervent patriots as well.

In any case, there were so few Catholics in the Colonies—perhaps ten thousand when war broke out, perhaps somewhat more, and mostly in Maryland and Pennsylvania—that they represented more of an unseen enemy than the neighbor next door for the vast majority of colonists. That was particularly true in New England, which was less ambivalent and more uniformly in support of the Revolution than any other region. For that matter, while anti-Catholicism might provide a sharp edge to revolutionary sentiment and be crudely exploited by patriotic opportunists, it never defined the essence of the rebellion—not in New England, and most certainly not anywhere else. The drive for self-determination, as defined by the Declaration of Independence, was by far the greater motivation. Nurtured in the Colonies for 150 years, this sentiment had its distant origins in a tiny congregation at Scrooby in southeast England, whose members first fled to Holland and later boarded the Mayflower, in order to establish a self-governing Christian society in the New World.

How Christian Revivalists Spread Democratic Values

Americans are the world's great social levelers. They aspire to wealth, but profess no awe of it. They admire deep learning, but rarely defer to it. They respect authority, but begrudge it any power. For more than two hundred years, visitors to the United States have regularly been struck by the conviction of even poor and unlucky Americans that they are, and deserve to be, masters of their destiny.

At the same time, despite this rugged individualism, foreign visitors have frequently found Americans unusually religious; and the most astute of these observers have also appreciated how these elements of the American personality fit together. "The Americans combine the notions of Christianity and of liberty so intimately in their minds that it is impossible to make them conceive the one without the other," wrote Alexis de Tocqueville.

This link between liberty and Christianity had existed since the arrival of the first settlers. It would be refreshed and strengthened in the first decades of the nineteenth century to a point never equaled, in all likelihood, before or since. Thanks to a remarkable collection of often ragtag itinerant revivalists preaching a message based on self-respect, personal responsibility to God, and fulfillment of individual potential, the nation's entire denominational landscape was soon turned upside down.

In 1776, Methodism had only a precarious handhold in the Colonies. Church members numbered little more than three thousand, the bulk of whom resided in Maryland and Virginia. Baptists were more plentiful, and indeed may already have overtaken the Anglicans, although they still lagged well behind the Congregationalists and Presbyterians. Yet Baptists and Methodists were on the march, appealing to the sort of populist instincts that before long would touch off an explosion in their membership. In a matter of a few decades, they would equal, then surpass the leading denominations of the colonial era—a fact that is less important to this story than the reasons why it occurred.

Americans today congratulate themselves on their ability to absorb the consequences of rapid change, but their predecessors of the early nineteenth century understood the meaning of real social anxiety. An exploding population pushed hundreds of thousands of people across the Appalachians and into relative isolation; cities tripled and quadrupled in size, or sprang up from nothing; land prices soared; the early factory system, that grinding oppressor, began its irresistible conquest of skilled artisans; small armies of men in such rootless occupations as canal building cast aside all social ties; and everywhere on the frontier Americans endured a diet of bleak monotony—corn meal and pork (or vice versa), and not always nearly enough of it.

Then, into this bracing scene burst hundreds of the most potent drumbeaters for democracy and the potential of the common man that this nation has ever known. They were the evangelists of the Second Great Awakening.

Theirs is a familiar trope in the American saga: entrepreneurial newcomers, fired by belief in their product and engaging in untiring salesmanship, manage to steal a large, underserved market from their lumbering, complacent competitors. These evangelists pushed Christianity in the United States (in contrast to what occurred in some parts of Europe) further away from the temptations of high culture and political power. Indeed, almost all important social movements in the first half of the nineteenth century were as explicitly populist as they were religious. Crusading revivalists sought out ordinary people wherever they lived, spoke to them on their own terms and in their own words, and infused them with a sense of their spiritual value and the primacy of conscience. Yet the accomplishments of these revivalists have been slighted by many historians, and are all but unknown to the general public.

They deserve better. "Not since the crusading vigor of the early Puritans or of first-generation Methodists had an English-speaking culture produced a generation of so many rootless, visionary young preachers," writes Norman O. Hatch in *The Democratization of American Christianity.* Indeed, "the wave of popular religious movements that broke upon the United States in the half century after independence did more to Christianize American society than anything before or since.... The eighteen hundred Christian ministers serving in 1775 swelled to nearly forty thousand in 1845. The number of preachers per capita more than tripled."[33]

Francis Asbury was a prototype of the new religious man. Arriving in America a few years before the Revolution, he quickly recognized opportunity in the expanding countryside and plunged into its vast reaches. As a self-appointed Methodist bishop (after 1788), Asbury spent the better part of three arduous decades crisscrossing the nation, logging thousands of miles a year against appalling obstacles, his possessions never exceeding what he could carry on a horse's back. A traveling salesman for God, he recruited a host of equally relentless circuit-riding preachers to minister to a burgeoning body of faithful. Hatch describes Asbury's creation as "a sort of religious military order"—shades of the Jesuits two centuries earlier—that was "bound together by strict rule and discipline under one leader."[34]

But if the circuit riders' organization was autocratic, their message was powerfully democratic and populist. Like that era's other dynamic religious movements of social outsiders—Baptists, Disciples of Christ, Latter Day Saints, Adventists—Methodist preachers assured their humble audiences that they were as capable as anyone, however well educated, of understanding the Gospel and walking in grace. Virtue and wisdom belonged to common folk—including women—no less than to college graduates. "The Methodists gave women extraordinary freedom to speak," Hatch says, "encouraging them to share their religious experiences in public."[35]

In the hands of the spellbinding evangelist Lorenzo Dow, such conviction became a thundering declaration of personal competence: "But if all men are 'BORN EQUAL' and endowed with unalienable RIGHTS by their CREATOR, in the blessings of life, liberty and the pursuit of happiness—then there can be no just reason, as a cause, why he may or should not think, and judge, and act for himself in matters of religion, opinion, and private judgment."

Camp meetings turned into "festivals of democracy," in the words of one contemporary. It was an apt description, given the participants' blunt disdain for all claims of learned expertise in religion. In this hothouse atmosphere, the most successful preachers were likely to be those who poured it on thick. "Larnin' isn't religion," declared one gifted stump speaker, "and eddication don't give a man the power of the Spirit. It is grace and gifts that furnish the real live coals from off the altar. St. Peter was a fisherman—do you think he ever went to Yale College?" As the famous Methodist circuit rider Peter Cartwright boasted, such rustic spokesmen "preached the Gospel with more success and had more seals to their ministry than all the sapient, downy D.D.'s in modern times."

"All of these movements," concludes Hatch, "challenged common people to take religious destiny into their own hands, to think for themselves, to oppose centralized authority."[36] Sometimes it seemed that the point was to oppose very nearly any authority at all except for the authority of God himself.

Yet when the revivalist later emerges in national lore, he has been given a fool's cap. In fact, there may be no figure in American culture so consistently ridiculed as the itinerant evangelist. He is alternatively a primitive rube or a smarmy buffoon—a force always of cheap emotion and intellectual reaction. He is also slightly sinister, we are to understand, since a certain type of naive listener actually takes him seriously.

In mocking the revivalist's cultural origins, however, the critics miss his essential nature: He is a dissenter and independent thinker par excellence. He breaks with what he considers to be (and often are) sterile, abstract formulations, in order to champion spontaneous experience in the service of conversion and faith. He is unafraid of—indeed, he welcomes—the scorn of elites, while he himself will brook no social distinctions. He is an unrelenting advocate of self-reliance in all matters involving the dictates of conscience.

In short, the Second Great Awakening buttressed Christianity's two-hundred-year American tradition as a force for diversity, dissent, individual autonomy, personal responsibility and moral equality. The nation's economy was passing through only the infant stages of capitalism, but it already boasted an unregulated market in religion. As historian Terry Bilhartz has quipped, "the price was right and the streets were filled with vendors."[37]

Religious revivalism never reached a majority of Americans, to be sure, but evangelical Christians exercised an influence far beyond their numbers. Indeed, the national identity and ethos of the nineteenth century were to a remarkable degree evangelical creations. "Earnest, intrusive, passionate, and disciplined, evangelical Christians eagerly made their affirmations those of the nation at large," explains Joyce Appleby.[38] Besides putting a pronounced emphasis on good works, they "wanted conversions to produce disciplined lives and self-mastery, the personal traits that made the revitalization of religion compatible with limited government and economic enterprise. . . . The unexpected responsiveness of the generation born after the Revolution to the revivalists' summons to a new life in Christ brought some measure of order to America's mobile society."[39]

It was evangelical Christians, above all Baptists and Methodists, who often made the first, belated religious overtures to African Americans. And blacks, free and slave, flocked to those denominations for the same reason that marginalized whites did:

the humblest man or woman was met with open arms. By the time the evangelical ministry in the South had shed most of its early reservations about slavery and allied itself with slaveholders, African-American preachers were already a force in their own right—and soon to become the main source of this nation's black leadership and champions for inclusion in the American Dream.

Evangelicals also organized the most determined effort of the early nineteenth century to defend Indian rights: a national campaign against President Andrew Jackson's brutal plan to confiscate the Cherokee Territory in Georgia and expel the natives from their land. It was an evangelical activist, the corresponding secretary for the American Board of Commissioners for Foreign Missions, who penned the essays that stirred opposition to the Indians' forced removal. Jeremiah Evarts insisted that "the Cherokees are human beings, endowed by their Creator with the same natural rights as other men," and that as human beings, they were "fellow-citizens with the saints and of the household of God." Evarts did not stop with moral declarations against the seizure of Indian lands; he also demolished the political and legal arguments behind the proposal. His essays were devoured by hundreds of thousands of his compatriots. Meanwhile, evangelical allies showered Congress with petitions pleading the Indians' cause.

It was evangelical missionaries, too, who defied the law against residing on Cherokee lands and chose to be arrested at the point of bayonets in order to push the Indians' case before the U.S. Supreme Court. Finally, it was men like Senator Theodore Frelinghuysen (New Jersey), whom John G. West Jr. calls "the nation's preeminent evangelical statesman,"[40] who provided the rhetorical firepower during the congressional debates in the fateful spring of 1830. (Rep. Davy Crockett, in the most admirable act of his public career, broke with Jackson on the Indian bill despite enormous pressure and political threats. Crockett's vote cost him his seat at the next election, but he expressed no regret, saying he voted as he had so as not to be ashamed "in the day of judgment.")

None of these efforts thwarted the eventual roundup of the Cherokees and their forcible relocation to Oklahoma in the infamous "Trail of Tears." Yet the Cherokee bill was controversial to begin with only because of the evangelical campaign, a grassroots effort that came within five votes in the House of defeating Jackson's scheme.

Evangelists were successful in extending their reach in such campaigns because they approached common people on their own terms and disdained social airs and credentials. Thus their frequent depiction as anti-intellectual. In fact, they were among the most ardent booksellers, newspaper hawkers and pamphleteers in history. Methodist circuit riders actually earned a hefty percentage of their meager salaries in commissions from the sale of religious books. A Methodist weekly, the *Christian Advocate and Journal,* quickly attracted more readers than any other newspaper in the country. The founder of the Disciples of Christ, Alexander Campbell, ran his own print shop, from which a lively torrent of religious publications flowed for years without pause—as from scores of similar shops in more than a hundred cities in the first half of the nineteenth century.

The revivals of the Second Great Awakening not only imbued men and women with a sense of their intellectual and spiritual competence, they also identified persuasion and individual example as means of achieving moral progress in society. "Religious benevolence was, it seems clear, the primary root of antebellum reform," writes Eric Foner.[41] There is no better example of this reformist urge, and of the way evangelical Christianity inspired wider civic participation, than the temperance movement.

How the Christian Temperance Movement Broadened American Democracy

To modern Americans, the antiliquor agitation of the early republic appears slightly comical, or at least of dubious purpose. Why should we honor a throng of self-appointed busybodies intent on curtailing their neighbors' pleasure? After all, temperance advocates never knew when to quit, or perhaps when to declare victory, pushing ultimately for the coercive Volstead Act in 1919 and the futile experiment in Prohibition that ensued.

Yet the original temperance movement in fact identified a social problem of lively interest: a great many Americans of the time were drunkards. The robust drinking style of the late colonial era, which might include a tankard of hard cider with breakfast, actually intensified through the first three decades of the nineteenth century. By 1830, Americans were drinking more per capita than ever before or since, and at least twice as much as today, and this staggering consumption was concentrated within perhaps half the male population. "By the 1820s there were noticeable changes in drinking patterns," notes W. J. Rorabaugh. "While many men continued to treat together in taverns, the old custom of drinking small amounts of alcoholic beverages regularly and frequently throughout the day was declining, and binges, whether communal or solitary, were increasing. It was the changing pattern of drinking ... that alarmed so many Americans."[42]

Christian ministers launched the temperance movement, churches sustained it, and moral appeals drove it to success. Not surprisingly, Methodist revivalists tended to lead the way, with the church's General Conference actually backing total abstinence in 1832. Yet many other denominations were active, too. Virtually all declared public inebriation to be sinful and chronic drunkenness to be a sign of depravity and likely damnation. This approach bore little resemblance to modern addiction counseling, but it worked. By 1840, per capita consumption had taken a dive. As Rorabaugh observes, "This period of rising interest in religion coincided with the first popular success of the campaign against alcohol. The two were inexorably linked."[43]

The heyday of the temperance movement, however, is associated with a slightly later period, following the Civil War. The reason: the indelible presence of the first mass women's movement in American history, which also began as a consciously Christian campaign. The spark was provided by an antiliquor lecture in a Presbyterian church in Hillsboro, Ohio, on December 23, 1873. The powder was the resolve of several dozen women who met the next day to organize a campaign against local liquor dealers. The resulting Women's Crusade that would spread from town to town during the next year was—like its better-known successor, the Woman's Christian Temperance Union (WCTU)—everywhere church-oriented and morally based.

Consider the process by which one of Hillsboro's leaders, Eliza Jane Thompson, decided to join the fray: "I turned the key, and was in the act of kneeling before God and His Holy Word, to see what would be sent me, when I heard a gentle tap at my door; upon opening it I saw my dear daughter with her little Bible open, and the tears coursing down her young cheeks, as she said, 'I opened to this, mother. It must be for you.'" The girl indicated Psalm 146, which says that "The Lord loves the righteous ... but the way of the wicked he brings to ruin...." This appeared to be a call to action, and Thompson responded.

In Hillsboro and dozens of other towns, prayer itself was deployed as a weapon. Saloons whose owners refused to sign a temperance pledge were occupied by women singing and praying the day long. These actions were, according to Barbara Leslie Epstein, "the first female sit-ins in American history, perhaps the first sit-ins of any variety."

In *Women and Temperance,* Ruth Bordin writes that "every meeting of which we have any record at which Crusades were organized and launched took place in Protestant churches."[44] The WCTU, which organized by national convention the following year, mirrored this tradition. Its first president, Annie Wittenmyer, not only edited the *Christian Woman* but had also founded the Methodist Home Missionary Society.

It is true that Wittenmyer's more famous successor, Frances Willard, eventually adopted a more therapeutic approach toward alcohol abuse, seeing the drunkard not as a moral reprobate but as a victim of disease and circumstance. At the same time, the WCTU gravitated to a broad agenda involving everything from working conditions to equal wages, culminating in Willard's embrace of Christian socialism. Yet the basis for this reform sentiment, right into the twentieth century, was female religious enthusiasm and the experience and confidence gained in church activity. No organization in this nation's history contributed more than the WCTU to women's growing sense of political independence and civic engagement, and it succeeded not in spite of Christianity, but because of it.

Christian activism also played a pivotal role in simultaneous efforts to extend the political franchise to women. A watershed moment in the early women's rights movement occurred, in fact, when American female abolitionists, including many devout Quakers, were denied entry to an antislavery gathering in England in 1840. By that time, Sarah Grimke had already published her *Letters on the Equality of the Sexes,* which developed biblical arguments for improving the status of women. Grimke (with her sister, Angelina) was among the first of many Christian feminists active in the decades before passage of the Nineteenth Amendment. Frances Willard, for example, maneuvered the WCTU into an endorsement of women's suffrage in the 1880s. And after 1900, two ardent Christians—Anna Howard Shaw, an ordained minister, and Carrie Chapman Catt—actually led the National American Woman Suffrage Association.

Not all Christian political activism was as successful, nor perhaps deserved to be. What Page Smith calls "the high tide of political radicalism in America"[45] was the surge of Populism in the late nineteenth century and its agrarian crusade, an often overtly Christian movement. When the Democratic Party co-opted the Populist plank calling for free coinage of silver in 1896, it simultaneously nominated a fundamentalist lion, William Jennings Bryan, as its standard-bearer. This leftist religious tradition was sustained in the early twentieth century in the Social Gospel of such Progressives as Walter Rauschenbusch. Yet the legacy of America's Third Great Awakening, of which the Social Gospel was a part, is not nearly as coherent as those of the first two great awakenings. This time revivalism split off into what the social scientist James Q. Wilson describes as "a deep political and cultural divide," with the larger mass movement led by such dazzling preachers as Billy Sunday.[46] Indeed, the next pivotal application of Christian ethics in the cause of American democracy did not occur until the 1950s, in the struggle for black civil rights.

How Christianity Inspired the Civil Rights Movement
Martin Luther King Jr. was not a civil rights leader who happened also to be a Baptist minister. Those two aspects of his identity were inseparable, as they were with the many other African-American preachers of the mid-twentieth century who led the fight for racial justice. "The doctrine they preached was a nonviolent doctrine," King himself explained in *Why We Can't Wait*. "It was not a doctrine that made their followers yearn for revenge but one that called upon them to champion change. It was not a doctrine that asked an eye for an eye but one that summoned men to seek to open the eyes of blind prejudice. The Negro turned his back on force not only because he knew he could not win his freedom through physical force, but also because he believed that through physical force he could lose his soul."[47]

In establishing the foundation of his movement, King singled out from history three examples of successful nonviolent agitation, including "the nonviolent resistance of the early Christians," which had "constituted a moral offensive of such overriding power that it shook the Roman Empire." This idea was no mere window dressing; it was central to his movement.

In Birmingham, for example, which King considered the "most segregated city in America," every local volunteer was required to sign a card pledging to follow the "Ten Commandments" of the nonviolent movement. Three of the first four commandments spoke directly to King's commitment to his faith: "1. MEDITATE daily on the teachings and life of Jesus.... 3. WALK and TALK in the manner of love, for God is love. 4. PRAY daily to be used by God in order that all men might be free."[48] If the campaign that dethroned Bull Connor's regime of terror wasn't stirred by Christian ideals, then it is difficult to imagine one that ever was.

King's vision of a morally rejuvenated America was suffused with religious imagery. As Stephen L. Carter notes in *The Culture of Disbelief,* "The leaders of the civil rights movement spoke openly of the commands of God as a crucial basis for their public activism. They made no effort to disguise their true intention: to impose their religious morality on others, on the dissenters who would rather segregate their hotels or lunch counters."[49] Yet the civil rights movement's political vocabulary, whose consonants and vowels were religious, is treated by many historians as little more than dramaturgy—as if the message were noble but the medium slightly embarrassing. The religious source of King's moral convictions can be obscured, however, only at the cost of misinterpreting utterly the truth of his life and his words.

"When we let freedom ring," he declared on August 28, 1963, in the most riveting American peroration since the final line of the Gettysburg Address, "when we let it ring from every village and every hamlet, from every state and every city, we will be able to speed up that day when all God's children, black men and white men, Jews and Gentiles, Protestants and Catholics, will be able to join hands and sing in the words of that old Negro spiritual, 'Free at last! Free at last! Thank God almighty, we are free at last!'"

How the Catholic Church Intervened to Save the Underclass
The American experiment has flourished in part because so many of its citizens have felt they have a stake in its success. But the process by which each wave of newcomers developed this civic commitment was not natural or foreordained. There have been close calls, times when the entire democratic proposition was in

jeopardy of fracturing into class and ethnic divisions of unbridge-able hostility—and perhaps none closer than when Irish immigrants arrived by the hundreds of thousands in the 1840s and 1850s. At times the Irish seemed like a hopelessly brutalized rabble that could never be transformed into mainstream Americans. And yet they were, thanks in large part to the Catholic Church.

It requires a measure of imagination for us to appreciate the magnitude of this achievement. The Irish peasants swept off their land by famine, discrimination and indifference were often ill equipped to succeed in their new American home. Uneducated and without skills—even their knowledge of farming was primitive—these immigrants included some of the most backward people in Europe. Some Irish melted into America without difficulty, but many others were nearly overwhelmed by culture shock. This was especially true of those trapped in the slums of cities such as New York and Boston. "New York's Irish truly formed an underclass," writes William J. Stern. "Every variety of social pathology flourished among them. Family life had disintegrated."[50] Theirs was an impressive roll call of vice and affliction: endemic drunkenness and addiction to opium and laudanum; flourishing prostitution and illegitimacy; children abandoned by the thousands to a nomadic existence on the streets; murderous gangs that preyed on their neighbors and on each other. The death rate among the Irish during their early years in America (as well as in British cities like Liverpool) universally shocked observers; it was social Darwinism before the term had been coined.

Yet without the intervention of the Catholic Church, the toll might have been immeasurably worse. For virtually the only ones willing to try to drain this swamp were priests and nuns. In New York City, Bishop John Hughes led the way, determined to instill into his rowdy flock a faith-based code of morals that could lift them off the floor. Besides founding numerous schools and churches in Irish neighborhoods, Hughes recruited priests and nuns who functioned as urban missionaries, dunning a message of self-control and self-help, sexual purity, temperance and mutual aid. No matter how little parishioners might have, Hughes insisted it was their Christian duty to contribute something to the assistance of others.

Meanwhile, he brought in groups such as the St. Vincent de Paul Society to wage battle against privation—not simply by providing alms, but by requiring work when possible in return for aid. The Society for the Protection of Destitute Catholic Children, formed with the bishop's support, targeted the legions of street urchins. Catholic nuns placed Irish domestics in the homes of the wealthy. Still another group Hughes helped prod into existence, the Irish Emigrant Society, not only functioned as an employment agency, but was the seed for what eventually became a prospering bank. Hughes himself died in 1863, but his strategy survived, and over time it worked. "Though just 30 or 40 years before, New Yorkers had viewed the Irish as their criminal class," writes Stern,

> by the 1880s and 1890s the Irish proportion of arrests for violent crime had dropped from 50 percent to less than 10 percent. The Irish were the pillars of the criminal justice system. Three-quarters of the police force was Irish. The Irish were the prosecutors, the judges and the jailers. Alcoholism and drug addiction withered away.... Many Irish sections in the city became known for their peacefulness, order and cleanliness—a far cry from the filth, violence and disease of the Five Points and Sweeney's Shambles of mid-century.... Irish family life, formerly so frayed and chaotic, became strong and nourishing. Irish children entered the priesthood or the convent, the professions, politics, professional sports, show business and commerce.[51]

Later Catholic immigrant groups did not, for the most part, arrive in such an utterly desperate state, yet they too benefited from what the historian Charles R. Morris has dubbed the church's "petit-bourgeois boot camp."[52] If any institution qualified as such a boot camp, it surely was the Catholic school, which also helped the Irish overcome the extraordinary discrimination and suspicion they faced.

Public schools in many cities in early-nineteenth-century America were religious schools, at least as we understand the term today. They were actually run by private Protestant societies, and the result was a curriculum filled with sectarianism that strayed into bigotry. Catholics and their faith weren't just ignored; they were derided in the crudest nativist terms. Reading assignments in New York City, for example, included *The Irish Heart,* which maintained that "the emigration from Ireland to America of annually increasing numbers, extremely needy, and in many cases drunken and depraved, has become a subject for all our grave and fearful reflection."

Catholics responded to such provocations in two ways. They supported and led campaigns to drive sectarian instruction from the public schools, and they resolved to build up a parallel system of schools of their own. In New York State, Bishop Hughes even raised the specter of an independent political movement of Irish Catholics. His threat was enough to bring the Democratic Party to heel, and in 1842 the New York legislature passed the Maclay Bill, which outlawed the grosser forms of sectarian instruction from public classrooms.

Meanwhile, Catholics dug deep into their pockets to finance a remarkable system of parochial schools. Whether the founding of those schools represented "the largest private enterprise of its kind in history," as Bishop Mark J. Hurley contends, the achievement was certainly staggering.[53]

By 1840 there were already upwards of 200 Catholic schools nationwide; the number would swell to more than 2,000 by 1884, when the bishops' Third Plenary Council of Baltimore mandated a school in every parish. This turned out to be an impossible goal, but the number of schools soared—to 3,300 by the turn of the century—in an effort to reach it. Even that figure was dwarfed by the great school-building binge stimulated by the surge of Catholic immigrants from Italy and Eastern Europe who arrived in the decades that followed.

Catholics didn't stop with construction of a private school system. They also built from scratch a parallel social service network: hospitals (540 by 1922, and some 600 still today) and orphanages, homes for the aged and infirm, as well as every variety of aid society. Most were staffed and run, as were the schools, by tens of thousands of women who had dedicated themselves to lives of service as nuns.

Had the Catholic Church not stepped in so determinedly in the nineteenth century—had the Irish underclass become a permanent fixture of urban life—there is no telling how American democracy might have evolved. Certainly the whole history of ethnic and interfaith relations would have been severely scarred, perhaps giving a recruitment boost to extremist political movements of the twentieth century. Instead, thanks to the church's efforts, America's story of expanding liberty eventually included millions of Catholic immigrants, too.

Conclusion

As the 2000 presidential campaign drew to a close, Senator Joseph Lieberman told an audience at the University of Notre Dame how grateful he felt, as an Orthodox Jew, for the "remarkable acceptance" he had experienced as a candidate for vice president. Yet even so, Lieberman added,

> There has been another equally eye-opening and less inspiring side to this experience. As public discussion moved from the fact of my faith to my interest in restoring a place for religion in public life, there was a wave of anxiety and apprehension. Much of that outpouring came from people who were concerned that I was coming dangerously close to the church-state dividing line because I have spoken the name of God in campaign speeches and suggested that religious faith can be a source of public morality. They seem to have forgotten that the Constitution promises freedom of religion, not freedom from religion. We are after all not just another nation, but "one nation under God."

Those chiding Lieberman for his declarations of faith included the Anti-Defamation League and the *New York Times*. The *Times* was particularly distressed that the senator may have offended "many highly ethical citizens who are not religious" when he declared that "George Washington warned us never to indulge the supposition 'that morality can be maintained without religion.' " The *Times* asserted that "Whenever religious matters are addressed, Lieberman should firmly and unequivocally reiterate his support for the separation of church and state."

At Notre Dame, Lieberman responded to this patronizing insistence that religious people have a special duty to declare their commitment to the Constitution.

> We are still arguably the most religiously observant people on earth and still share a near universal belief in God. But you wouldn't know it from our national public life today. The line between church and state is an important one and has always been critical for us to draw, but in recent years we have gone far beyond what the Framers ever imagined in separating the two. So much so that we have practically banished religious values and religious institutions from the public square and constructed a "discomfort zone" for even discussing our faith in public settings—ironically making religion one of the few remaining socially acceptable targets of intolerance.

The best evidence for Lieberman's thesis may be the fact that he is virtually the only politician of national stature who could have made it and not been ridiculed and marginalized professionally as a result. In the eyes of militant secularists, Orthodox Judaism is a form of cultural exotica—retrograde but unthreatening. Lieberman may have detected a "wave of anxiety and apprehension" at his professions of faith, but an evangelical politician uttering almost the exact same words would have been struck by a tsunami. No doubt this realization explains in part why even evangelical Christians identified with Lieberman's Republican opponents rushed to defend his language. As Lieberman himself has said, what separates Americans today "seems to be not our different denominations and faith practices, but faith itself.... We are a society of the religious and the secular, where practicing Jews and Christians and Muslims often have more in common with each other than with their non-believing peers."

Ultimately, this social division is the source of the anti-Christian caricature this book has sought to refute. While most nonbelievers have no particular ax to grind with Christianity, the secular orthodoxy of many major American institutions—from Hollywood and the federal courts to important elements of academia and the press—holds that religious belief is a worrisome phenomenon, at once slightly ludicrous and menacing, that must be kept at bay. And so the dark summary of historical Christianity is repeated at every opportunity, as if to shame the devout into silence.

"People will not look forward to posterity," Edmund Burke said, "who never look backward to their ancestors." In America today, the study of history has been so downgraded that when seniors at fifty-five highly rated colleges were surveyed recently by the Roper Organization, only 34 percent could identify George Washington as the American general at the battle of Yorktown. And fewer than half recognized the significance of Valley Forge or words from the Gettysburg Address. "History is a discipline in decline," laments Oscar Handlin, the Harvard University author of many influential historical works. "There is a profound ignorance not only among students, but among their teachers as well."[1]

The Roper survey, aptly titled *Losing America's Memory: Historical Illiteracy in the Twenty-first Century,* also discovered that more than three-fourths of the colleges did not require so much as a single history course for graduation. No wonder that even many educated people have difficulty debunking, or even recognizing, a sound-bite caricature of the Christian past—particularly when the one-sided portrayal is reinforced by Christian denominations themselves guiltily offering repentance.

The Southern Baptists, for example, have apologized for once supporting slavery and segregation. The Evangelical Lutheran Church has expressed regret for the anti-Semitic writings of Martin Luther. The United Methodists have even issued a formal apology for the actions of a lay preacher, Col. John Chivington, who led a massacre of Cheyenne and Arapaho Indians in nineteenth-century Colorado.

When it comes to formal apologies, however, no institution on earth has matched the output of the Roman Catholic Church under Pope John Paul II. Since his election in 1978, John Paul II has asked forgiveness or publicly apologized on behalf of the church no fewer than a hundred times, according to John Thavis of Catholic News Service.[2] The pope has acknowledged lapses in the church's treatment of Africans, Native Americans, women and other Christian churches. He has described the Crusades as mistakes, condemned the intolerance and violence of the Inquisition, asked God's forgiveness for the suffering of Jews at Christian hands, spoken out regarding the church's checkered relationship with slavery, and condemned the treatment of Galileo. This long march of mea culpas culminated in the year 2000 with a 19,000-word document, "Memory and Reconciliation: The Church and the Faults of the Past," a sweeping recitation of the sins of two millennia.

Some of the faithful have criticized what they see as an orgy of apology, but in fact the acknowledgment of sin before and against God—the internal examination of oneself and disclosure of fault—is a non-negotiable obligation of Christian faith. Self-examination also offers (or so Christian tradition teaches) such practical benefits as the formation of a stronger conscience and possible reconciliation with those who have been wronged. It is perhaps only natural that a religion so dedicated to the admission of personal imperfection should produce leaders uniquely willing to confront the ignoble episodes of the past.

But if knowledge of such dark episodes in the history of Christianity is essential, it is also corrosive if it is the *only* knowledge of the past that most people possess. History provides us with our identity; it is the collective memory of who we are and what we were. If a religious tradition is seen only as an unbroken embarrassment, there is no reason to care whether it survives, and every reason to hope that it does not.

Whether they realize it or not, however, Americans have no need to pore over historical works to appreciate an example of the more hopeful side of the Christian legacy. They merely have to look back on their own experience, for the generation of which they are a part has lived through a turning point that was decisively influenced by the conscious application of Christian ethics— a pivotal moment when the sordid business of the secular status quo was disrupted and then shattered, in the words of Richard John Neuhaus, "by an appeal to religiously based public values."[3] This was the collapse of communism in Eastern Europe, which began with a nonviolent campaign in Poland led in large part by people of Christian faith.

To be sure, the Polish Communist regime in 1978 was already beleaguered by terrible economic woes. Yet there was nothing inevitable about its retreat into marshal law three years later, or its surrender to democracy in 1989, making Poland the first of the Soviet satellites to break free. The fact that the Polish people sundered the Iron Curtain as quickly as they did—blasting a hole through which the entire Eastern Bloc piled through—is a credit to Karol Wojtyla and the inspiration he provided as the first Polish pope.

It would be difficult to exaggerate the electrifying effect of the pope's 1979 visit to Poland, just a few months after his election to the office. "It was as though a magician from a distant land had alighted in Poland and broken the evil spell that held its people in thrall," writes Joseph Shattan in *Architects of Victory: Six Heroes of the Cold War*.[4] Everywhere the pope went, he exhorted immense throngs to be resolute, hopeful, unyielding—and peaceful. "You must be strong, dear brothers and sisters," he would tell them. "You must be strong with the strength which comes from faith.... I ask that you never despair, never grow weary, never become discouraged; ... that you always seek strength in Him, where so many generations of our mothers and fathers found it ... that you never lose that freedom of the spirit for which He has liberated man."

The pope spoke of "inalienable rights" and "political self-determination" to a people for whom such things seemed impossible dreams. And he did so always with a Christian motif. "Crestfallen Communists had to listen as thousands of Silesian miners sang out 'Christ has conquered, Christ is king, Christ commands our lives,' " explains Thomas Bokenkotter in *Church and Revolution*. "It was nothing less than a Polish Pentecost, a moral renewal and an incomparable spiritual experience that restored to the Polish people a sense of their nationhood."[5]

As the world would later learn, this was not a case of the pope being carried away by an emotional return home. His assertiveness was part of a deliberate strategy adopted almost from the outset of his papacy. It was hinted at in his inaugural sermon when he intoned three times the words that would become his signature phrase: "Be not afraid!"

Solidarity emerged one year later in this religious atmosphere. Alexander Solzhenitsyn later remarked, "Let us not be mistaken: Solidarity inspired itself not by socialism but by Christianity"—a fact apparent to nearly every visitor to the Lenin Shipyard in Gdansk at the time of its historic strike. Lech Walesa, the strike leader, described his religious faith as "my peace and my strength" and invariably sported a picture of the Black Madonna of Czestochowa on his lapel. (Later, after his release from eleven months of detention, he would make a pilgrimage to Czestochowa.) Images of the pope, the cross and the Virgin Mary were ubiquitous at the shipyard; all three appeared on its gates.

The Poles had struck against their Communist masters before— in 1956, 1970 and 1976—each time in bloody, violent futility. This time, however, was different. The workers began their strikes committed to Christian nonviolence and maintained that com-mitment throughout.

"It is hard to think of any previous revolution," writes Timo-thy Garton Ash, "in which ethical categories and moral goals have played such a large part; not only in the theory but also in the practice of the revolutionaries, not only at the outset but through-out the revolution. . . . This extraordinary record of non-violence, this majestic self-restraint in the face of many provocations, dis-tinguished the Polish revolution from previous revolutions."[6]

The pope's second trip to Poland, in 1983, was only slightly less seismic than the first. After the imposition of martial law by General Jaruzelski in December 1981 and the outlawing of Soli-darity, the church had become the focus of Polish hopes and ideals. It was the only institution the regime dared not crush outright, yet there was some question whether Cardinal Jozef Glemp would be up to the task of maintaining pressure for democratic reform and human rights. The pope settled the matter in his subtle but unyielding style. The church would not foment violence, but it would not accept the status quo, either. He instructed the massive crowds who turned out once again for him to "call good and evil by name." He told them to forgive, but warned that "to forgive does not mean to resign from truth and justice." He talked of fun-damental human rights, and of Poland's destiny as a sovereign nation "between East and West." In an essay written at the time, Timothy Garton Ash already recognized the finality of what had begun to unfold. "This transformation of consciousness," he said of the pope's somber second visit, "this moral revolution, is a last-ing achievement of the pope and Solidarity. . . . Though the police rule the streets, this country cannot be 'normalized'—i.e., returned to Soviet norms. Though the totalitarian Communist system remains in outward form, in reality it is still being dismantled from within."[7]

George Weigel, who wrote the authoritative biography of the pope, argues that "a serious case can be made for Pope John Paul II as the man who most singularly embodie[d] humanity's trials and triumphs in the twentieth century."[8] At the very least, the pope has demonstrated the continuing relevance of Christian ethics and their adaptability to a democratic-capitalist age. It wasn't so many decades ago, after all, that Catholic popes were still insist-ing that "error has no rights"—that error might be tolerated, but hardly given the same free rein as church-defined truth. Yet John Paul II quickly "emerged as the world's most important and effective advocate of freedom and democracy," according to the president of Freedom House, the New York–based organization that tracks the status of liberty around the globe.[9]

"Even the Chinese government has acknowledged the democratizing force of Christianity," according to two scholars writing in the *National Interest.* "Noting the role of Christian churches in the downfall of the Warsaw Pact in 1992, an official party organ urged that to avoid a similar fate the regime must 'strangle the baby while it is still in the manger.'" As Allen Hertzke and Daniel Philpott go on to explain, the Chinese anxiety is not misplaced. "Contrary to secular intellectuals' image of Christianity as backward or colonial," they write, "its indigenous growth outside the West is one of the signal democratizing forces around the globe today."[10]

For the pope, of course, freedom and democracy were not ends in themselves. They were means by which men and women could seek virtue and truth. They were also means by which the pope could reinvigorate a truly ancient Christian commitment—a commitment whose liberating implications have been a major theme of this book. As he wrote to a friend in 1968, "The evil of our times consists in the first place in a kind of degradation, indeed in a pulverization, of the fundamental uniqueness of each human person. This evil is even more of the metaphysical order than of the moral order. To this disintegration planned at times by atheistic ideologies we must oppose, rather than sterile polemics, a kind of 'recapitulation' of the inviolable mystery of the person."

It is safe to say that fewer Americans appreciate the role of John Paul II in the fall of communism than the number who correctly lay the blame for the Inquisition on the popes of the Middle Ages. And while there is nothing wrong with remembering the evil that men do, there is something altogether perverse in consistently disregarding the good that men do. The history of Christianity is replete with the likes of John Paul II and the members of Solidarity, men and women whose faith inspired them to accomplishments every bit as worthy of our memory. The "inviolable mystery of the person"—and hence the dignity of one and all—is not just a Holy Grail for our time. It is a message embedded in the Gospels, embellished by early church teachings, and called upon to counter blind oppression and inhumanity throughout two millennia of both stained and shining history. So long as humans are human, this message will never lack for opportunity to work its wonders on the heart.

Notes

Introduction

1. Martin E. Marty with Jonathan Moore, *Politics, Religion and the Common Good* (San Francisco: Jossey-Bass, 2000), 1.
2. Quoted in Stephen L. Carter, *The Culture of Disbelief: How American Law and Politics Trivialize Religious Devotion* (New York: Basic Books, 1993), 51.
3. Ibid.
4. Stanley Kurtz, "The Wall's Expansion," *National Review online,* 22 May 2001, http://www.nationalreview.com/comment/ comment-kurtz052201.shtml.
5. Thomas C. Reeves, "Not So Christian America," *First Things,* October 1996.
6. Roger Finke and Rodney Stark, *The Churching of America, 1776–1990: Winners and Losers in Our Religious Economy* (New Brunswick: Rutgers University Press, 1992), 202.

Chapter 1: Christianity and Progress

1. Elaine Pagels, *The Origin of Satan* (New York: Vintage Books, 1995), 37.
2. Robin Lane Fox, *Pagans and Christians* (New York: Alfred A. Knopf, Inc., 1987), 311.
3. Rodney Stark, *The Rise of Christianity* (San Francisco: HarperSanFrancisco, 1997), 106.
4. Regine Pernoud, *Those Terrible Middle Ages! Debunking the Myths* (San Francisco: Ignatius Press, 2000), 103.
5. Wayne A. Meeks, *The First Urban Christians: The Social World of the Apostle Paul* (New Haven: Yale University Press, 1983), 71.

6. Thomas Cahill, *Desire of the Everlasting Hills: The World Before and After Jesus* (New York: Doubleday, 1999), 141.
7. A. N. Wilson, *Paul: The Mind of the Apostle* (New York: W. W. Norton & Co., 1997), 140.
8. Robert L. Wilken, *The Christians as the Romans Saw Them* (New Haven: Yale University Press, 1984), 124.
9. Henry Chadwick, *The Early Church* (London: Penguin, 1993), 72.
10. Pagels, *The Origin of Satan,* 115.
11. Quoted in Bertrand Russell, *History of Western Philosophy* (London: George Allen & Unwin Ltd., 1948), 350.
12. Ramsay MacMullen, *Christianizing the Roman Empire, A.D. 100–400* (New Haven: Yale University Press, 1984), 54.
13. Wayne Meeks, *The Origins of Christian Morality* (New Haven: Yale University Press, 1993), 2–3.
14. Fox, *Pagans and Christians,* 591.
15. Ibid., 668.
16. Christopher Dawson, *The Making of Europe: An Introduction to the History of European Unity* (London: Sheed & Ward, 1932), 36.
17. Peter Brown, *Late Antiquity* (Cambridge, Mass.: The Belknap Press of Harvard University Press, 1998), 24.
18. Wilken, *The Christians as the Romans Saw Them,* 201.
19. Russell, *History of Western Philosophy,* 602.
20. Richard Fletcher, *The Barbarian Conversion: From Paganism to Christianity* (New York: H. Holt & Co., 1998), 30.
21. Dawson, *The Making of Europe,* 42.
22. Fletcher, *The Barbarian Conversion,* 29.
23. Isaiah Berlin, *Four Essays on Liberty* (London: Oxford University Press, 1969), 129.
24. Charles Taylor, *Sources of the Self: The Makings of the Modern Identity* (Cambridge, Mass.: Harvard University Press, 1989), 131–33.
25. Elaine Pagels, *Adam, Eve and the Serpent* (New York: Random House, 1988), 117.
26. Thomas Cahill, *How the Irish Saved Civilization* (New York: Doubleday, 1995), 65.
27. Chadwick, *The Early Church,* 222.
28. Garry Wills, *Saint Augustine* (New York: Viking, 1999), 102.
29. Paul Marshall, "Keeping the Faith: Religion, Freedom, and International Affairs," *Imprimis,* March 1999, 4.
30. David S. Landes, *The Wealth and Poverty of Nations: Why Some Are So Rich and Some So Poor* (New York: W. W. Norton & Co., 1998), 35.
31. Fletcher, *The Barbarian Conversion,* 45.
32. Chadwick, *The Early Church,* 248–49.
33. Cahill, *How the Irish Saved Civilization,* 181.

34. Quoted in Christopher Dawson, *Religion and the Rise of Western Culture* (New York: Sheed & Ward, 1950), 57.
35. Paul Johnson, *A History of Christianity* (New York: Atheneum, 1987), 149.
36. Fletcher, *The Barbarian Conversion*, 191.
37. H. R. Ellis Davidson, *Gods and Myths of Northern Europe* (London: Penguin Books, 1990), 71.
38. Patrick Collinson, "Religion and Human Rights: The Case of and for Protestantism," in *Historical Change and Human Rights: The Oxford Amnesty Lectures, 1994* (New York: Basic Books, 1995), 34.
39. Landes, *The Wealth and Poverty of Nations*, 40.
40. Dawson, *Religion and the Rise of Western Culture*, 175.
41. Paul Johnson, "Laying Down the Law," *Wall Street Journal,* 10 March 1999.
42. Ibid.
43. Tom Bethell, *The Noblest Triumph: Property and Prosperity through the Ages* (New York: St. Martin's Press, 1998), 85.
44. Ibid., 80.
45. Russell, *History of Western Philosophy,* 450.
46. Antony Black, "Christianity and Republicanism: From St. Cyprian to Rousseau," *American Political Science Review,* September 1997, 650.
47. Ibid.

Chapter 2: Christianity and Slavery

1. Paul Johnson, *A History of Christianity* (New York: Atheneum, 1987), 437.
2. Robert William Fogel, *The Rise and Fall of American Slavery* (New York: W. W. Norton & Co., 1991), 205.
3. James Walvin, *Black Ivory: A History of British Slavery* (Washington, D.C.: Howard University Press, 1994), 195.
4. Milton Meltzer, *Slavery: A World History* (New York: Da Capo Press, Plenum Publishing, 1993), 91.
5. J. P. V. D. Baldson, *Romans and Aliens* (Chapel Hill: University of North Carolina Press, 1979), 80.
6. Wayne A. Meeks, *The First Urban Christians: The Social World of the Apostle Paul* (New Haven: Yale University Press, 1983), 64.
7. Regine Pernoud, *Those Terrible Middle Ages! Debunking the Myths* (San Francisco: Ignatius Press, 1977), 85.
8. Johnson, *A History of Christianity,* 437.
9. David Brion Davis, *Slavery and Human Progress* (New York: Oxford University Press, 1984), 131.
10. *The Columbia History of the World,* ed. John A. Garraty and Peter Gay (New York: Harper & Row, 1972), 894.

11. Hugh Thomas, *The Slave Trade* (New York: Simon & Schuster, 1997), 541.
12. Ibid., 495.
13. Walvin, *Black Ivory,* 304.
14. Fogel, *The Rise and Fall of American Slavery,* 212.
15. Davis, *Slavery and Human Progress,* 139.
16. Thomas, *The Slave Trade,* 797.
17. Ibid., 495.
18. Fogel, *The Rise and Fall of American Slavery,* 218.
19. Ibid., 219.
20. Thomas, *The Slave Trade,* 556.
21. Both Mill and Toqueville quoted in Davis, *Slavery and Human Progress,* 110–11.
22. Fogel, *The Rise and Fall of American Slavery,* 203–4.
23. Herbert S. Klein, *Slavery in the Americas* (Chicago: Ivan R. Dee, 1989), 41.
24. John B. Boles, ed., *Masters and Slaves in the House of the Lord: Race and Religion in the American South, 1740–1870* (Lexington: University Press of Kentucky, 1988), 5.
25. Johnson, *A History of Christianity,* 370–71.
26. Walvin, *Black Ivory,* 185.
27. Rebecca Merrill Groothuis, *Women Caught in the Conflict: The Culture War between Traditionalism and Feminism* (Eugene, Oregon: Wipf & Stock Publishers, 1994), 36.
28. John G. West, *The Politics of Revelation and Reason: Religion and Civic Life in the New Nation* (Lawrence: University Press of Kansas, 1996), 114.
29. Randy J. Sparks, "Religion in Amite County, Mississippi, 1800–1861," in *Masters and Slaves in the House of the Lord,* ed. Boles, 79.
30. Clarence L. Mohr, "Slaves and White Churches in Confederate Georgia," in *Masters and Slaves in the House of the Lord,* ed. Boles, 157.
31. Stanley Elkins, *Slavery: A Problem in American Institutional and Intellectual Life,* 2nd ed. (Chicago: University of Chicago Press, 1969), 182.
32. James M. McPherson, *Battle Cry of Freedom: The Civil War Era* (New York: Oxford University Press, 1988), 8.
33. Ibid., 88–89.
34. Fogel, *The Rise and Fall of American Slavery,* 323.
35. Walvin, *Black Ivory,* 193.
36. Elkins, *Slavery,* 71.
37. Ibid., 68.
38. Davis, *Slavery and Human Progress,* 12.
39. Walvin, *Black Ivory,* 196.
40. Boles, *Masters and Slaves in the House of the Lord,* 10.

41. Eugene D. Genovese, *Roll, Jordan, Roll: The World the Slaves Made* (New York: Pantheon Books, 1974), 232.
42. Quoted in ibid., 253.
43. Ibid., 254.
44. Meltzer, *Slavery: A World History,* 216.
45. William Loren Katz, *Breaking the Chains: African American Slave Resistance* (New York: Atheneum, 1990), 76.
46. Orlando Patterson, *The Ordeal of Integration* (Washington, D.C.: Civitas/Counterpoint, 1997), 105.
47. Johnson, *A History of Christianity,* 436.
48. Victor B. Howard, *Religion and the Radical Republican Movement, 1860–1870* (Lexington: University Press of Kentucky, 1990), 89.
49. Charles Jacobs, "History Will Judge Clinton Harshly for His Silence on Sudan," *Boston Globe,* 12 February 2000, A15.

Chapter 3: Christianity and Science
1. Stanley L. Jaki, *Science and Creation: From Eternal Cycles to an Oscillating Universe* (New York: Science History Publications, 1974), viii.
2. Jaroslav Pelikan, *The Christian Tradition,* vol. 1, *The Emergence of the Catholic Tradition (100–600)* (Chicago: University of Chicago Press, 1971), 50. Pelikan remarks that "Most of the generous things which the church fathers said about paganism applied to the philosophers." Ibid., 66.
3. Quoted in Jaroslav Pelikan, *The Excellent Empire* (San Francisco: Harper & Row, 1987), 111.
4. Ibid., 24.
5. Paul Johnson, *A History of Christianity* (New York: Atheneum, 1987), 6.
6. Shirley Jackson Case, *The Origins of Christian Supernaturalism* (Chicago: University of Chicago Press, 1946), v.
7. Quoted in Daniel Boorstin, *The Discoverers* (New York: Harry N. Abrams, 1983), 37.
8. Pelikan, *The Christian Tradition,* 281.
9. Ibid., 281–82.
10. Robert Nisbet, *History of the Idea of Progress* (New York: Basic Books, 1980), 47.
11. Ibid., 76.
12. Lynn White Jr., "Medieval Europe Foresaw Planes, Cars, Submarines," *Smithsonian,* October 1978, 115.
13. Arnold Pacey, *The Maze of Ingenuity, Ideas and Idealism in the Development of Technology* (Cambridge, Mass.: MIT Press, 1992), 27.
14. David S. Landes, *The Wealth and Poverty of Nations: Why Some Are So Rich and Some So Poor* (New York: W. W. Norton & Co., 1998), 58.

15. D. S. L. Cardwell, *Turning Points in Western Technology* (New York: Science History Publications, 1972), 7.
16. Ibid., 211.
17. Frederick F. Cartwright, *Disease and History: The Influence of Disease in Shaping the Great Events of History* (New York: Thomas Y. Crowell Co., 1972), 38.
18. Jaki, *Science and Creation*, 36.
19. Jean Gimpel, *The Medieval Machine: The Industrial Revolution of the Middle Ages* (New York: Holt, Rinehart & Winston, 1976), 13.
20. Quoted in Stanley L. Jaki, *Cosmos in Transition: Studies in the History of Cosmology* (Tucson: Pachart Publishing, 1990), 246.
21. Boorstin, *The Discoverers*, 723–24.
22. Gimpel, *The Medieval Machine*, 63.
23. Lynn White Jr., *Medieval Technology and Social Change* (New York: Oxford University Press, 1962), 76.
24. Quoted in Michael Novak, "How Christianity Created Capitalism," *Wall Street Journal*, 23 December 1999.
25. Pacey, *The Maze of Ingenuity*, 12.
26. Landes, *The Wealth and Poverty of Nations*, 58.
27. Arnold Pacey, *Technology in World Civilization: A Thousand-year History* (Cambridge, Mass.: MIT Press, 1990), 44.
28. Gimpel, *The Medieval Machine*, 1.
29. Boorstin, *The Discoverers*, 61–62.
30. A. C. Crombie, *The History of Science from Augustine to Galileo* (New York: Dover, 1995), 184.
31. Ibid., 243.
32. White, *Medieval Technology*, 134.
33. Gimpel, *The Medieval Machine*, 146.
34. Crombie, *The History of Science*, 68–69.
35. Pacey, *The Maze of Ingenuity*, 23.
36. Williston Walker, Richard A. Norris, David W. Lotz and Robert T. Handy, *A History of the Christian Church* (New York: Charles Scribner's Sons, 1985), 327.
37. Thomas Bokenkotter, *A Concise History of the Catholic Church* (New York: Image Books/Doubleday, 1990), 146.
38. Alfred North Whitehead, *Science and the Modern World* (New York: Macmillan, 1925; reprint, The Free Press, 1997), 11–12.
39. Marie Boas Hall, *The Scientific Renaissance, 1450–1630* (New York: Dover, 1994), 309.
40. Francis X. Rocca, "Looking to Heaven, Gazing at the Stars," *Wall Street Journal*, 19 October 1999.
41. Boas Hall, *The Scientific Renaissance*, 88.
42. Whitehead, *Science and the Modern World*, 184.

43. John L. Heilbron, *The Sun in the Church* (Cambridge, Mass.: Harvard University Press, 1999), 202–3.
44. Ibid., 203.
45. Boas Hall, *The Scientific Renaissance,* 342.
46. Heilbron, *The Sun in the Church,* 3.
47. Ibid., 88.
48. Ibid., 151.
49. Ibid., 22.
50. Johnson, *A History of Christianity,* 334.
51. Boorstin, *The Discoverers,* 607.
52. John Habgood, *Truths in Tension: New Perspectives on Religion and Science* (New York: Holt, Rinehart & Winston, 1964), 36.
53. Boorstin, *The Discoverers,* 697.
54. Habgood, *Truths in Tension,* 67.
55. Jeffrey Burton Russell, *Inventing the Flat Earth: Columbus and Modern Historians* (New York: Praeger, 1991), 71.
56. John Polkinghorne, *Belief in God in an Age of Science* (New Haven: Yale University Press, 1998), 5.
57. Russell, *Inventing the Flat Earth,* 38.
58. Ibid., 2.
59. Ibid., 26.
60. Ibid., 11.
61. Jaki, *Science and Creation,* 293.
62. Laurence R. Iannoccone, "Introduction to the Economics of Religion," *Journal of Economic Literature,* September 1998, 1471.
63. Polkinghorne, *Belief in God,* 5.
64. Ibid., 6.
65. Gregg Easterbrook, "Science Sees the Light," *New Republic,* 12 October 1998, 26.
66. Kim A. McDonald, "Science Confronts the Ultimate Question," *Chronicle of Higher Education,* 12 May 1993.
67. Quoted in Gregg Easterbrook, *Beside Still Waters: Searching for Meaning in an Age of Doubt* (New York: William Morrow & Co., 1998), 78–79.
68. Easterbrook, "Science Sees the Light," 27.
69. Easterbrook, *Beside Still Waters,* 113.
70. Ibid., 77.
71. Quoted in Polkinghorne, *Belief in God,* 12.
72. Niles Eldredge, *The Triumph of Evolution and the Failure of Creationism* (New York: W. H. Freeman & Co., 2000), 169.
73. Stephen Jay Gould, *Rocks of Ages: Science and Religion in the Fullness of Life* (New York: Ballantine, 1999), 210.
74. Whitehead, *Science and the Modern World,* 192.

75. Quoted in *The Intellectuals Speak Out about God,* ed. Roy Abraham Varghese (Dallas: Lewis & Stanley, 1984), 50.
76. Habgood, *Truths in Tension,* 150–51.
77. Polkinghorne, *Belief in God,* 77.

Chapter 4: Christianity and the Slaughter of the Innocents
1. Roland H. Bainton, *Christian Attitudes toward War and Peace: A Historical Survey and Critical Re-evaluation* (New York: Abingdon Press, 1960), 54.
2. Ibid., 53.
3. Richard Fletcher, *The Barbarian Conversion: From Paganism to Christianity* (New York: H. Holt & Co., 1998), 122.
4. Bainton, *Christian Attitudes toward War,* 103.
5. James Turner Johnson, *The Holy War Idea in Western and Islamic Traditions* (University Park: Penn State University Press, 1997), 111–12.
6. Stephen Neill, *A History of Christian Missions* (New York: Penguin Books, 1986), 97
7. Jonathan Riley-Smith, in *First Things,* March 2000, 20–23.
8. Neill, *A History of Christian Missions,* 98.
9. Piers Paul Read, *The Templars* (New York: St. Martin's Press, 1999), 311.
10. Ibid.
11. John Hale, *The Civilization of Europe in the Renaissance* (New York: Touchstone, 1995), 137.
12. Johnson, *The Holy War Idea,* 31.
13. David Martin, *Does Christianity Cause War?* (Oxford: Clarendon Press, 1997), 104.
14. Quoted in James Turner Johnson, "Onward, Christian Soldiers?" *First Things,* December 1998, 45–48.
15. Johnson, *The Holy War Idea,* 112.
16. David S. Landes, *The Wealth and Poverty of Nations: Why Some Are So Rich and Some So Poor* (New York: W. W. Norton & Co., 1998), 76.
17. John Hemming, *Red Gold: The Conquest of the Brazilian Indians, 1500–1760* (Cambridge, Mass.: Harvard University Press, 1978), 473.
18. Ibid., 451.
19. Sydney Ahlstrom, *A Religious History of the American People* (New Haven: Yale University Press, 1972), 861.
20. Quentin Skinner, *The Foundations of Modern Political Thought,* vol. 2 (New York: Cambridge University Press, 1978), 169.
21. Robert Royal, *1492 and All That* (Washington, D.C.: Ethics and Public Policy Center, 1992), 75–76.
22. Quoted in ibid., 87–88.
23. Hugh Thomas, *Conquest: Montezuma, Cortes, and the Fall of Old Mexico* (New York: Simon & Schuster, 1993), xiv.

24. Ibid., 26.
25. Keith Windschuttle, *The Killing of History* (San Francisco: Encounter Books, 2000), 66.
26. Henry Kamen, *The Spanish Inquisition: A Historical Revision* (New Haven: Yale University Press, 1998), 59–60.
27. Ibid., 203.
28. Ibid., 45.
29. Ibid., 50.
30. Arthur Quinn, *A New World* (Boston: Faber & Faber, 1994), 163–64.
31. Christy G. Turner and Jacqueline A. Turner, *Man Corn: Cannibalism and Violence in the Prehistoric American Southwest* (Salt Lake City: University of Utah Press, 1999), 131.
32. Quoted in James Bishop Jr., "Bones of Contention," *High Country News,* 25 October 1999.
33. Lawrence H. Keeley, *War Before Civilization: The Myth of the Peaceful Savage* (New York: Oxford University Press, 1996), 18.
34. Ibid., 19.
35. Thomas, *Conquest,* 592–93.
36. Shepard Krech III, *The Ecological Indian: Myth and History* (New York: W. W. Norton & Co., 1999), 80.
37. See Stephane Courtois, Nicolas Werth, Jean-Louis Panne, Adrzej Paczkowski, Karel Bartooek and Jean-Louis Margolin, *The Black Book of Communism: Crimes, Terror, Repression,* trans. Jonathan Murphy and Mark Cramer (Cambridge, Mass.: Harvard University Press, 1999).
38. Regine Pernoud, *Those Terrible Middle Ages! Debunking the Myths* (San Francisco: Ignatius Press, 1977), 138.
39. Martin, *Does Christianity Cause War?* 204–5.
40. Quoted in Johnson, *The Holy War Idea,* 98.
41. Bainton, *Christian Attitudes toward War,* 65.

Chapter 5: Christianity and the Third Reich

1. J. S. Conway, *The Nazi Persecution of the Churches* (New York: Basic Books, 1968), 140.
2. Richard Grunberger, *The Twelve-Year Reich: A Social History of Nazi Germany, 1933–1945* (New York: Holt, Rinehart & Winston, 1971), 445.
3. Conway, *The Nazi Persecution,* 194.
4. Grunberger, *The Twelve-Year Reich,* 446.
5. John F. Morley, *Vatican Diplomacy and the Jews during the Holocaust* (New York: KTAV Publishing, 1980), 145.
6. Conway, *The Nazi Persecution,* 296.
7. Thomas F. X. Noble, "A Tendentious Telling," *First Things,* May 2001, 59–63.

8. Quoted in Liz McMillen, "The Uniqueness of the Holocaust," *Chronicle of Higher Education,* 22 June 1994.

9. James Bentley, *Martin Niemoller* (New York: The Free Press, 1984), 91.

10. Renate Wind, *Dietrich Bonhoeffer: A Spoke in the Wheel* (Grand Rapids: William B. Eerdmans, 1992), 70.

11. Conway, *The Nazi Persecution,* 9.

12. William J. O'Malley, S.J., "The Priests of Dachau," *America,* 14 November 1987, 352.

13. Robert Royal, *The Catholic Martyrs of the Twentieth Century: A Comprehensive World HIstory* (New York: Crossroad, 2000), 132.

14. Ronald Rychlak, "A Different Read: Vatican Chronicles," *Brill's Content,* April 2000.

15. Eamon Duffy, *Saints and Sinners* (New Haven: Yale University Press, 1997), 263–64.

16. John Cornwell, "Hitler's Pope," *Vanity Fair,* October 1999, 182.

17. Robert S. Wistrich, "The Pope, the Church, and the Jews," *Commentary,* April 1999, 26.

18. Ronald J. Rychlak, *Hitler, the War and the Pope* (Huntington, Indiana: Our Sunday Visitor, 2000), 213.

19. Morley, *Vatican Diplomacy,* 45.

20. Robert A. Graham, "How to Manufacture a Legend: The Controversy over the Alleged 'Silence' of Pope Pius XII in World War II," *Pius XII and the Holocaust* (Milwaukee: Catholic League for Religious and Civil Rights, 1988), 16.

21. Philip Friedman, *Their Brothers' Keepers* (New York: Holocaust Library, 1978), 58.

22. See Question 15 in "The Vatican and the Holocaust: A Preliminary Report Submitted to the Holy See's Commission for Religious Relations with the Jews and the International Jewish Committee for Interreligious Consultations," by the International Catholic-Jewish Historical Commission, October 2000.

23. Pierre Blet, S.J., *Pius XII and the Second World War, According to the Archives of the Vatican* (New York: Paulist Press, 1999), 185.

24. Joseph Lichten, Introduction to "Pius XII's Defense of Jews and Others: 1944–45," *Pius XII and the Holocaust,* 35.

25. Rychlak, *Hitler, the War and the Pope,* 222.

26. Blet, *Pius XII and the Second World War,* 63.

27. William D. Rubinstein, "The Devil's Advocate," *First Things,* January 2000, 39.

28. William D. Rubinstein, *The Myth of Rescue: Why the Democracies Could Not Have Saved More Jews from the Nazis* (London: Routledge, 1997), 69 and 73.

29. Ibid., 101.

30. Michael Novak, "Pius XII as Scapegoat," *First Things,* August/September 2000.
31. Deborah E. Lipstadt, "The Failure to Rescue and Contemporary American Jewish Historiography of the Holocaust: Judging from a Distance," in *The Bombing of Auschwitz: Should the Allies Have Attempted It?* (New York: St. Martin's Press, 2000), 228.
32. David S. Wyman, *The Abandonment of the Jews: America and the Holocaust, 1941–1945* (New York: Pantheon Books, 1984), 189.
33. Ibid., 311.
34. Friedman, *Their Brothers' Keepers,* 49.
35. Wyman, *The Abandonment of the Jews,* 232.
36. Philip P. Hallie, *Lest Innocent Blood Be Shed: The Story of the Village of Le Chambon and How Goodness Happened There* (New York: Harper & Row, 1979), 46.
37. Friedman, *Their Brothers' Keepers,* 153.

Chapter 6: Christianity and Charity

1. Arnaud C. Marts, *Philanthropy's Role in Civilization* (New York: Harper & Brothers, 1953), 79.
2. John McManners, ed., *The Oxford Illustrated History of Christianity* (Cambridge: Oxford University Press, 1990), 37.
3. Rodney Stark, *The Rise of Christianity* (San Francisco: HarperSanFrancisco, 1997), 212.
4. Robin Lane Fox, *Pagans and Christians* (New York: Alfred A. Knopf Inc., 1987), 324.
5. Stark, *The Rise of Christianity,* 86.
6. Michel Riquet, *Christian Charity in Action* (New York: Hawthorn Books, 1961), 55.
7. Stark, *The Rise of Christianity,* 75.
8. Quoted from Demetrios J. Constantelos, *Byzantine Philanthropy and Social Welfare* (New Brunswick, New Jersey: Rutgers University Press, 1968), 153.
9. E. J. Mayeaux Jr., M.D., *A History of Western Medicine and Surgery* (Shreveport: Louisiana State University Medical Center, 1989), http://lib-sh.lsumc.edu/fammed/grounds/history.html.
10. Riquet, *Christian Charity in Action,* 116.
11. Ibid., 89.
12. Richard Fletcher, *The Barbarian Conversion: From Paganism to Christianity* (New York: H. Holt & Co., 1998), 155.
13. Christopher Dawson, *The Making of Europe: An Introduction of the History of European Unity* (London: Sheed & Ward, 1932), 270.
14. Henri Daniel-Rops, *Monsieur Vincent: The Story of St. Vincent de Paul* (New York: Hawthorn Books, 1961), 76.

15. Riquet, *Christian Charity in Action,* 160.
16. McManners, ed., *Oxford Illustrated History,* 217.
17. Ibid.
18. Lewis W. Spitz, *The Protestant Reformation* (New York: Harper & Row, 1985), 375.
19. Leland Ryken, *Worldly Saints: The Puritans As They Really Were* (Grand Rapids: Zondervan, 1986), 175.
20. Mary Oates, *The Catholic Philanthropic Tradition in America* (Bloomington: Indiana University Press, 1995), 69.
21. Marts, *Philanthropy's Role in Civilization,* 37.
22. David Ho, "Donations to Charities Rise 13 Percent," *Rocky Mountain News,* 30 October 2000, 25A.
23. Quoted in Independent Sector homepage: http://www.independentsector.org/.
24. Quoted in "Cheap States and Cheapskates," *Rocky Mountain News,* 14 December 1997, 1B.
25. Laurence R. Iannoccone, "Introduction to the Economics of Religion," *Journal of Economic Literature,* September 1998, 1469.
26. Oates, *The Catholic Philanthropic Tradition,* 171.
27. Diane Winston, *Red-Hot and Righteous: The Urban Religion of the Salvation Army* (Cambridge, Mass.: Harvard University Press, 1999), 95.
28. Edward H. McKinley, *Marching to Glory: The History of the Salvation Army in the United States* (New York: Harper & Row, 1980), 7.
29. Winston, *Red-Hot and Righteous,* 235.
30. Ibid., 9.

Chapter 7: Christianity and the Environment

1. Stanley L. Jaki, *Patterns or Principles and Other Essays* (Wilmington: Intercollegiate Studies Institute, 1995), 39.
2. Joyce Burnette and Joel Mokyr, "The Standard of Living through the Ages," in *The State of Humanity,* ed. Julian L. Simon (Cambridge: Blackwell, 1995), 136.
3. David S. Landes, *The Wealth and Poverty of Nations: Why Some Are So Rich and Some So Poor* (New York: W. W. Norton & Co., 1998), 174–79.
4. Leland Ryken, *Worldly Saints: The Puritans As They Really Were* (Grand Rapids: Zondervan, 1990), 33.
5. Laurence R. Iannoccone, "Introduction to the Economics of Religion," *Journal of Economic Literature,* September 1998, 1475.
6. Rene Dubos, *The Wooing of Earth* (New York: Scribner, 1980), 64–66.
7. Shepard Krech III, *The Ecological Indian: Myth and History* (New York: W. W. Norton & Co., 1999), 147–49.
8. Ibid., 213.

9. Quoted in Robert Whelan, *Wild in Woods: The Myth of the Noble Eco-Savage* (London: Institute of Economic Affairs, 1999), 41.
10. Andrew C. Isenberg, *The Destruction of the Bison: An Environmental History, 1750–1920* (New York: Cambridge University Press, 2000), 93–122.
11. Quoted in "Gold Spelled Tribes' Doom," *Denver Post,* 5 April 1999, 6B.
12. B. L. Turner and K. W. Butzer, "The Columbian Encounter and Land-Use Change," *Environment* 34, no. 8 (October 1992), 42.
13. Krech, *The Ecological Indian,* 120.
14. Louis S. Warren, "Seeing the People for the Trees: The Promise and Pitfalls of Indian Environmental History," *OAH Magazine of History,* Spring 1996, 19.
15. J. David Bleich, "Judaism and Animal Experimentation," *Animal Sacrifices: Religious Perspectives on the Use of Animals in Science* (Philadelphia: Temple University Press, 1986), 61–62.
16. Lewis Regenstein, *Replenish the Earth* (New York: Crossroad, 1991), 19.
17. Jaki, *Patterns or Principles,* 39.
18. William Edward Hartpole Lecky, *History of European Morals, from Augustus to Charlemagne* (New York: D. Appleton & Co., 1898), 171.
19. Ibid., 161.
20. Paul Johnson, *The Birth of the Modern: World Society, 1815–1830* (New York: HarperCollins, 1991), 719.
21. Dubos, *The Wooing of Earth,* 13.
22. Quoted in ibid., 15.
23. *Catechism of the Catholic Church* (Liguori, Missouri: Liguori Publications, 1994), 580.
24. Andrew Linzey, "The Place of Animals in Creation: A Christian View," in *Animal Sacrifices,* 124–25.

Chapter 8: Christianity and Democracy

1. Page Smith, *Rediscovering Christianity: A History of Modern Democracy and the Christian Ethic* (New York: St. Martin's Press, 1994), 62.
2. E. Digby Baltzell, *Puritan Boston and Quaker Philadelphia: Two Protestant Ethics and the Spirit of Class Authority and Leadership* (New York: The Free Press, 1979), 125.
3. Kevin Phillips, *The Cousins' Wars: Religion, Politics, and the Triumph of Anglo-America* (New York: Basic Books, 1999), 27.
4. Smith, *Rediscovering Christianity,* 69.
5. Paul Johnson, *A History of Christianity* (New York: Atheneum, 1987), 422.

6. Stephen Foster, *Their Solitary Way: The Puritan Social Ethic in the First Century of Settlement in New England* (New Haven: Yale University Press, 1971), 156.
7. Ibid., 169.
8. Ibid., 165.
9. Patricia U. Bonomi, *Under the Cope of Heaven* (New York: Oxford University Press, 1986), 29.
10. Bryan F. LeBeau, *The Story of the Salem Witch Trials* (Upper Saddle River, New Jersey: Prentice Hall Inc., 1998), 198–204.
11. R. H. Tawney, *Religion and the Rise of Capitalism* (New York: Harcourt, Brace & Co., 1926), 165.
12. Ibid.
13. Sydney Ahlstrom, *A Religious History of the American People* (New Haven: Yale University Press, 1972), 124.
14. M. Stanton Evans, *The Theme Is Freedom: Religion, Politics, and the American Tradition* (Washington, D.C.: Regnery, 1994), 201.
15. Bernard Bailyn, *The Ideological Origins of the American Revolution* (Cambridge, Mass.: The Belknap Press of Harvard University Press, 1967), 32.
16. Ellis Sandoz, *A Government of Laws: Political Theory, Religion, and the American Founding* (Baton Rouge: Louisiana State University Press, 1989), 100–1.
17. William Warren Sweet, *Religion in the Development of American Culture, 1765–1840* (New York: Charles Scribner's Sons, 1952), 85.
18. Richard Brookhiser, *Founding Father: Rediscovering George Washington* (New York: The Free Press, 1996), 146.
19. John G. West Jr., *The Politics of Revelation and Reason: Religion and Civic Life in the New Nation* (Lawrence: University Press of Kansas, 1996), 36.
20. Johnson, *A History of Christianity,* 427.
21. Ibid.
22. Alan Heimert, *Religion and the American Mind: From the Great Awakening to the Revolution* (Cambridge, Mass.: Harvard University Press, 1966), 14.
23. Ibid., 13.
24. Bonomi, *Under the Cope of Heaven,* 157–58.
25. Sweet, *Religion in the Development of American Culture,* 36.
26. Roger Finke and Rodney Stark, *The Churching of America, 1776–1990: Winners and Losers in Our Religious Economy* (New Brunswick, New Jersey: Rutgers University Press, 1992), 39.
27. Ahlstrom, *A Religious History,* 347.
28. Bonomi, *Under the Cope of Heaven,* 186.
29. Ibid., 216.

30. Perry Miller, "From Covenant to Revival," in *The Shaping of American Religion,* ed. James Ward Smith and A. Leland Jamison (Princeton: Princeton University Press, 1961), 341.

31. Phillips, *The Cousins' Wars,* 168–69.

32. Miller, "From Covenant to Revival," 343.

33. Nathan O. Hatch, *The Democratization of American Christianity* (New Haven: Yale University Press, 1989), 3–4.

34. Ibid., 82.

35. Quoted from "Evangelicalism and American Life: A Conversation with Nathan Hatch, Grant Wacker, and Hanna Rosin," *Center Conversations* (Washington, D.C.: Ethics and Public Policy Center, July 2000).

36. Hatch, *The Democratization of American Christianity,* 58.

37. Terry D. Bilhartz, *Urban Religion and the Second Great Awakening: Church and Society in Early National Baltimore* (Cranbury, New Jersey: Associated University Presses, 1986), 139.

38. Joyce Appleby, *Inheriting the Revolution: The First Generation of Americans* (Cambridge, Mass.: The Belknap Press of Harvard University Press, 2000), 193.

39. Ibid., 204.

40. West, *The Politics of Revelation and Reason,* 187.

41. Eric Foner, *Politics and Ideology in the Age of the Civil War* (New York: Oxford University Press, 1980), 65.

42. W. J. Rorabaugh, *The Alcoholic Republic: An American Tradition* (New York: Oxford University Press, 1979), 169.

43. Ibid., 210.

44. Ruth Bordin, *Women and Temperance: The Quest for Power and Liberty, 1873–1900* (Philadelphia: Temple University Press, 1982), 29.

45. Smith, *Rediscovering Christianity,* 167.

46. James Q. Wilson, "Body and Soul," *Commentary,* June 2000, 68.

47. Martin Luther King Jr., *Why We Can't Wait* (New York: Signet Classic, 2000), 21.

48. Ibid., 51.

49. Stephen Carter, *The Culture of Disbelief: How American Law and Politics Trivialize Religious Devotion* (New York: Basic Books, 1993), 229.

50. William J. Stern, "How Dagger John Saved New York's Irish," *City Journal,* Spring 1997.

51. Ibid.

52. Charles R. Morris, *American Catholic: The Saints and Sinners Who Built America's Most Powerful Church* (New York: Times Books, 1997), 111.

53. Mark J. Hurley, *The Unholy Ghost: Anti-Catholicism in the American Experience* (Huntington, Indiana: Our Sunday Visitor, 1992), 47.

Conclusion

1. Quoted in Andrea Billups, "Washington's History a Mystery to Collegians," *Washington Times*, 21 February 2000.
2. John Thavis, "Sharing the Burden of Fault," *Denver Catholic Register*, 15 March 2000, 7.
3. Richard John Neuhaus, "The Vulnerability of the Naked Square," *Good Order: Right Answers to Contemporary Questions* (New York: Simon & Schuster, 1995), 59.
4. Joseph Shattan, *Architects of Victory: Six Heroes of the Cold War* (Washington, D.C.: The Heritage Foundation, 1999), 208.
5. Thomas Bokenkotter, *Church and Revolution: Catholics in the Struggle for Democracy and Social Justice* (New York: Image Books/Doubleday, 1998), 547.
6. Quoted in Ibid., 564.
7. Timothy Garten Ash, *The Uses of Adversity: Essays on the Fate of Central Europe* (New York: Random House, 1989), 60.
8. George Weigel, "John Paul II and the Crisis of Humanism," *First Things*, December 1999, 31–36.
9. Adrian Karatnycky, "Democratic Church," *National Review*, 4 May 1998, 38.
10. Allen D. Hertzke and Daniel Philpott, "Defending the Faiths," *National Interest*, Fall 2000, 78.

ACKNOWLEDGMENTS

Many people provided valuable suggestions and assistance during this project, but a special thanks must go to three: to Peter Collier, for giving the idea a chance and helping to keep it focused; to Carol Staswick, for her unfailingly meticulous and intelligent editing; and to Douglas Groothuis, for so much wise advice.

Vincent Carroll
Rocky Mountain News

INDEX

Ottoboni, Pietro, 76
Ozanam, Frederick, 151

Pacelli, Eugenio. *See* Pius XII
Pacey, Arnold, 62, 65–66, 70–71
pacificism, 90–91, 111
paganism: and animals, 170–71;
    and charity, 140, 143, 146–47;
    ethics, 3, 9; fate, 58–61; neopa-
    ganism, 115–17, 109, 121; and
    supernatural, 58–59; view of
    Christians, 8, 143, 144, 146
Pagels, Elaine, 3, 6, 14
papacy: antimodernism, 57, 79;
    on bullfights, 173; Crusades, 91;
    on indigenous peoples, 102;
    learning, 58; on Nazism,
    114–15, 126, 128–36; on reli-
    gious war, 94; on science, 54;
    vs. secular powers, 21; on slav-
    ery, 29
parables, 141–42
Parents' Television Council, xiv
Parliament, 36–38
Pastors' Emergency League,
    122–23
Patrick, St., 26
Patterson, Orlando, 50
Paul III, 102
Paul of Tarsus (apostle), 4, 5; on
    slavery, 28, 42
Peabody, George, 157
Peace and Truce of God, 95
Pelikan, Jaroslav, 58, 59–60
Penn, William, 97, 184
Penrose, Roger, 82
Perkins Institute for the Blind, 158
Perkins, William, 153
Pernoud, Regine, 5, 29, 109,
Peters, Rudolph, 110

philanthrophy. *See* charity
Phillips, Kevin, 180, 190
Philpott, Daniel, 211
Picking up the Pieces (film), 140
Pitt, William, 35, 38
Pius V, 173
Pius IX, 79
Pius X, 57
Pius XI, 126
Pius XII: accusations against, viii,
    114–15, 132, 133; on bullfight-
    ing, 173; on communism, 133;
    concordat, 125; resistance to
    Nazism; 128–35; protection of
    Jews, 130–34
Plato, 59
Pliny the Younger, 8
Poland, 118–19, 208–10
politics: church vs. state, 10–15,
    20–22, 205–6; "civic religion,"
    xi; Religious Right, ix–x; *see also*
    democracy
Polkinghorne, John, 78, 81, 85
Ponting, Clive, 163
populism, 192–95, 200
Pournarpoulos, G. C., 148
poverty: as ideal, 142, 143, 151
Presbyterians, 157, 190
Preysing, Konrad von, 124, 130
progress: idea of, 60–61
Prohibition, 197
property, 22
Protestantism: anti-Catholic prej-
    udice, 190–81, 203; and capital-
    ism, 166–67; on Copernicus,
    56; and education, 152; individ-
    ual conscience, 187; and liter-
    acy, 166; on natural world,
    163–64; on saints, 62; vs. slav-
    ery, 41–42

scholasticism, 22–23, 71–72
schools: parochial, 203–4
science: astronomical revolution, 73–77; attitude behind, 57–64; clergy in, 73, 76–77; design principle, 81–83; medieval invention, 64–71; medieval philosophy, 71–73; as opposed to religion, 78–80; religious believers in, 73, 76–78, 80–81, 84–85; resistance to, 56–57, 74–75
Scopes Trial, 80
Second Lateran Council, 95
Seneca, 60
"Sensation" (exhibit), xiii
Sepulveda, Juan Gines de, 102
Seton, Elizabeth Ann, 154–55
Sewall, Gilbert T., 177
Sewall, Samuel, 41
Sharp, Granville, 31–32
Shattan, Joseph, 209
Shaw, Anna Howard, 200
Sheldrake, Rupert, 164
Siegel, Eric, xiii
Sierra Club, 164
Simon Wiesenthal Center, 136
Sixtus IV, 105
slavery: in Americas, 97, 98; in antiquity, 6, 27–28; in Bible, 28, 42; debates over, 101–2; economics of, 33–34; in Latin America, 48–49; in Middle Ages, 29; modern, 51–52; as natural, 31; opposition to, 26–27, 31–47; religious rationale, 40–41, 42–43; ubiquity of, 26, 29–30, 100; in U.S., 40–41
slaves: religion among, 47–50
Smith, Brian K., 86

Smith, Page, 180, 200
Smithsonian Institution, 164
Social Gospel, 200
Solidarity, 209–10
Solzhenitsyn, Alexander, 209
Somerset, James, 33
Soviet Union, 117
Spanish colonies, 96–102
Spanish Inquisition, 104–6
Spanish missions, 96–100
Sparks, Randy, 43
Stalin, Joseph, 51, 117
Stannard, David, 87
Stark, Rodney, xvii, 4, 142–43, 145–46, 188
Stauffenberg, Klaus von, 124
Stephen, James, 38
Stepinac, Aloysius, 132
Stern, William J., 202, 203
Stoics, 3, 9
Stowe, Harriet Beecher, 47
St. Vincent de Paul Society, 151, 202
Sudan, 52, 110
Sunday, Billy, 79, 200
Swaggert, Jimmy, 140
Sweet, W. W., 185, 188
Syllabus of Errors, 79

Tamerlane, 92
Tappan, Arthur, 45
Tappan, Lewis, 25, 45
Tawney, R. H., 182
Taylor, Charles, 13–14
Taylor, Myron, 133
technology: medieval, 65–69; and well-being, 165–66
television, xiv, 139–40; evangelists on, 140
temperance movement, 197–99

Weld, Theodore Dwight, 45–46
Wells, H. G., 161
Wesley, John, 32, 34, 37
West, Elliott, 169–70
West, John G., 43, 196
Westfall, Richard S., 56
White, Andrew Dickson, 55, 79, 80
White, Lynn, 62, 65, 162–63
Whitefield, George, 32, 186
Whitehead, Alfred North, 72–73, 74, 84
Wilberforce, William, 35–39, 174
Wilhoit, Cleveland, xv
Wilken, Robert L., 5, 9
Willard, Frances, 199
William and Mary College, 156
Williams, Roger, 180, 184
Wills, Garry, 14–15, 86
Wilson, A. N., 5
Wilson, James Q., 200
Wind, Renate, 124
Windschuttle, Keith, 104
Winston, Diane, 160, 161

Winthrop, John, 153, 184
Wistrich, Robert S., 130
witch trials, 181–82
Witherspoon, John, 185
Wittenmyer, Annie, 199
Wojtyla, Karol. *See* John Paul II
Wolowska, Marta, 138
Woman's Christian Temperance Union, 198–200
women: abolitionism, 46–47; activism, 198–200; in early church, 4–5; rights of, xiii–xiv, 199–200
Wood, Forrest, 26
work, sanctity of, 166, 167
Wurm, Theophil, 136
Wyman, David S., 135–36

Yale, Elihu, 156
Yale University, 156
YMCA, 158
Yugoslavia, 95